AFRICAN AMERICAN WOMEN
SPEAK OUT ON
ANITA HILL–
CLARENCE THOMAS

AFRICAN AMERICAN WOMEN SPEAK OUT ON ANITA HILL– CLARENCE THOMAS

EDITED BY
GENEVA SMITHERMAN

 WAYNE STATE UNIVERSITY PRESS   DETROIT

Library of Congress Cataloging-in-Publication Data

African American women speak out on Anita Hill-Clarence Thomas / edited
  by Geneva Smitherman.
      p.   cm. — (African American life series)
  Includes bibliographical references and index.
  ISBN 0-8143-2530-0 (pbk. : alk. paper)
    1. Afro-American women.   2. Sexual harassment of women—United
States.   3. Sex role—United States.   4. Hill, Anita.   5. Thomas,
Clarence, 1948–   .   I. Smitherman-Donaldson, Geneva, 1940–
II. Series.
E185.86.A3344   1995
305.48'89073—dc20   94-48645

Designer: Mark C. Howell

AFRICAN AMERICAN LIFE SERIES

*A complete listing of the books in this series can be found at the back
of this volume.*

General Editors	Toni Cade Bambara	Wilbur C. Rich
	Author and Filmmaker	Wellesley College
	Geneva Smitherman	Ronald W. Walters
	Michigan State University	Howard University

Contents

Introduction

GENEVA SMITHERMAN

In the annals of Black women's history, October 11, 1991, will stand as a watershed, a metaphorical marker of the intersection of race, gender, class. On that day, African American law professor Anita Faye Hill, of the University of Oklahoma, appeared before the U.S. Senate Judiciary Committee charging that African American judge Clarence Thomas sexually harassed her between 1981 and 1983 when she worked for him at the Department of Education and the Equal Employment Opportunity Commission. Her allegations occasioned the reopening of the Senate confirmation hearing to assess Thomas's suitability for the U.S. Supreme Court. On October 16, 1991, Judge Clarence Thomas became Justice Clarence Thomas by a Senate vote of 52 to 48, the smallest margin of confirmation for any Supreme Court justice in U.S. history.

The Hill-Thomas controversy resulted in a unique and extraordinarily complex moment in U.S. history, the reverberations of which will continue to resound for years to come. From October 11 until 2:00 A.M. on October 14, when the hearing concluded, this dramatic event unfolded on national television, in prime time, becoming the catalyst for wide-ranging debate and discussion of women's rights, gender issues in the workplace, sexual stereotypes, male insensitivity, white male political hegemony, gender and class conflict in the Black community, class and race tensions in the U.S. women's movement, the absence of diversity in persona and thought in the nation's elected bodies and governance system, the Black leadership crisis, and the future direction and survival of African Americans.

Other Supreme Court nominees have been subjected to rigorous and controversial scrutiny before the U.S. Senate and the American public, and Thomas was not the first person of color to sit on the Court, that "first" having been established by African American Thurgood Marshall, a champion of civil rights and the legal architect of *Brown* v. *Board of Education*, the 1954 Supreme Court decision that mandated the desegregation of schools. Nor was sexual harassment in the workplace a new issue, its legal history having been established during the previous decade. What made the Hill-Thomas case unique was the confluence of the "invisible" man and woman on national television, raising the issue of sexual harassment before an all-white, male, highly "visible" elected political body. And that both Hill and Thomas were Black political conservatives who had overcome poverty and racism in their ascent to positions of prominence; that Thomas was married to a white woman, attorney Virginia Lamp Thomas, whose presence was also highly "visible"; that Hill was a reluctant witness who publicly presented her case only after two reporters, one of them a white female, National Public Radio's Nina Totenberg, broke the story; that graphic details about pornographic narratives and references revived historical stereotypes about Black sexuality; that the parade of witnesses exposed millions of white Americans to the ideological and class diversity of Black America; that Thomas', countercharge of "high-tech lynching" and "Is she or isn't she?" (lying, that is) became frequent discussion themes among everyday people on buses and subways, in beauty and barbershops, at 7-11's and Mickey D's. These factors catapulted the Hill-Thomas controversy beyond the legalities of sex harassment to a societal phenomenon of mammoth proportions.

8

Since October 1991, Thomas has retreated to the background and solitude of the Supreme Court, but Hill has made numerous public appearances and speeches. A few bizarre incidents playing off the hearings' symbolic trappings have received national attention. Numerous local and national forums and publications have addressed the social and political issues spotlighted by the controversy. Businesses and corporate institutions have begun to review and/or revise their sexual harassment policies and to hold training seminars and forums on harassment for their employees and executives. On the front of electoral politics, an unprecedented number of twenty-one Black women ran for the U.S. House of Representatives in 1992. In Illinois, a Democrat, Carol Moseley-Braun, created a major upset by winning the U.S. Senate race and carving out a place in history as the first Black woman senator. In fact, the record number of African and European American women elected to Congress in 1992 has been dubbed "The Anita Hill Class": four women elected to the Senate and twenty-four to the House. The name "Anita Hill" has become a metaphor for women's issues and has introduced new terminology into the national discourse—as in, "Let's 'Anita Hill' the childcare issue."

Hill's media appearances have ranged from "60 Minutes" (with Ed Bradley, January 2, 1992) to an interview by *Essence*, the Black women's magazine (March 1992). Her speaking appearances have included an audience of several hundred female state legislators at a national convention in San Diego (November 1991), a fifty-dollar-per-person sell-out fundraiser for a domestic violence shelter in southeastern Michigan (September 1992), and audiences numbering more than one thousand at university lecture halls around the country.

The list of bizarre incidents includes a skit with a man in blackface and curly wig posing as and satirizing Anita Hill at the Monmouth, New Jersey, Bar's Christmas party in 1991, and the suspension of a Harvard Medical School Black male student for an assault on his white male classmate when he arrived at the school's annual Halloween party dressed in blackface as Thomas, along with his white female classmate in blackface as Hill. In retrospect, these incidents are perhaps no more bizarre than the invocation of "erotomania" by the Senate Judiciary Committee to explain away Hill's charges. This rare psychological disorder—which, according to the experts, afflicts women primarily—is characterized by a woman's delusions that she is having an affair with a man of superior social status.

Books generated by the Hill-Thomas case thus far number eight, counting this one. In-depth articles in journals and magazines have been numerous, particularly during 1992. A double issue of *Black Scholar* (Winter 1991–Spring 1992, now in book form) featured brief prepared statements by African American male and female leaders, activists, and scholars. *Essence* ("A House Divided," January 1992) featured reactions from "21 influential African Americans"—academics, writers, filmmaker Spike Lee, and the "raptivist" Sister Souljah. *Tikkun* (January–February 1992) published a roundtable discussion between African and European American male and female scholars and intellectuals on the topic "sexuality after Thomas/Hill." Hill appeared on the cover of *People* one week, in the story "Sex and the Boss" (October 28, 1991), and Clarence and Virginia Thomas appeared on the cover another week, in the story "How We Survived" (November 11, 1991). *Ms.*'s January–February 1992 issue featured a cover photograph of legions of women marching and the story "Rage + Women = Power." *Glamour's* March 1992 issue featured the cover byline and story "Why Women Are Mad As Hell." The etymology of *crush*, what Hill allegedly had on Thomas, a discussion of the penis as the "dong" from *Long Dong Silver*, the pornographic video Thomas allegedly discussed with Hill,[1] and other "linguistic and grammatical reverberations" generated by the Thomas hearing were taken up by William Safire in his weekly language columns for the

9

New York Times Magazine. Editorial commentaries and journalistic essays have appeared in all the major newspapers, as well as in *The Nation, Emerge, The American Spectator*—the list seems endless.

Because what *Essence* called the "Hill-Thomas mess" is not simply about a man and a woman on the outs, but at bottom, concerns power relations within and across what Andrew Hacker called "two nations . . . separate, hostile, unequal" (1992), attention to the Hill-Thomas case will continue far beyond Andy Warhol's proverbial fifteen minutes.

African American Women in Defense of Ourselves

During both phases of the hearings, in the panoply of voices opining in the mainstream media, one strained to hear the sound of African American women. Though central to this controversy, they had been silenced throughout the progress of the hearings. A month later, on November 17, 1991, "African American Women in Defense of Ourselves," a full-page statement signed by 1,603 Black women, appeared in the *New York Times*. It also appeared in seven African American newspapers. (See Barbara Ransby's essay in this volume.) This national effort to bring the voice of African American women before the American public was a historic moment, introducing a new saga about the old boundaries of race, gender, and class in the United States.

10   As phase two of the Thomas hearings was coming to a close, I conceived of this book as an avenue for articulating the impact and meaning of this historic event on the African American community. Given the race-sex-class configuration of the Hill-Thomas case, there was never any question in my mind that the contributors had to be Black women. I issued the call for essays through the Black women's grapevine, through the network that had formed around the "African American Women in Defense of Ourselves" campaign, and through other word-of-mouth channels that have served African Americans for generations. In talking with women about the pieces they would write, I deliberately chose not to impose an overarching theme, leaving each contributor at liberty to select the angle of vision that fit her particular lens. We had been silenced once throughout this controversy. As the editor, I was concerned that I not be the source of yet another level of silencing. The contributions are thus varied, both in length and in approach.

The book is structured to give voice to African American women offering reflections as well as in-depth analyses. Several of the pieces were conceived shortly after the hearings and capture the poignancy and immediacy of that historical moment, both for Black women and for other groups. The analytical probings, most of which were written over a period of several months after the hearings, render the broader ramifications and the future impact on the African American community and the nation. Unlike other journal collections and books on Hill-Thomas, this book has neither males nor European American women as contributors. This absence is not an oversight but the result of a deliberate design to focus on the historically silenced voice of the Black woman in the United States— a marginalization continued in the neglect of African American women during the Thomas hearings.

The voices presented here are those of activists, writers, journalists, and scholars across disciplines. There is a practitioner of the healing arts and a cartoonist. In the ways of our foremothers, we are multifaceted, most of us operating in several spheres simultaneously. We range from sharecroppers' daughters to those who grew up in privileged surroundings. We reflect variety in the status of our relationships: married, unattached, divorced, partners. Several of us are mothers of daughters and sons, and our ages range from thirty-something to eighty-something. Although we are the living embodiment of race-gender-class questions, we are often "asked in a thousand ways, large and small, to take sides against ourselves, postponing a confrontation in one arena to address an equally urgent task in another" (Bray 1991, p. 2). While the voices and perspectives presented here are diverse, the unifying motif throughout is our dual concern for the survival and development of African-American women *simultaneous with* what Alice Walker called the "survival whole" of our people—and, ultimately, of all marginalized groups and progressive people.

11

It is critical to understand not only where Black women are but also where we are not. Many people were puzzled by the fact that of all race-gender groups, support for Hill was lowest among Black women. A progressive critique of the Hill-Thomas phenomenon demands that we deplore the assault upon Hill's dignity and the racist, sexist treatment accorded her as an African American woman who refused to continue her silence about gender subordination and sexual harassment. Simultaneously, we must acknowledge Hill's ideological reality as an African American, as a person with poverty origins, and as a woman. She did, after all, put professional accomplishment over principle, by her own acknowledgment speaking out only after her career was "on solid ground." When she indicated in the "60 Minutes" interview with Ed Bradley that she was a Democrat, it was a surprise to many people, her politics, particularly as manifested in her upward climb to professional success, appearing to lie clearly outside the parameters of liberalism. Indeed, the image of Hill that emerged during the hearings and in news reports was that of a conservative who had supported Judge Robert Bork for the Supreme Court and whose political line closely paralleled that of Thomas.

We should give Hill props for courage and grace under pressure, and we should acknowledge and applaud her role in this dramatic motion of history. She opened a window for examining the nexus of race, gender, and class politics. Yet we must remember that such an examination was not on her personal agenda, nor was concern about race-gender-class the motivation for her coming forth. As bell hooks has stated, "it was never clear what Hill intended by her disclosure. . . . She never really stated an agenda. . . . Hill's performance suggests that she brought to the hearings misguided faith in a system that has rarely worked for women seeking justice" (1992, p. 19). Nor, we may add, has this system worked well for African American males, or the poor of any hue. Thus, it behooves us to be wary of the current trend, particularly pronounced among European American women, to fetishize Hill.

Notwithstanding personal motivation and personal histories—intriguing matters, to be sure—our mission as African American women is to keep our eyes on the prize. In our deliberations here, we have sought to understand for ourselves, and to clarify for our community and this nation, the meaning and symbolic significance of the Hill-Thomas phenomenon at this historical moment in the United States. Hill-Thomas catapulted to the foreground of life in these United States the objective realities of blackness-whiteness, maleness-femaleness, poverty-privilege, and race, class, and gender oppression and subordination. Black women grappled with the dilemma posed, on the one hand, by Hill—a Black woman charging the (age-old) sexual harassment of Black women, who did not appear to be a progressive or a Black Womanist[2] or a Black feminist— and, on the other hand, by Thomas—a Black man charging the (age-old) lynching of Black men by white men, who was neither a race man[3] nor a political progressive. African American women's struggle to resolve these ideological contradictions is the subject of Barbara Ransby's overview of the "African American Women in Defense of Ourselves" campaign in "A Righteous Rage and a Grassroots Mobilization." As one of the three initial organizers of this collective response by Black women nationwide, a longtime community activist, and a scholar of African American history, Ransby is uniquely situated to narrate the story of this campaign.[4]

Because of the social deterioration and economic ravages of Black communities across the nation, society's failure to deliver on the promises African Americans struggled for during the 1960s, the alarming increase in the number of Black female-headed poverty households, and the backlash against affirmative action—all of which have characterized the national scene since 1980—the contemporary era has been deemed the "Second Reconstruction" (e.g., Marable 1989). Yet it would be a misreading of history to assert that the struggles of the 1960s have not borne fruit. In African America, there is now a burgeoning, unparalleled middle class. Of all the Ph.D.'s in the history of Black Americans, 80 percent were awarded between 1960 and 1980 (Blackwell 1981). And Black women have made substantial social and economic gains since the 1960s, having benefited more from gender-based policies than from racial policies (Giddings 1984). Hill and Thomas's overcoming poverty backgrounds, achieving law degrees from Yale University, and attaining professional success in their fields reflects the 1960s legacy that created an environment for the flowering of the talents of African American women and men and European-American women. Yet Hill and Thomas's seeming indifference to this legacy revived debates about "double consciousness" (Du Bois 1903), renewed discussions about race men and historical struggles against white male supremacy, and introduced into this dialogue within the race the issue of the role of Black women in what Marable calls this "Post-Black" era.

Margaret Walker Alexander, Harriette Pipes McAdoo, and Dianne M. Pinderhughes provide thoughtful reflections on these complex issues. Alexander poses her reflection in the form of a question. "Whose 'Boy' Is This?" she asks. McAdoo captures her reflective thinking by employing as metaphor the literal historical reality of "The Circling of the Wagons." Pinderhughes reflects that these issues represent "Faults in the Movement" and that the Hill-Thomas controversy may be considered symbolic of "The End of One Era and the Beginning of Another."

Situating the society's view of women within the Judeo-Christian tradition and biblical metaphors, Nettie Jones offers us "Anita at the Battle of the Bush: Thomas on the Hill: Dark Town Strutters Ball." She chronicles the intrusion of this dramatic event into her personal theological world and presents her views and those of fellow clergy on the Hill-Thomas case. Also employing otherworld metaphors, Toi Derricotte indicates that Hill-Thomas brought to her mind her poem "On the Turning Up of Unidentified Black Female Corpses," which she wrote as a reaction to excavations being conducted in New York City. And journalist Susan Watson used such metaphorical constructs as "the devil," "born-again black," and "wretched spectacle" in her daily coverage of the hearings for the *Detroit Free Press*.

Issues of race and gender are inextricable from the question of class. The status of the women writing in this volume cannot presently be characterized as working-class, though several grew up in working-class and what Wilson (1989) would label under-class backgrounds. Although this volume has no "everyday" Black women as contributing authors, their voices and views are represented here in the interviews conducted and analyzed by Gwendolyn Etter-Lewis, the forums and group discussions analyzed by Beverly Grier, and the economic analyses and historical assessment of sexual harassment by Julianne Malveaux. Etter-Lewis's "High-Tech Lynching on Capitol Hill: Oral Narratives from African American Women" analyzes the language used by Black women in their stories about sexual harassment and the Hill-Thomas controversy, finding that these women reflected a grasp of the complexity of gender *and* race and a feeling that the entire Black community was on trial. Grier attempts to

13

make sense of the divergent responses of Black women she interacted with as participant-observer, noting that the women seemed to split along the lines of age, education, and occupation. Malveaux reminds us that even though professional women are the ones who have recently come out with sexual harassment complaints and issues, the earliest recorded cases were "from the bottom of the occupational hierarchy, not the top." She addresses the situation of working- (and under-) class women, such as African American Brenda Patterson, laid off in 1982 after months of harassment, who filed a lawsuit against her employers; and household workers of color, such as the immigrant Peruvian Mrs. Cordero, who worked for Clinton attorney general nominee Zoe Baird for minimum wages. Posing issues of equal pay, genuine welfare reform (as opposed to "welfare scapegoating"), health care, and employment benefits for the women who comprise two-thirds of those working for poverty wages, Malveaux concludes that the question after "The Year of the Woman" is the same as that posed by Sojourner Truth in 1852: "Ain't I a woman?"

Lest we forget those Black women in our history who were sexually exploited "For Pleasure, Profit, and Power," Darlene Clark Hine narrates the abuse of Harriet Jacobs, Celia the slave, and Joan Little. She links these women's histories to Hill as symbolic reminders that vis-à-vis white males, Black males, and white women, the Black woman still is not "free and considered fully human." Angela Y. Davis's "Clarence Thomas as 'Lynching Victim'" reflects on Hill's courageous role in bringing this historical issue to the fore, not only for African American women but also for Chicana women and other women of color. Davis concludes that the Hill-Thomas drama problematized and has forever altered the way African Americans construct ourselves as a community.

Contending that the Black woman's quest for wholeness is thwarted by the masculinization of Black history as well as by the de-racialization and de-classing of Black women, Elsa Barkley Brown recalls her father's political cartoons depicting the lynching of Black men *and* women. Her "Imaging Lynching: African-American Women, Communities of Struggle, and Collective Memory" calls for a "re-remembering" of history that is inclusive of women of all social classes. Rosalind B. Griffin addresses the medical-legal dimensions of imaging in "A Forensic Psychiatrist Reflects on Sexual Harassment." Utilizing a psychoanalytic paradigm to deconstruct female and male dimensions of sexual abuse, she concludes with a clinical vignette from her private practice that demonstrates a Black woman's successful and empowering challenge to sexual harassment.

Patricia Coleman-Burns's "Social and Political Thought on Anita Hill from the Feminist and Black Communities: The Scapegoat and the Sacrificial Lamb" provides a schematic to categorize and explicate public reactions to the Hill-Thomas controversy. Her Burkeian analysis concludes with an explanation and a caution: Race loyalty must not obfuscate sexism and classism within the race, and preoccupations with white supremacy must not blind us to the machinations of gender and class bias outside the race. While Coleman-Burns focuses on political and ideological factors behind public discourse on Hill-Thomas, Linda Susan Beard concentrates on the literary language used to talk about the controversy. Her "Of Metaphors and Meaning: Language, Ways of Knowing, Memory Holes, and a Politic Recall" demonstrates that to make sense of this cataclysmic event, the public's only recourse was to the language of imaginative literature.

Essays by Denise Troutman-Robinson and Geneva Smitherman discuss the communication styles used in the hearings. Troutman-Robinson's "The Tongue or the Sword: Which Is Master?" compares the discourse style of Hill with that of the senators in terms of the linguistic symbols of power in communication between men and women. She concludes that (at least within the European-American rhetorical tradition) Hill held the upper hand. Exploring the linguistic manifestations of what Linda F. Williams calls the new bifurcation of African America, Smitherman contrasts the language of Hill and Thomas as a sociolinguistic case study of African and European American rhetorical styles. Her "Testifyin, Sermonizin, and Signifyin" argues that Thomas seized the rhetorical advantage by exploiting the African American Verbal Tradition, and thus there is a need for African American women to address the linguistics of leadership.

Addressing the complexity of race-gender-class issues as reflective of a "crisis in Black leadership," Linda F. Williams begins with the moment of Thomas's nomination by President Bush and locates the Hill-Thomas phenomenon within recently developed class tensions and age-old sexism in African America. Through Williams's examination of the reactions of African American male and female leadership and of Black responses in poll data, in both phases of the hearings, we begin to see that Blacks' contradictory reactions to Hill-Thomas represent the failure of African American leadership to adapt to changing conditions, and thus the "era that's ending" is that of current Black leadership. In the Black tradition of "laughing to keep from crying," Barbara Brandon offers her reflections on race-gender-class in the form of two cartoons that appeared during the Hill-Thomas "mess." Her "Where I'm Coming From" nationally syndicated characters speak to the issues in Black women's own inimitable style.

Here, then, are our voices: twenty African American women on the Anita Hill-Clarence Thomas phenomenon and its meaning and significance for African Americans and the nation. This book represents a continuation of African American women voicing ourselves in our quest to add a new chapter to the saga about race, gender, and class politics in the United States.

Notes

1. Surprisingly, my prediction that the porno video market would capitalize on the publicity given to the old *Long Dong Silver* film apparently will not come to pass. For weeks after the hearings ended, I tried in vain to find the *Long Dong Silver* video. I went through the porno sections in several video stores in two major cities and in Michigan's capital before I finally located it. My curiosity piqued, I rushed home with the video, only to be sorely disappointed by the appearance on my television screen of a gap-toothed, very unsexy, ordinary-looking Black man with a silly grin on his face, having uninspired sex while sporting a wide-brimmed country hat. This is what was supposed to arouse Hill to passion?!
2. A Womanist is rooted in the Black community and committed to the survival and development of that community and herself as a woman at the same time (Smitherman, 1994). The term was first used and popularized by Alice Walker, who appropriated *womanist* from the African American English word *womanish* (also *womlish*). Walker writes: "Womanist . . . From the black folk expression of mothers to female children, 'You acting womanish,' i.e., like a woman. . . . Wanting to know more and in greater depth than is considered 'good' for one. . . . Acting grown up. . . . Interchangeable with another black folk expression: 'You trying to be grown.' Responsible. In charge. *Serious*" (1983, p. xi).
3. The term *race man* (also *race woman*) refers to a person who is devoted to and promotes African American culture and staunchly defends Blacks and Black causes and issues. The expression dates back to the early 1900s. Consult Smitherman (1994) for more details.
4. The other two initial organizers were Elsa Barkley Brown and Deborah King. See Brown's essay in this volume.

References

Blackwell, James. *Mainstreaming Outsiders: The Production of Black Professionals*. Bayside, N.Y.: General Hall, 1981.

Bray, Rosemary. "Taking Sides Against Ourselves." *New York Times Magazine*, Nov. 11, 1991, pp. 1–4.

Du Bois, W. E. B. *Souls of Black Folk*. New York: Fawcett, 1903.

Giddings, Paula. *When and Where I Enter: The Impact of Black Woman on Race and Sex in America*. New York: Morrow, 1984.

Hacker, Andrew. *Two Nations*. New York: Scribner's, 1992.

hooks, bell. "A Feminist Challenge: Must We Call All Women Sister." Z, Feb. 1992, pp. 19–22.

Marable, Manning. "African-American or Black? The politics of cultural identity." *Black Issues in Higher Education*, April 13, 1989, p. 72.

Smitherman, Geneva. *Black Talk: Words and Phrases from the Hood to the Amen Corner*. Boston: Houghton Mifflin, 1994.

Walker, Alice. *In Search of Our Mother's Gardens*. New York: Harcourt Brace, 1983.

Wilson, Julius W. "The Underclass: Issues, Perspectives, and Public Policy." *Annals of the American Academy of Social Science*. 1989.

On the Turning Up
of Unidentified Black
Female Corpses

TOI DERRICOTTE

Moving his three acres with a tractor,
a man notices something ahead—a mannequin—
he thinks someone threw it from a car. Closer
he sees it is the body of a Black woman.

The medics come and turn her with pitchforks.
Her gaze shoots past him to nothing. Nothing
is explained. How many Black women
have been turned up to stare at us blankly.

In weedy fields, off highways,
pushed out in plastic bags,
shot, knifed, unclothed partially, raped,
their wounds sealed with a powdery crust.

Last week on TV, a gruesome face, eyes bloated shut.
No one will say "She looks like she's sleeping," ropes
of blue-black slashes at the mouth. Does anybody
know this woman? Will anyone come forth? Silence

like a backwave rushes into that field
where, just the week before, four other Black girls

had been found. The gritty image hangs in the air
just a few seconds, but it strikes me,

a Black woman, there is a question being asked
about my life. How can I
protect myself? Even if I lock my doors,
walk only in the light, someone wants me dead.

Am I wrong to think
if five white women had been stripped,
broken, the sirens would wail until
someone was named?

Is it any wonder I walk over these bodies
pretending they are not mine, that I do not know
the killer, that I am just like any woman—
if not wanted, at least tolerated.

Part of me wants to disappear, to pull
the earth on top of me. Then there is this part
that digs me up with this pen
and turns my sad black face to the light.

Statement of Anita F. Hill to the Senate Judiciary Committee October 11, 1991

M r. Chairman, Senator Thurmond, members of the committee, my name is Anita F. Hill, and I am a professor of law at the University of Oklahoma. I was born on a farm in Okmulgee County, Oklahoma, in 1956. I am the youngest of thirteen children. I had my early education in Okmulgee County. My father, Albert Hill, is a farmer in that area. My mother's name is Irma Hill. She is also a farmer and a housewife.

My childhood was one of a lot of hard work and not much money, but it was one of solid family affection, as represented by my parents. I was reared in a religious atmosphere in the Baptist faith, and I have been a member of the Antioch Baptist Church in Tulsa, Oklahoma, since 1983. It is a very warm part of my life at the present time.

For my undergraduate work, I went to Oklahoma State University and graduated from there in 1977. I am attaching to this statement a copy of my résumé for further details of my education.

I graduated from the university with academic honors and proceeded to the Yale Law School where I received my J.D. degree in 1980. Upon graduation from law school, I became a practicing lawyer with the Washington, D.C., firm of Wald, Hardraker, and Ross.

The ellipses indicate repetitions and/or restatements that have been deleted to facilitate reading fluency. Otherwise, this is an exact transcription of Professor Anita F. Hill's statement to the Senate Judiciary Committee.—*Ed.*

In 1981, I was introduced to now-Judge Thomas by a mutual friend. Judge Thomas told me that he was anticipating a political appointment, and he asked if I would be interested in working with him. He was, in fact, appointed as assistant secretary of Education for civil rights. After he had taken that post, he asked if I would become his assistant, and I accepted that position.

In my early period there, I had two major projects. The first was an article I wrote for Judge Thomas's signature on the education of minority students. The second was the organization of a seminar on high-risk students which was abandoned because Judge Thomas transferred to the EEOC, where he became the chairman of that office.

During this period at the Department of Education, my working relationship with Judge Thomas was positive. I had a good deal of responsibility and independence. I thought he respected my work and that he trusted my judgment. After approximately three months of working there, he asked me to go out socially with him.

What happened next and telling the world about it are the two most difficult . . . experiences of my life. It is only after a great deal of agonizing consideration . . . and a great number of sleepless nights that I am able to talk of these unpleasant matters to anyone but my close friends.

I declined the invitation to go out socially with him and explained to him that I thought it would jeopardize what at the time I considered to be a very good working relationship. I had a normal social life with other men outside of the office. I believed then, as now, that having a social relationship with a person who was supervising my work would be ill advised. I was very uncomfortable with the idea and told him so.

I thought that by saying no and explaining my reasons, my employer would abandon his social suggestions. However, to my regret, in the following few weeks, he continued to ask me out on several occasions. He pressed me to justify my reasons for saying no to him. These incidents took place in his office or mine. They were in the form of private conversations which would not have been overheard by anyone else.

My working relationship became even more strained when Judge Thomas began to use work situations to discuss sex. On these occasions, he would call me into his office for reports on education issues and projects, or he might suggest that because of the time pressures of his schedule, we go to lunch to a government cafeteria. After a brief discussion of work, he would turn the conversation to a discussion of sexual matters.

His conversations were very vivid. He spoke about acts that he had seen in pornographic films involving such matters as women having sex with animals and films showing group sex or rape scenes. He talked about pornographic materials depicting individuals with large penises or large breasts involved in various sex acts. On several occasions, Thomas told me graphically of his own sexual prowess.

Because I was extremely uncomfortable talking about sex with him at all and particularly in such a graphic way, I told him that I did not want to talk about these subjects. I would also try to change the subject to education matters or to nonsexual personal matters such as his background or his beliefs. My efforts to change the subject were rarely successful.

Throughout the period of these conversations, he also, from time to time, asked me for social engagements. My reaction to these conversations was to avoid them by eliminating opportunities for us to engage in extended conversations. This was difficult because at the time I was his only assistant at the Office of Education . . . Civil Rights.

During the latter part of my time at the Department of Education, the social pressures and his conversation of offensive behavior ended. I began both to believe and hope that our working relationship could be a proper, cordial, and professional one.

When Judge Thomas was made chair of the EEOC, I needed to face the question of whether to go with him. I was asked to do so, and I did. The work itself was interesting, and at that time it appeared that the sexual overtures, which had so troubled me, had ended. I also faced the realistic fact that I had no alternative job. While I might have gone back to private practice, perhaps in my old firm or at another, I was dedicated to civil rights work, and my first choice was to be in that field. Moreover, the Department of Education itself was a dubious venture. President Reagan was seeking to abolish the entire department.

For my first months at the EEOC, where I continued to be an assistant to Judge Thomas, there were no sexual conversations or overtures. However, during the fall and winter of 1982, these began again. The comments were random and ranged from pressing me about why I didn't go out with him to remarks about my personal appearance. I remember his saying that someday I would have to tell him the real reason that I wouldn't go out with him.

He began to show displeasure in his tone and voice and his demeanor and his continued pressure for an explanation. He commented on what I was wearing in terms of whether it made me more or less sexually attractive. The incidents occurred in his inner office at the EEOC.

One of the oddest episodes I remember was an occasion in which Thomas was drinking a Coke in his office. He got up from the table at which we were working, went over to his desk to get the Coke, looked at the can, and asked, "Who has put pubic hair on my Coke?" On other occasions, he referred to the size of his own penis as being larger than normal, and he also spoke on some occasions of the pleasures he had given to women with oral sex.

At this point, late 1982, I began to feel severe stress on the job. I began to be concerned that Clarence Thomas might take out his anger with me by degrading me or not giving me important assignments. I also thought that he might find an excuse for dismissing me.

In January of 1983, I began looking for another job. I was handicapped because I feared that, if he found out, he might make it difficult for me to find other employment, and I might be dismissed from the job I had. Another factor that made my search more difficult was that . . . this was during a period of a hiring freeze in the government. In February of 1983, I was hospitalized for five days on an emergency basis for acute stomach pains, which I attributed to stress on the job.

Once out of the hospital, I became more committed to finding other employment and sought further to minimize my contact with Thomas. This became easier when Allison Duncan became office director, because most of my work was then funneled through her, and I had contact with Clarence Thomas mostly in staff meetings.

In the spring of 1983, an opportunity to teach at Oral Roberts University opened up. I . . . taught an afternoon session and seminar at Oral Roberts University. The dean of the university saw me teaching and inquired as to whether I would be interested in . . . pursuing a career in teaching, beginning at Oral Roberts University. I agreed to take the job in large part because of my desire to escape the pressures I felt at the EEOC due to Judge Thomas.

When I informed him that I was leaving in July, I recall that his response was that now I would no longer have an excuse for not going out with him. I told him that I still preferred not to do so. At some time after that meeting, he asked if he could take me to dinner at the end of the term. When I declined, he assured me that the dinner was a professional courtesy only, and not a social invitation.

I reluctantly agreed to accept that invitation, but only if it was at the very end of a working day.

On, as I recall, the last day of my employment at the EEOC in the summer of 1983, I did have dinner with Clarence Thomas. We went directly from work to a restaurant near the office. We talked about the work I had done, both at Education and at the EEOC. He told me that he was pleased with all of it except for an article and speech that I had done for him while we were at the Office for Civil Rights. Finally, he made a comment that I will vividly remember. He said that if I ever told anyone of his behavior that it would ruin his career. This was not an apology, nor was it an explanation. That was his last remark about the possibility of our going out or reference to his behavior.

In July of 1983, I left the Washington, D.C., area and have had minimal contact with Judge Clarence Thomas since. I am, of course, aware from the press that some questions have been raised about conversations I had with Judge Clarence Thomas after I left the EEOC. From 1983 until today, I have seen Judge Thomas only twice. On one occasion,

I needed to get a reference from him, and on another, he made a public appearance in Tulsa.

On one occasion, he called me at home, and we had an inconsequential conversation. On one occasion, he called me without reaching me, and I returned the call without reaching him, and nothing came of it. I have, on at least three occasions, been asked to act as a conduit to him for others.

I knew his secretary, Diane Holt. We had worked together at both EEOC and Education. There were occasions on which I spoke to her, and on some of these occasions, undoubtedly, I passed on some casual comment to then-Chairman Thomas. There were a series of calls in the first three months of 1985, occasioned by a group in Tulsa which wished to have a civil rights conference. They wanted Judge Thomas to be the speaker and enlisted my assistance for this purpose.

I did call in January and February to no effect, and finally suggested to the person directly involved, Susan Cahall, that she put the matter into her own hands and call directly. She did so in March of 1985. In connection with that March invitation, Ms. Cahall wanted conference materials for the seminar, and some research was needed. I was asked to try to get the information and did attempt to do so.

There was another call about a possible conference in July of 1985. In August of 1987, I was in Washington, D.C., and I did call Diane Holt. In the course of this conversation, she asked me how long I was going to be in town, and I told her. It is recorded in the message as August 15. It was, in fact, August 20. She told me about Judge Thomas's marriage, and I did say congratulate him.

It is only after a great deal of agonizing consideration that I am able to talk of these unpleasant matters to anyone except my closest friends. As I've said before, these last few days have been very trying and very hard for me, and it hasn't just been the last few days this week. It has actually been over a month now that I have been under the strain of this issue.

Telling the world is the most difficult experience of my life, but it is very close to having to live through the experience that occasioned this meeting. I may have used poor judgment early on in my relationship with this issue. I was aware, however, that telling at any point in my career could adversely affect my future career. And I did not want early on to burn all the bridges to the EEOC.

As I said, I may have used poor judgment. Perhaps I should have taken angry or even militant steps, both when I was in the agency, or after I left it. But I must confess to the world that the course that I took seemed the better, as well as the easier approach.

I declined any comment to newspapers, but later when Senate staff asked me about these matters, I felt I had a duty to report. I have no personal vendetta against Clarence Thomas. I seek only to provide the committee with information which it may regard as relevant.

It would have been more comfortable to remain silent. I took no initiative to inform anyone. But when I was asked by a representative of this committee to report my experience, I felt that I had to tell the truth. I could not keep silent.

Statement of Clarence Thomas to the Senate Judiciary Committee October 11, 1991

Mr. Chairman, Senator Thurmond, members of the committee. As excruciatingly difficult as the last two weeks have been, I welcome the opportunity to clear my name today. No one other than my wife and Senator Danforth, to whom I read this statement at 6:30 A.M., has seen or heard this statement. No handlers, no advisers.

The first I learned of the allegations by Professor Anita Hill was on September 25, 1991, when the FBI came to my home to investigate her allegations. When informed by the FBI agent of the nature of the allegations and the person making them, I was shocked, surprised, hurt, and enormously saddened. I have not been the same since that day.

For almost a decade my responsibilities included enforcing the rights of victims of sexual harassment. As a boss, as a friend, and as a human being, I was proud that I had never had such an allegation leveled against me, even as I sought to promote women and minorities into nontraditional jobs.

In addition, several of my friends who are women have confided in me about the horror of harassment on the job or elsewhere. I thought

---

The ellipses indicate repetitions and/or restatements that have been deleted to facilitate reading fluency. Otherwise, this is an exact transcription of Judge Clarence Thomas's statement to the Senate Judiciary Committee.—*Ed.*

I really understood the anguish, the fears, the doubts, the seriousness of the matter. But since September 25, I have suffered immensely as these very serious charges were leveled against me. I have been wracking my brains and eating my insides out, trying to think of what I could have said or done to Anita Hill to lead her to allege that I was interested in her in more than a professional way, and that I talked with her about pornographic or X-rated films.

Contrary to some press reports, I categorically denied all of the allegations and denied that I ever attempted to date Anita Hill when first interviewed by the FBI. I strongly reaffirm that denial.

Let me describe my relationship with Anita Hill. In 1981, after I went to the Department of Education as an assistant secretary in the Office of Civil Rights, one of my closest friends from both college and law school, Gil Hardy, brought Anita Hill to my attention. As I remember, he indicated that she was dissatisfied with her law firm and wanted to work in government. Based primarily, if not solely, on Gil's recommendation, I hired Anita Hill.

During my tenure at the Department of Education, Anita Hill was an attorney adviser who worked directly with me. She worked on special projects, as well as day-to-day matters. As I recall, she was one of two professionals working directly with me at the time. As a result, we worked closely on numerous matters. I recall being pleased with her work product and the professional, but cordial, relationship which we enjoyed at work. I also recall engaging in discussions about politics and current events. Upon my nomination to become chairman of the Equal Employment Opportunity Commission, Anita Hill, to the best of my recollection, assisted me in the nomination and confirmation process. After my confirmation, she and Diane Holt, then my secretary, joined me at EEOC. I do not recall that there was any question or doubt that she would become a special assistant to me at EEOC, although as a career employee, she retained the option of remaining at the Department of Education.

At EEOC, our relationship was more distant and our contacts less frequent as a result of the increased size of my personal staff and the dramatic increase and diversity of my day-to-day responsibilities. Upon reflection, I recall that she seemed to have had some difficulty adjusting to this change in her role. In any case, our relationship remained both cordial and professional.

At no time did I become aware, either directly or indirectly, that she felt I had said or done anything to change the cordial nature of our relationship. I detected nothing from her or from my staff, or from Gil Hardy, our mutual friend, with whom I maintained regular contact. I am certain that had any statement or conduct on my part been brought to my attention, I would remember it clearly because of the nature and seriousness of such conduct as well as my adamant opposition to sex discrimination and sexual harassment. But there were no such statements.

In the spring of 1983, Mr. Charles Kothe contacted me to speak at the law school at Oral Roberts University in Tulsa, Oklahoma. Anita Hill, who is from Oklahoma, accompanied me on that trip. It was not unusual that individuals on my staff would travel with me occasionally. Anita Hill accompanied me on that trip primarily because this was an opportunity to combine business and a visit to her home.

As I recall, during our visit at Oral Roberts University, Mr. Kothe mentioned to me the possibility of approaching Anita Hill to join the faculty at Oral Roberts University Law School. I encouraged him to do so and noted to him, as I recall, that Anita Hill would do well in teaching. I recommended her highly, and she eventually was offered a teaching position.

Although I did not see Anita Hill often after she left EEOC, I did see her on one or two subsequent visits to Tulsa, Oklahoma. And on one visit, I believe she drove me to the airport. I also occasionally received telephone calls from her. She would speak directly with me or with my secretary, Diane Holt. Since Anita Hill and Diane Holt had been with me at the Department of Education, they were fairly close personally, and I believe they occasionally socialized together. I would also hear about her through Linda Jackson, then Linda Lambert, whom both Anita Hill and I met at the Department of Education, and I would hear of her from my friend, Gil.

Throughout the time that Anita Hill worked with me, I treated her as I treated my other special assistants. I tried to treat them all cordially, professionally, and respectfully, and I tried to support them in their endeavors and be interested in and supportive of their success. I had no reason or basis to believe my relationship with Anita Hill was anything but this way until the FBI visited me a little more than two weeks ago.

I find it particularly troubling that she never raised any hint that she was uncomfortable with me. She did not raise or mention it when considering moving with me to EEOC from the Department of Education, and she'd never raised it with me when she left EEOC and was moving on in her life. And, to my fullest knowledge, she did not speak to any other women working with or around me who would feel comfortable enough to raise it with me, especially Diane Holt, to whom she seemed closest on my personal staff. Nor did she raise it with mutual friends, such as Linda Jackson and Gil Hardy.

This is a person I have helped at every turn in the road since we met. She seemed to appreciate the continued cordial relationship we had since day one. She sought my advice and counsel, as did virtually all of the members of my personal staff.

During my tenure in the executive branch as a manager, as a policymaker, and as a person, I have adamantly condemned sex harassment. There is no member of this committee or this Senate who feels stronger about sex harassment than I do. As a manager, I made every effort to

27

take swift and decisive action when sex harassment raised or reared its ugly head. The fact that I feel so very strongly about sex harassment and spoke loudly at EEOC has made these allegations doubly hard on me. I cannot imagine anything that I said or did to Anita Hill that could have been mistaken for sexual harassment.

But with that said, if there is anything that I have said that has been misconstrued by Anita Hill or anyone else to be sexual harassment, then I can say that I am so very sorry, and I wish I had known. If I did know, I would have stopped immediately, and I would not, as I've done over the past two weeks, have to tear away at myself, trying to think of what I could possibly have done. But I have not said or done the things that Anita Hill has alleged. God has gotten me through the days since September 25, and he is my judge.

Mr. Chairman, something has happened to me in the dark days that have followed since the FBI agents informed me about these allegations. And the days have grown darker as this very serious, very explosive, and very sensitive allegation—or these sensitive allegations—were selectively leaked in a distorted way to the media over the past weekend. As if the confidential allegations themselves were not enough, this apparently calculated public disclosure has caused me, my family, and my friends enormous pain and great harm. I have never in all my life felt such hurt, such pain, such agony. My family and I have been done a grave and irreparable injustice.

During the past two weeks, I lost the belief that if I did my best, all would work out. I called upon the strength that helped me get here from Pin Point, and it was all sapped out of me. It was sapped out of me because Anita Hill was a person I considered a friend, whom I admired and thought I had treated fairly and with the utmost respect. Perhaps I could have . . . better weathered this if it was from someone else. But here was someone I truly felt I had done my best with. Though I am by no means a perfect person . . . I have not done what she has alleged, and I still don't know what I could possibly have done to cause her to make these allegations.

When I stood next to the president in Kennebunkport being nominated to the Supreme Court of the United States, that was a high honor; but as I sit here before you, 103 days later, that honor has been crushed. From the very beginning, charges were leveled against me from the shadows, charges of drug abuse, anti-Semitism, wife beating, drug use by family members, that I was a quota appointment, confirmation conversion, and much, much more. And now, this.

I have complied with the rules. I responded to a document request that produced over 30,000 pages of documents, and I have testified for five full days under oath. I have endured this ordeal for 103 days. Reporters sneaking into my garage to examine books I read. Reporters and interest groups swarming over divorce papers looking for dirt. Unnamed people starting preposterous and damaging rumors. Calls all over the country specifically requesting dirt. This is not American; this is Kafkaesque. It has got to stop. It must stop for the benefit of future nominees and our country. Enough is enough.

I'm not going to allow myself to be further humiliated in order to be confirmed. I am here specifically to respond to allegations of sex harassment in the workplace. I am not here to be further humiliated by this committee or anyone else, or to put my private life on display for prurient interests or other reasons. I will not allow this committee or anyone else to probe into my private life. This is not what America is all about. To ask me to do that would be to ask me to go beyond fundamental fairness.

Yesterday I called my mother. She was confined to her bed, unable to work and unable to stop crying. Enough is enough.

Mr. Chairman, in my forty-three years on this earth, I have been able, with the help of others and with the help of God, to defy poverty, avoid prison, overcome segregation, bigotry, racism, and obtain one of the finest educations available in this country, but I have not been able to overcome this process. This is worse than any obstacle or anything that I have ever faced.

Throughout my life, I have been energized by the expectation and the hope that in this country, I would be treated fairly in all endeavors. When there was segregation, I hoped there would be fairness one day or someday. When there was bigotry and prejudice, I hoped that there would be tolerance and understanding someday.

Mr. Chairman, I am proud of my life, proud of what I have done, and what I have accomplished, proud of my family. And this process, this process is trying to destroy it all. No job is worth what I have been through, no job. No honor in my life has been so debilitating. Confirm me if you want. Don't confirm me if you are so led, but let this process end. Let me and my family regain our lives.

I never asked to be nominated. It was an honor. Little did I know the price, but it is too high.

I enjoy and appreciate my current position, and I am comfortable with the prospect of returning to my work as a judge on the U.S. Court of Appeals for the D.C. Circuit, and to my friends there. Each of these positions is public service, and I have given at the office. I want my life and my family's life back, and I want them returned expeditiously. I have experienced the exhilaration of new heights, from the moment I was called to Kennebunkport by the president to have lunch, and he nominated me. That was the high point. At that time, I was told eye-to-eye that, "Clarence, you made it this far on merit. The rest is going to be politics." And it surely has been.

There have been other highs. The outpouring of support from my friends of long standing; a bonding like I have never experienced with my old boss, Senator Danforth; the wonderful support of those who have

29

worked with me. There have been prayers said for my family and me by people I know and people I will never meet, prayers that were heard and that sustained not only me but also my wife and my entire family.

Instead of understanding and appreciating the great honor bestowed upon me, I find myself here today defending my name, my integrity, because somehow select portions of confidential documents dealing with this matter were leaked to the public.

Mr. Chairman, I am a victim of this process. My name has been harmed. My integrity has been harmed. My character has been harmed. My family has been harmed. My friends have been harmed. There is nothing this committee, this body, or this country can do to give me my good name back. Nothing.

I will not provide the rope for my own lynching or for further humiliation. I am not going to engage in discussions, nor will I submit to roving questions of what goes on in the most intimate parts of my private life or the sanctity of my bedroom. These are the most intimate parts of my privacy, and they will remain just that, private.

30

WHERE I'M COMING FROM copyright 1991 Barbara Brandon. Dist. by UNIVERSAL PRESS SYNDICATE.
Reprinted with permission. All rights are reserved.

Observations of a Journalist on the Wretched Spectacle

SUSAN WATSON

Boys Will Be Boys While Women Suffer (October 11, 1991)

About twenty-five years ago, when Anita Hill was a little girl living near Tulsa, Oklahoma, and Clarence Thomas was a teenager, a former editor at the *Detroit Free Press* walked by me in the newsroom one evening.

As casually as you please, he blew in my ear.

He didn't say anything. He didn't touch me with his hand or brush against me. He didn't threaten to relegate me to a life of rewriting news releases if I didn't respond to his overture. He just held my eyes a few seconds and continued on his way.

He probably considered the incident a joke or forgot about it seconds later, but I didn't. I felt cheapened and humiliated. I also felt guilty. I figured that I must have done something wrong to trigger his actions.

I puzzled over which aspect of my behavior led him to believe he could be so familiar with me.

I didn't raise a stink because I was new to the job. Back then, a rugged male camaraderie existed in this newsroom and probably every other newsroom across the country. Women were almost interlopers. We walked a tightrope between being a "lady" and being a tough, street reporter.

If you were considered a crybaby in a skirt, you wouldn't get very far.

Trapped in a Catch-22

I raged about the incident to a girlfriend, but if I mentioned it to another editor—and I'm not 100 percent certain I did—I mentioned it casually. I didn't want to make waves; I wanted to get good bylines. The man who made my life miserable that summer night also had the power to end my career.

I continued to work for that editor. He didn't repeat his behavior. Perhaps someone told him to cut it out; perhaps he decided to blow in his wife's ear.

The editor left the paper a few years later. Up until his departure, I was polite to him. On a few occasions when our dinner breaks coincided, we sat at the same table in the building's restaurant. Still, I was haunted by a nagging uneasiness around him.

Nearly a quarter-century later, Anita Hill's sexual harassment charges against Clarence Thomas spilled out in the press. I felt a flush of humiliation all over again.

And when Thomas's supporters attacked Hill's credibility because she didn't make an instant fuss over his alleged sexual advances, I became furious. I found myself giving all the reasons why she—or was it I—would keep quiet.

Twenty-five years ago, fifteen years ago, even ten years ago, women had everything to lose and nothing to gain by complaining about sexual harassment, particularly if it involved what was considered harmless behavior—flirting, making risque comments, or making a pass.

Allegations Kept Secret

A woman who complained vigorously likely would be taunted that she couldn't take a joke.

And if the "boys will be boys" attitude of the male-only Senate Judiciary Committee is any indication, sexual harassment is still being trivialized, at least by certain members of the Senate.

The committee members knew about Hill's allegations during the hearings but decided, after the FBI took conflicting statements from Hill and Thomas, to keep them secret.

They could have, and they should have, delayed the vote on the nomination and launched a full-scale investigation. Even if Hill had proved to be an unwilling witness, she should have been subpoenaed, if necessary.

But that didn't happen, of course.

Even in 1991, Anita Hill—Yale graduate, lawyer, professor—had about as much credibility on this issue as I had back in the mid-'60s. In fact, she may have had even less, since my nemesis cleaned up his act.

Hill's charges would have been buried if someone hadn't recognized what those senators refused to see: Charges of sexual harassment must be taken seriously.

Whether the accused is a candidate for the highest court in the land or an editor at a big-city newspaper, the days of winking at "boyish" pranks and sexual innuendos must end now—not another twenty-five years from now.

Testimony Was a Tragedy for Role Models (October 12, 1991)

WASHINGTON—At first it seemed like a cross between a porno flick and a bad lesson in how not to run a government.

Supreme Court nominee Clarence Thomas, the target of sex harassment charges by Oklahoma law professor Anita Hill, raged against the nomination system that, he said, has spun out of control and damaged his family, his friends, and himself.

"No job is worth what I have been through," he said. Then, in a move that had reporters sitting on the edge of their seats, Thomas came within a sentence of telling the senators to take the Supreme Court job and shove it. Instead, he told the Senate Judiciary panel to "let this process end. Let me and my family regain our lives."

Minutes after his impassioned opening statement, Thomas was replaced on the witness seat by Hill, who faced a table of dark-suited men and talked about sexual harassment she allegedly encountered when working for Thomas. She spoke in graphic terms, repeating what she said were references by Thomas to a Coke can with pubic hair on it, male sexual organs, bestiality, mammary glands, group sex, and rape.

And only a few minutes into her testimony, it was clear that what was happening on Capitol Hill Friday was more than sex, lies, and bad government. It was a tragedy. No one could claim victory—not Thomas, who denied the charges, and not Hill, who, with her seventy-nine-year-old mother looking on, talked graphically about sex and pornography.

For hour after hour, Hill explained why she chose to continue working for Thomas even after he allegedly made sexual overtures. Republican committee member Arlen Specter tried to lead her into a minefield with questions about her relationship with Thomas. Committee chair Joseph Biden tried to lead her to safety with questions about why she was reluctant to go public with her charges and why she called Thomas on the telephone after leaving her job as his assistant at the Equal Employment Opportunity Commission.

In the end, there was no safety.

Hill and Thomas, who both came from relatively poor, hardworking backgrounds and managed to succeed in their chosen field, wound up permanently scarred.

Even if Thomas is named to the Supreme Court, a cloud of doubt will follow him for the rest of his career. He will not be able to rule on a sexual harassment or sex discrimination case without being shadowed by memories of this day. Thomas was presented to the nation by President George Bush as a man of integrity and character. In fact, he had more character than legal experience.

Now that character is riddled with holes.

And the same is true for Hill. According to most accounts, she built a fine reputation as a person of character. By Friday evening, she had been portrayed as a scorned woman with a near-fatal attraction for Thomas.

The real tragedy is that both of these people, Hill and Thomas, represent many of the things we seek for our children, particularly our African American children.

They worked hard. They didn't give in to adversity. They steered clear of the pitfalls that befall so many of our young.

And now, when both should be at or approaching the peak of their careers, they wind up on national television, hurling well-spoken charges at each other in front of the American public.

It was enough to make you either want to cry—or wash your hands.

35

The Devil, Smarmy Senator Says: Hearings on Thomas Degenerate (October 13, 1991)

Day Two of Sex, Lies, and Incredibly Bad Government, also known as the reopened confirmation hearings on Supreme Court nominee Clarence Thomas.

I have this overwhelming urge to slap the living daylights out of each and every member of the Senate Judiciary Committee. In fact, at one point in Saturday morning's testimony—around the time that Republican committee member Orrin Hatch of Utah held up a copy of *The Exorcist* and suggested that Anita Hill's testimony about pubic hair and Coke cans was drawn from page 70 of the book—I wished I had remembered my umbrella. I could have used it to bash those bumbling boobs across their smarmy senatorial seats.

The hearings are an exercise in wretched excess. Like most exercises, they were necessitated by the Judiciary Committee's mind-boggling refusal to take seriously Anita Hill's allegations of sexual harassment.

After all, these were charges against a man nominated to sit on the highest court in the land.

Had any of the fourteen male members of the committee had more than the sense it takes to knot a tie, this graphic and gut-wrenching public testimony could have been avoided. Private sessions could have elicited the same information—without all the TV cameras and reporters. The senators could have taken the time to evaluate the charges, rather than rush to get the nomination to the full Senate floor. But that didn't happen.

These $125,000-plus wonders initially brushed aside Hill's charges. Now those same charges threaten to pillory them as well as the accused.

Senatorial Angst

And the committee members now have the unmitigated gall to pretend that they are upset, offended, and saddened by the spectacle that they wrote, staged, and directed.

One after another, these politicians pull their chins, furrow their brows, and talk about the harm done to both Hill and Thomas.

Then some of those conveniently pious senators, Joe Biden and Orrin Hatch in particular, exhibit an almost prurient interest in the scatological details of Anita Hill's testimony.

Gimme a break, guys. Is this some kind of contest to see who can say "breasts" or "penis" the most times in one hearing?

On Saturday, Hatch, who is a Thomas supporter, recounted with minute detail Hill's most graphic allegations about Thomas. Punctuating each question about sex or anatomy with a disingenuous sigh or specious apology, Hatch put on a bravura performance. His voice rose in anger, quivered in indignation, and softened in disbelief. What a piece of work.

Then Hatch made a clumsy effort to portray the poised law professor as a puppet of wild-eyed liberals who will go to any lengths to destroy conservatives.

Hatch did manage to turn a point to his advantage when he introduced a 1988 sexual harassment lawsuit that referred to the same pornographic film character allegedly mentioned to Hill by Thomas. But then he turned into a fool by whipping out a copy of *The Exorcist* to bolster his puppet theory.

Biden wasn't any better.

After Hill's opening statement, which stunned the audience with its specificity, Biden pressed the woman for more and more details. He exhibited what appeared to be a relentless—and somewhat embarrassing for spectators—curiosity about function, frequency, and anatomy.

And he spent almost as much time defending himself against charges that he botched the earlier hearings as he did questioning Hill.

All in all, Day Two was another disaster, and my biggest regret was that I didn't have my trusty old bumbershoot with me. Just think of the public good I could have done.

Cutline: U.S. Sen. Orrin Hatch holds up *The Exorcist*, a book about driving out the devil, from which he read during hearings Saturday. Hatch suggested the book inspired some details of Anita Hill's account of harassment.

Sen. Alan Simpson, R-Wyo., and Sen. Edward Kennedy, D-Mass., confer on Saturday. The hearings are to resume today.

Hours of Questions, No Resolution: Nominee Ran, Couldn't Hide from Bork (October 14, 1991)

Day Three of Sex, Lies, and Incredibly Bad Government, also known as the Senate Judiciary Committee's confirmation hearings into Clarence Thomas's nomination to the U.S. Supreme Court.

Sometimes truth really is stranger than fiction, particularly in politics.

Take these hearings, for example.

The Bush White House mapped out a careful strategy to get Appeals Court Judge Clarence Thomas confirmed. At the crux of the strategy was one word that summed up everything the White House wanted Thomas to steer clear of.

That one word was *Bork*.

In 1988, U.S. Appeals Court Judge Robert Bork's amazing candor and his controversial legal opinions cost him his chance to take a seat on the Supreme Court. When asked a question, he gave an answer. And it wasn't a mamby-pamby, wishy-washy answer. His answers landed with the force of a slug of lead.

That word was *Borked*, a pithy little verb that means having your hopes shot out of the water.

Opponents of Thomas, another conservative, wanted to Bork him because of his earlier statements attacking affirmative action and quotas. Some women's groups wanted to Bork him because they feared he would join the antiabortion forces on the high court.

Well, the best Borkers of them—civil rights leaders, labor leaders, and feminist leaders—weren't able to derail Thomas's nomination.

White House strategists, painfully aware of what happened in 1988, hit upon the "Invisible Nominee" theory. Nominees, including Thomas, would cloak their views in so much ambiguity that no one would know how they felt about anything, except perhaps the weather.

Thomas seemed Bork-proof. He ducked and dodged so much during his initial round of confirmation hearings that he couldn't be pinned down on anything—except his love for his dear departed grandfather.

Then, surprise of all surprises, on the eve of his confirmation by the full Senate, Clarence Thomas was Borked.

And the person who fired what could be the fatal shot at him was none other than a prim and proper former Republican administration mid-level bureaucrat named Anita Hill, a woman who thought the world of Robert Bork.

Hill met Bork when she was a law student at Yale and took one of his classes. She later rallied to his defense when others castigated him.

Thomas's confirmation, which looked like a sure thing, became clouded in doubt when the public learned that Hill, who worked for Thomas in two federal agencies, accused Thomas of sexually harassing her on both of those jobs.

In other words, despite everything the White House did to protect Thomas, he was Borked.

And it wasn't by a wild-eyed women's libber. Not by a prochoicer. Not by the combined forces of the liberal civil rights establishment.

No way.

The man was Borked by an educated African American female attorney, a Black Urban Professional, a Buppy if you will, who looked on the surface amazingly similar to Thomas himself.

Both graduated from Yale; both came from rural backgrounds; both found a place for themselves in a Republican administration; both had strong family ties.

From everything that's been said about Hill, she'd be the last person the anti-Thomas forces would choose to launch the Bork missile.

38

And yet she did—with what could be deadly accuracy.

It's like I said, truth really is stranger than fiction.

Cutline: Judge Susan Hoerschner reads an opening statement as Ellen Wells, John Carr, and Joel Paul wait to testify on behalf of law professor Anita Hill before the Senate Judiciary Committee on Sunday.

In a show of support for Supreme Court nominee Clarence Thomas, former colleagues are sworn in Sunday . . . J. C. Alvarez, Nancy Elizabeth Fitch, Diane Holt, and Phyllis Berry Myers.

Divided Senate Faces Agonizing Vote: The Winners of These Are Clear Losers (October 15, 1991)

Day Four of Sex, Lies, and Incredibly Bad Government, also known as the reopened confirmation hearings of U.S. Supreme Court nominee Clarence Thomas.

Now that the Senate Judiciary Committee has concluded its hearings into Anita Hill's charges against Thomas, the time has come to announce the winners of the first, and I hope the last, Watson Awards for the most memorable—or most forgettable—moments in the hearings.

To paraphrase a line heard in every awards ceremony: Remember, there are no winners here, only losers.

Without further ado . . .

The "I Would Kill Myself Before I Went Out with This Man" Award goes to John Doggett III, the Austin, Texas, businessman and casual acquaintance of Hill. Doggett monopolized the final hours of the hearings with his pompous posturing about his education, his community service, his irresistible charm over women, and his uncanny ability to tell by the look on Anita Hill's face that she wanted his body and had sexual fantasies about him and other men.

The "I Would Quit My Job and Try to Get on General Assistance in Michigan Before I Shared an Office with Them" Award goes to former Equal Employment Opportunity Commission employees J. C. Alvarez and Phyllis Berry Myers. Alvarez and Myers, who testified Sunday night on Thomas's behalf, obviously disliked Hill so much that it's a wonder she got out of the EEOC alive. Alvarez practically called Hill an uppity you-know-what, who acted "a little holier than thou." Myers, who sat ramrod straight during her testimony, vacillated between gushing like a lovestruck schoolkid over Thomas and accusing Hill of having a crush on the man.

The "I Know Your Mother's Watching This Program" Award goes to John Carr, a New York corporation lawyer who briefly dated Hill in the early '80s. Asked by committee chairman Joseph Biden to describe their relationship, Carr responded: "I guess I would say we didn't get but so far."

The "Earth-to-Space: Is Anybody in There" Award goes to Alabama Senator Howell Heflin for his incredibly sensitive and enlightened definition of date rape. "Date rape is where people go out on dates and rape occurs," he said.

The "Born-Again Black" Award, also known as the "Look Ma, I'm Still Black" Award, goes to Judge Clarence Thomas, the conservative former EEOC chairman, for his stirring oration about the devastating effect of American racism on black males. Thomas spent his professional career downplaying the role of racism on blacks. When he was hit with Hill's sexual harassment charges, he suddenly became the victim of a high-tech lynching.

The "Sometimes It's Better to Burn Your Bridges Behind You Even If You Don't Know How to Swim" Award goes to Anita Hill. Her series of telephone calls to Thomas after she left the EEOC came back to haunt her.

The "Speak Clearly So Mommy Can Hear What You're Saying" Award also goes to Anita Hill for her perfect pronunciation of the name of porno film star Long Dong Silver while her mother sat behind her. Hill charged that Thomas mentioned Silver's physical attributes to her.

39

The "Absolutely, Positively, Totally Dumbest Question Ever Asked" Award to Iowa Senator Charles Grassley. After sitting through allegations that Thomas was a foul-mouthed, sexually aggressive bully, Grassley asked Thomas what Thomas's grandfather would have advised him.

The "Don't Get Me in the Middle of This" Award goes to Senator Edward Kennedy of Massachusetts, who, while briefly presiding over the hearings in Biden's absence, was caught in the middle of an argument between Heflin and Senator Orrin Hatch of Utah. The subject of the argument: date rape. One of Kennedy's nephews has been charged with raping a woman he had just met.

The "I Don't Believe You Said That" Award goes to Alvarez, the former EEOC employee and Hill coworker. Alvarez said Hill leveled the charges against Thomas to get publicity. She's becoming "the Rosa Parks of sexual harassment," Alvarez snapped.

The "Best Single Moment of the Hearings" Award goes to 2:01 A.M. Monday, when Biden gaveled the disgraceful sessions to a close.

Thomas Calls for Healing: For Everyone's Sake, Let's Hope He Told the Truth (October 16, 1991)

I believe Anita Hill, but I hope she's lying through her teeth.

I hope that newly confirmed U.S. Supreme Court Associate Justice Clarence Thomas is every bit the fair, honest, decent, and sensitive man that his supporters claim. I hope, as someone recently said, that he is indeed a man who possesses a feminist's understanding of women's issues.

And most of all, I hope that Clarence Thomas never sexually harassed any coworker or employee. I hope he didn't ask any female employee about the size of her breasts, comment on the shape of someone's behind, discuss dirty movies, pressure female coworkers for dates, or brag about his anatomy or his endurance.

I hope he didn't do any of those things, because, if he did, the truth will come out. It always does, sooner or later. And the effects of such a revelation would send shock waves through the nation and make the recently concluded hearings seem mild by comparison.

Not only would Thomas's credibility be ruined—and it wasn't that strong to begin with—but the integrity of the highest court in the land also would be impugned.

The outcome of any case in which he was involved, particularly cases involving women's rights, sexual harassment, or racial discrimination, immediately would be called into question. Cries of foul play would rend the air. In the case of particularly close votes, few would feel that justice had been done.

We would witness the kind of judicial upheaval that you would have to measure on the Richter scale. And the upset in the nation's judicial system, from the highest court to the township magistrate's office, would be nothing compared to the explosions on the political scene.

There would be hell to pay for those politicians who saw fit to trash Hill in order to rescue Thomas's reputation. Even those politicians who voted for confirmation because they believed that Thomas deserved the benefit of the doubt will be called to task.

I can hear the protests now. "In matters as crucial as this," the argument will go, "the benefit of the doubt should have gone not to Thomas but to the nation." The dictates of common sense should have made those politicians send the President back to the drawing board for another, less controversial nominee.

If Anita Hill isn't lying, our troubles have just begun.

Biases Would Deepen

Men and women will be at each other's throats, and you'll see blood, not bruises. Feminists will charge that the male-dominated Senate initially ignored Hill's accusations because she is a woman.

There's more. The strained relations between Blacks and whites in this country will become even more strained, more bitter. If Anita Hill isn't a bald-faced liar or a crazy person, then Thomas engaged in the worst kind of racial politics to get his Supreme Court seat. If the unflappable Oklahoma law professor isn't a liar, then Thomas unleashed under oath a thunderstorm of charges about racism and intolerance just to cover his own egregious behavior.

Blacks who justifiably raise a cry of racism or intolerance could be met with more scorn than usual. A protest over racial discrimination could be met more frequently with an arched eyebrow and a look that said, "You're just trying to pull a Clarence Thomas on me."

Those Blacks, particularly conservative Blacks, who supported Thomas would be called political opportunists who willingly put on blinders to help him get his seat.

As much as I believe Anita Hill's testimony, as much as I was impressed by her composure, her calm, and her rock-steady presentation, I still hope that she is lying.

I hope that Clarence Thomas's categorical denial, which was cloaked in flaming racial rhetoric, is true.

Because if it isn't, we ain't seen nothing yet.

While Homeless Live on Streets, Nation Lives a Fantasy (October 20, 1991)

It was Tuesday morning, and I was looking out the window of the cab that was taking me to Capitol Hill for the Senate vote on Clarence Thomas's nomination to the U.S. Supreme Court.

The driver cruised down one boulevard after another, past elegant marble buildings with shiny brass fixtures.

I wasn't paying attention to the scenery. I was thinking about all the psychological mumbo jumbo that had been bandied about during the closing days of the tortured process.

Words like *delusional* and *schizophrenic* had bounced off the richly marbled walls of the hearing room. Under sparkling chandeliers, Anita Hill was described as a woman who fell victim to her own improbable romantic hallucinations.

Soft whispers about fantasies tiptoed up graceful federal stairways. Everyone seemed preoccupied with that one woman's psychological well-being—or the lack of it.

Liar, Then a Schizophrenic

People who couldn't spell the word *schizophrenic* suddenly funnel billions of dollars into foreign countries while citizens here go jobless and hungry. The White House speaks of economic recovery while the country grapples with a recession. We ignore poverty and homelessness at our feet.

Surely, that kind of behavior makes us as a nation just as delusional as that dancing man, just as socially disconnected and just as swept up by fantasy.

42   I only hope that now that Anita Hill's detractors have had their say about her so-called emotional problems, those same people will turn their attention to the emotional problems of this country. After all, any nation that can pretend that its poor and sick do not exist obviously isn't playing with a full deck.

A Wretched Spectacle (December 16, 1991)

At the conclusion of the second round of the Clarence Thomas confirmation hearings—the sessions where Anita Hill leveled those sexual harassment charges—I gave out eleven awards for the most memorable moments in the hearings.

If you missed the awards, the categories included topics like the "I Would Kill Myself Before I Went Out with This Man" Award. That prize went to that incredibly pompous Texas executive who said he could tell by the look on Hill's face that she wanted his body.

A reader from Fenton said I should have added a twelfth award. As M.K. wrote: "The 'Sorry I Can't Hear You Because My Mind Is Already Made Up' Award goes to Susan Watson, for refusing to consider any possibility whatsoever that circumstances could be anything other than exactly what Anita Hill claims."

Dear M.K., my mind wasn't completely made up, but I still accept your award with deep appreciation. And I want to thank the members of the Senate Judiciary Committee, also known as the "You Don't Have to Have a Brain to Be Elected to Office" Club, for making this honor possible. Without their incredibly stupid refusal to take seriously Hill's charges when they first learned of them, the public might not have been subjected to such a wretched spectacle, and the Watson Awards might not exist.

43

African American Women In Defense of Ourselves

As women of African descent, we are deeply troubled by the recent nomination, confirmation and seating of Clarence Thomas as an Associate Justice of the U.S. Supreme Court. We know that the presence of Clarence Thomas on the Court will be continually used to divert attention from historic struggles for social justice through suggestions that the presence of a Black man on the Supreme Court constitutes an assurance that the rights of African Americans will be protected. Clarence Thomas' public record is ample evidence this will not be true. Further, the consolidation of a conservative majority on the Supreme Court seriously endangers the rights of all women, poor and working class people and the elderly. The seating of Clarence Thomas is an affront not only to African American women and men, but to all people concerned with social justice.

We are particularly outraged by the racist and sexist treatment of Professor Anita Hill, an African American woman who was maligned and castigated for daring to speak publicly of her own experience of sexual abuse. The malicious defamation of Professor Hill insulted all women of African descent and sent a dangerous message to any woman who might contemplate a sexual harassment complaint.

We speak here because we recognize that the media are now portraying the Black community as prepared to tolerate both the dismantling of affirmative action and the evil of sexual harassment in order to have any Black man on the Supreme Court. We want to make clear that the media have ignored or distorted many African American voices. We will not be silenced.

Many have erroneously portrayed the allegations against Clarence Thomas as an issue of either gender or race. As women of African descent, we understand sexual harassment as both. We further understand that Clarence Thomas outrageously manipulated the legacy of lynching in order to shelter himself from Anita Hill's allegations. To deflect attention away from the reality of sexual abuse in African American women's lives, he trivialized and misrepresented this painful part of African American people's history. This country, which has a long legacy of racism and sexism, has never taken the sexual abuse of Black women seriously. Throughout U.S. history Black women have been sexually stereotyped as immoral, insatiable, perverse; the initiators in all sexual contacts—abusive or otherwise. The common assumption in legal proceedings as well as in the larger society has been that Black women cannot be raped or otherwise sexually abused. As Anita Hill's experience demonstrates, Black women who speak of these matters are not likely to be believed. In 1991, we cannot tolerate this type of dismissal of any one Black woman's experience or this attack upon our collective character without protest, outrage, and resistance.

As women of African descent, we express our vehement opposition to the policies represented by the placement of Clarence Thomas on the Supreme Court. The Bush administration, having obstructed the passage of civil rights legislation, impeded the extension of unemployment compensation, cut student aid and dismantled social welfare programs, has continually demonstrated that it is not operating in our best interests. Nor is this appointee. We pledge ourselves to continue to speak out in defense of one another, in defense of the African American community and against those who are hostile to social justice no matter what color they are. No one will speak for us but ourselves.

A Righteous Rage and a Grassroots Mobilization

BARBARA RANSBY

———————————————————————————————

The Senate hearings surrounding
the confirmation of Clarence Thomas to the U.S. Supreme Court, especially that part of the hearings involving Anita Hill's allegations of sexual
harassment, were among the major media events of the decade. Every
major newspaper ran daily front-page coverage, often including verbatim
transcripts of witnesses' testimony. Editorials examined even the most
obscure angles of the topics at hand. The electronic media were even
more obsessed, with some channels offering gavel-to-gavel coverage of
the day-long proceedings and others rearranging schedules to offer extended news broadcasts highlighting the details of each day's events. Yet
in the midst of this media orgy, an obvious set of voices was consistently
muted or overlooked. These were the voices of Black Feminists, or Womanists, who, in contrast to the painfully superficial commentators and ill-
informed theorists masquerading as analysts, could have synthesized most
of the complex issues of race, class, and gender raised by the hearing.
But the mainstream media would have none of it. Aside from a few one-
line quotes in lengthy news stories or articles in the alternative press, a
Black feminist/Womanist viewpoint was sorely absent from the national
debate. Voices of Black women who for decades have struggled to address the concerns of Black women and redress the injustice of racial and
sexual oppression highlighted so graphically by the mistreatment of Hill
were wholly ignored. Where were the interviews with the likes of Barbara

Smith, Audre Lourde, Mary Frances Berry, Angela Davis, Gloria Hull, June Jordan, or any of dozens of other prominent African American feminist/Womanists one could name? In fact, it was this blatant and inexcusable exclusion of Black Womanists and feminists from the national dialogue on an issue that impinged so dramatically on our lives that inspired some of us to launch the campaign to carve out a public forum for our views—even if we had to purchase that forum with the meager resources we could collectively muster. The theme of the mobilization and the title of the ad campaign almost flowed naturally. What were we? "African American Women in Defense of Ourselves."

Armed only with our frustration, our rage, and the hope and confidence that many other women of African descent shared our sentiments, Elsa Barkley Brown, Deborah King, and I initiated a campaign to mobilize Black women to break the imposed silence on this issue. Sexism on the one side and racism on the other had served to suffocate Black women's voices. There was no place for our anger or our insights. Ironically, an event that made a single Black woman more visible to more people than at any time in our recent memory simultaneously signified our collective invisibility. Given the artificial way in which most observers dichotomized the issues underlying the hearings as having to do with *either* race or gender, Hill was rendered raceless, and thus Black women's unique experience as both African Americans and women was disregarded. In light of this larger picture, our goal became to get as many Black women as we could, within a very short time span, to sign onto a statement that would challenge the distorted view of Black public opinion being offered by the mainstream media, expand the parameters of the debate, and serve as a catalyst for future efforts. We wanted specifically to speak out in opposition to the sexual abuse and degradation of black women, including that of Hill, to condemn what we felt certain were misogynist and reactionary policies and practices by Thomas, and to dispel any erroneous notions that he enjoyed ubiquitous support among Black women. We decided that since the *New York Times* is one of the most widely distributed papers in the nation and often leads the way in setting the tone for distorted and biased coverage, this is where we needed to insist that an alternative voice be heard. In addition, since we were as eager to enter the internal dialogue within the Black community as we were to offer an alternative perspective in the national media, we decided to put the statement in seven African American papers across the country as well. The statement appeared in the *Chicago Defender*, the (New York) *City Sun*, the *Los Angeles Sentinel*, the *San Francisco Sun Reporter*, the *D.C. Spotlight*, the *Carolinian*, and the *Atlanta Inquirer*. It was published in letter form in the *Amsterdam News*, and portions of it have been reprinted in *Essence* and *The Black Scholar*.

A Call to the Community of African American Women

As we initially drafted and redrafted the statement, trying to be as precise and forceful as possible, we grappled with the conflicting realities of limited space on the one hand and the need to fill so many voids in the popular dialogue on the other. There were the constant dual pressures of wanting to say more but having to say less. I remember one conversation with Elsa Brown, in particular, regarding the section of the statement that discusses the negative stereotypes concerning Black women's sexuality. In one of my more pragmatic moods, I insisted that we needed to be more succinct, and therefore we should simply say, "African American women have been negatively stereotyped," and leave it at that. People would know what we meant, I reasoned. But in her calm, determined manner, Elsa insisted that we really had to spell it out. She was right. The result was the passage that read: "Throughout U.S. history, Black women have been sexually stereotyped as immoral, insatiable, perverse; the initiators of all sexual contacts—abusive or otherwise." The passage ultimately, I think, helped to counter the invisibility others were attempting to impose on us and demanded that the flesh-and-blood reality of our history and our lives be acknowledged.

Another conscious effort on our part to be proactive, and not simply defensive, was in the construction of the introductory paragraph. This was largely Deborah King's influence, as I recall. Deborah was concerned, and we all agreed, that we should underscore that our opposition to Thomas extended well beyond the single issue of sexual harassment. Based on his record on a range of social issues, he had proven himself to be antagonistic not only to some narrowly defined set of "women's issues," abstracted from their racial, class, or political contingencies, but also to the interests of all those concerned with social justice in the broadest sense. Taking such an inclusive stance was an extension of the long-standing Black Womanist tradition of embracing multiple visions of change simultaneously through the lens of our multiple yet inextricably related identities as members of an oppressed racial group, a subjugated sex, and, more often than not, an exploited class. In essence, the statement attempted to carve out a vision and critique that was self-consciously progressive on multiple fronts.

I think we also successfully resisted the tendency to deify Hill, the individual, as the patron saint of Black womanhood. While we supported Hill and admired her personal courage on this issue, from what we knew at the time of her politics on other equally relevant issues, there were serious differences that could not be glossed over for the sake of political expediency in one immediate circumstance. In rushing to Hill's defense,

47

we were not prepared to leave behind those who have been the principal victims of the Reagan-Bush assault on poor people of color—a war in which Hill, it appeared, had served loyally on the wrong side. While many women who called or wrote to sign onto the statement were motivated largely by personal concern for Hill, others were explicit in their insistence that the statement be general rather than a personal endorsement of Hill as a martyr or symbolic leader of our efforts. In her astute essay published in *Black Scholar*, Joy James (1992) effectively outlines the potential problems and contradictions inherent in such heroine construction, especially in this case. For men, the fact that such humiliating and malicious treatment could be meted out to Hill, without respite, was only a small measure of the abusive treatment poor Black women receive on a daily basis and therefore, in principle, needed to be opposed. It is treatment we can expect more of in the future, if we do not take seriously the task of mobilizing ourselves as Black women to be vocal and visible forces for change in the present as we have been in the past. Therefore, it was essential not only that we express our outrage at the mistreatment of Hill but also that we express our rage at the assault on poor and working-class Black women who suffer the brunt of oppression in our society. Specifically, when we were asked if the campaign should be characterized as Black female academicians coming to the aid of a colleague, we emphatically said no. We were speaking out as women of African descent, and we consciously tried to transcend as many barriers as possible in making our collective statement.

Responses to Our Call

A few criticisms and a number of weaknesses notwithstanding, the response we received to our ad campaign was overwhelmingly positive. In the first few days of the campaign, we sent out letters and faxes and made phone calls to friends, colleagues, and fellow activists across the country. We obtained a post office box and a voice-mail answering service. The responses came pouring in. Some women who called our voice-mail wept openly and exclaimed the sense of relief they felt at hearing an affirmation of their anger and an articulation of their views. On another level, the tactic of a signature ad served a very useful purpose. Unlike an opinion piece written by a single author, one who is deemed worthy of publication by the editorial elites, the ad allowed hundreds of women to feel ownership of the statement, to vent their anger and their rage in a public forum. And while we invited contributions to cover the cost of the ad, no woman's name was excluded if she could not afford to make such a contribution, and we made that point clear.

Within the course of a week, the process of mobilizing support and raising funds for the campaign became a grassroots effort that took on a life of its own, fairly independent of the three of us who had initiated it. Hundreds of women came to feel that the statement was *their* statement. Some called to suggest changes, lawyers provided solicited and unsolicited legal advice on liability concerns, and, most importantly, the ad became a stimulus for numerous discussions and debates. Some of the questions raised included: Should Black women publicly criticize a "brother"? Was a white publication the forum for such a criticism? Was voicing our sentiments a political act or a futile after-the-fact gesture? Were we being divisive? And could the money for the ad be better spent? We grappled seriously with all of these concerns and concluded several things. First, it was not our decision to argue out the issue of sexual harassment in the mainstream media; that process was already occurring. Whether or not the national media was the most appropriate venue was a moot point. At the same time, however, which voices were being heard in that public debate was not moot, and our voices were being systematically excluded. I personally reflected on the phrase "speaking truth to power" which graces the masthead of the *City Sun*, a Black-run newspaper in New York City. Breaking silence, naming a problem, pushing open the narrow limits of the dialogue is a first, but necessary, step in the larger process of political mobilization and action. In terms of the money spent on the ad, we clearly did not see the purchase of a platform for our views as an endorsement of or act of support for the *New York Times*. Rather, we saw the biased coverage in papers like the *Times* as the very impetus for our action. Furthermore, tens of thousands of Black people across the country spend tens of thousands of dollars annually for the dubious privilege of reading the *New York Times*. For our expenditure, on at least one occasion, we would see our own viewpoint aired in the paper's pages, in our own words, and not in words imposed on us as a refraction of someone else's view of who we are and what we think, feel, and need.

49

The campaign lasted about six weeks. During that time, the outpouring of support from women of African descent across the nation helped to strengthen old alliances for some of us and served as the starting point for new relationships and bonds of sisterhood for others. It also revealed an invisible but potentially powerful national network of Black women that already existed. Within a few short weeks, sister-to-sister connections were being made all across the country, from New York to San Francisco and multiple points in between. To listen each day to the voices of female callers and to hear women, most of whom I did not know, speak in words and emotions that were my own was an empowering and affirming experience, especially given the current conservative political climate in which women like us often feel under assault from racism, sexism, and classism on a daily basis. The rapidity with which the word got out and the level of consensus among the signators reveal a shared sense of community among Black women, born of a common set of experiences and reflective of a great deal of diversity at the same time.

In addition to relying on preexisting local groups of Black women to publicize the ad campaign, we relied primarily on word-of-mouth. And fortunately, many of us had big enough mouths to yell the message far and wide. After the initial outreach was made, a ripple effect took over. Letters were rewritten and circulated to additional networks of like-minded friends and colleagues. Women in offices and departments got together, collected funds, and sent their contributions and lists of names in a single batch. Announcements were made in classes, at conferences, in churches, and at meetings as a way of recruiting more support for the campaign. At the height of the campaign, we were receiving more than 150 calls and several dozen letters a day. Of course, with no organizational structure in place to handle the volume of responses and to do bookkeeping and clerical tasks associated with a large and short-term mobilization, the campaign was a grassroots effort in the best political sense and a logistical nightmare in the worst practical sense. In any case, we were proud of the result. As Barbara Smith said to me recently: "This was the first time women of African descent mobilized so quickly and broadly to respond directly to a national political issue in a visible and public way." While not earth-shaking or inherently revolutionary, it was an important landmark in Black women's political history.

Another important component of the campaign and a source of strength was the support we received from allies who were not African-American women. In fact, the initial outreach for the campaign was conducted on two fronts simultaneously. While Deborah, Elsa, and I circulated a letter addressed primarily to other Black women, Tom Holt, a history professor at the University of Chicago and former Civil Rights activist, made a similar appeal to Black men to lend moral and financial support to the campaign as a matter of principle and an act of solidarity. Several individual European American women also launched fund-raising initiatives on our behalf. A few of them generously provided bridge loans to enable us to make our publication deadline before all the individual checks from signators and supporters had cleared. These allies acted from a position of respect which recognized the importance and political significance of a statement conceived and executed by women of African descent. This was especially true since at the center of the fray was the abusive treatment of a Black woman, and our collective response was being distortedly portrayed as either quiet acquiescence to this affront, a tacit endorsement of it, or a proxy protest orchestrated by European-American women. This context made our particular statement all the more essential. To those who supported our effort who are not women of African descent, we are very grateful. Moreover, it is the type of selfless support offered by brothers like Tom Holt and sisters too numerous to name which promises to form the foundation for future principled coalitions between men and women and between whites and people of color— coalitions based on mutual respect, shared vision, and an appreciation for oppressed communities to enjoy a margin of autonomy in our political organizing efforts.

Where Do We Go From Here?

The fundamental question at this juncture is: Which way forward? Since the culmination of the ad campaign in November 1991, there have been numerous discussions and debates, on local and national levels, about how to follow through on our promise that the mobilization would be not a one-shot deal but a catalyst for future action. Groups of women in some key cities took the initiative to convene follow-up meetings on their own. In Chicago, a group of about thirty women who came together as a result of the ad has been meeting on a monthly basis since January 1992. Other groups have begun meeting in Philadelphia, New York, and San Francisco. Similar meetings are planned in other cities. Some of the suggestions that have emerged ranged from the formation of a loose national network of African-American women and the establishment of some method for maintaining contact with one another, to the formation of a national organization of progressive African American women. Another suggestion is the creation of a Black women's writing collective which would submit articles to various publications on issues of concern to Black women.

Whatever strategies we employ, we need to think of formulating a national agenda for liberation that defines race, class, and gender as inextricably linked variables. Vicky Crawford (1992) urges us to tap the "cultural memory of Black women's resistance and struggle . . . to form networks . . . and to keep things stirring" (p. 17). Maya Angelou (1992), who, ironically, supported Thomas when he was first nominated, insightfully suggested that we "need to haunt the halls of history and listen anew to the ancestors' wisdom." Melba Boyd (1992) insists that we define "a Black woman's justice [as] a people's justice" (p. 27). And, finally, Marcia Ann Gillespie (1992) concludes a poignant article in *Ms.* with the following message:

> It's time Black women stopped dancing around and avoiding speaking out on issues of rape and sexual violence, on incest, on femicide, on the misogyny that pervades our community. We need to make it clear once and for all that Black men are not the only ones endangered in the United States of America. The only script we will follow is the one we write, or the one that acknowledges our existence, our truths. We speak in tongues. We will be heard. (p. 43)

51

References

Angelou, Maya. "The Black Community Speaks Out on the Racial and Sexual Politics of Thomas vs. Hill." In *Court of Appeal*, ed. Robert Chrisman. New York: Ballantine, 1992.

Boyd, Melba. "Collard Greens, Clarence Thomas, and the High-tech Rape of Anita Hill."
    In *Court of Appeal*, ed. Robert Chrisman. New York: Ballantine, 1992.
Crawford, Vicky. "On the Clarence Thomas hearings." In *Court of Appeal*, ed. Robert
    Chrisman. New York: Ballantine, 1992.
Gillespie, Marcia A. "We Speak in Tongues." *Ms.* (Jan.–Feb. 1992): 43.
James, Joy. "On Anita Hill–Clarence Thomas." In *Court of Appeal*, ed. Robert Chrisman.
    New York: Ballantine, 1992.

Social and Political Thought on Anita Hill from the Feminist and Black Communities: The Scapegoat and the Sacrificial Lamb

PATRICIA COLEMAN-BURNS

Like other red-letter benchmarks 53
in history, such as *Brown* v. *Board of Education, Roe* v. *Wade*, the assassinations of Malcolm X and Martin Luther King, Jr., the rebellions of the 1960s and those in Los Angeles in 1992, the Clarence Thomas hearings and the Hill-Thomas controversy have had a profound impact on society. Life in these United States around gender issues and human relationships, particularly for the political left, will never be the same. The discussions around the event were varied and highly controversial. Interestingly enough, the greatest differences occurred within those communities most directly affected by the controversy, the African American and feminist communities. For white women who tended to make a gender-only analysis, the question of whom to believe was clear: Anita Hill. Many African Americans, female and male, feminists and nonfeminists who considered themselves "progressive" around Black women's issues and racism gave support to the "sister" with little equivocation. For African Americans, male and female, who tended not to believe Hill but to believe Thomas, or who believed Hill but were silent, race and race pride were paramount. Key to understanding these extremely passionate and polarized analyses is recognizing that each perspective identifies a different external enemy or enemies, and that each reveals different internal contradictions. The question is whether the intersection of gender, race, and class accounts for the varied analyses of external and internal enemies

within each of the affected communities. The answer may facilitate the understanding of the significance of the Hill-Thomas controversy to the social and political history and thought of the feminist and African American communities, specifically, and to the United States in general.

The purpose of this essay is to analyze representative rhetoric that emerged from the feminist and Black intellectual communities in response to the Hill-Thomas conflict. The methodology combines a social movement and Black rhetorical genre approach to political ideologies with a Burkeian approach for examining the metaphorical "enemy," the "scapegoat," and the "sacrificial lamb," as defined through each ideological perspective. The interplay and intersection of race, gender, and class provide a schematic within which the rhetorical drama of the controversy unfolds. Key to the Burkeian analysis are the concepts of the contradiction between internal and external struggle, purification, and transformation. First, each perspective is identified and defined rhetorically in terms of the concepts of gender, race, and class. Second, the external "enemy" will be named for each perspective. Third, the metaphors of purification through scapegoating will be identified and the internal enemy named. Finally, the essay will provide rhetorical strategies for mitigating the tensions between the perspectives and suggest possible ways in which the Hill-Thomas debate can be a point for advancing the whole society toward fundamental change, rather than a backward movement caused by polarization and retrenchment of social forces.

54

Gender, Race, and Class

The most significant emerging theoretical and ideological contribution of the Hill-Thomas controversy to social and political thought is its provision for examination and clarification of the intersection of gender, race, and class as dominant themes. From the parochial perspective of the media, the 1992 Democratic National Convention, European Americans, and particularly feminists, one would conclude that the meaning of Anita Hill—that is, the collective social consciousness—had already been defined as a historic watershed in the women's movement. At least half a dozen times during the July 1992 Democratic National Convention in New York City, the name of Professor Anita Hill was invoked as an example of the rising activism of U.S. women. The crossover of issues between gender and race boundaries so often sought in the social, economic, and political arenas was easily achieved in electoral politics through an African American woman who had become the heroine of many, but primarily of European American, middle-class, "liberal" feminists. However, once again, even in a discussion around an African American male and female, the major perspective tended to exclude the Black voice, or to make that perspective marginal, rather than being inclusive and viewing the African American perspective as central.

So there were two "feminist" perspectives. One tended to be European American, making a gender analysis. The other tended to be African American, making an analysis that reflected the intersection of gender and race. But there was also a grassroots perspective, steeped in race pride and class victimization, which was particularly antifeminist. Was there some common ground around which these three perspectives could come together to inform an advanced analysis of racism, classism, and sexism issues generated by the Hill-Thomas event? The difference in the response of all three of these cohorts—the African American masses, European and African American feminists, and the African American intellectual left—can be most cogently understood by examining how the perspectives form a social and political thought paradigm. The genre of social and political thought of feminists and African Americans provides for the exploration of several other perspectives and paradigms of analysis, particularly among the African American masses, as a way of understanding the convoluted nature of the Hill-Thomas controversy. This genre can be utilized to examine the various perspectives, not only based on whether they make a gender-only, race-and-gender, or race-only analysis, but on the basis of attitudes toward change and the status quo, and on possible avenues for change. These attitudes can be defined as "political tendencies" (Coleman-Burns 1992).

Political tendencies represent a particular predisposition toward understanding one's reality and are particularly useful in understanding a person's or a group's nuances of thought among the collective whole. These represent subtle distinctions within ideas, belief systems, and ideologies. Political positions analyzing issues of public policy are excellent tools for locating a person's or a group's political tendency. Tendencies can be generally located on a continuum by plotting various positive or negative attitudes toward change and the existing order (see Fig. A). Therefore, we can locate a group or individual to the left or to the right of center by surveying attitudes on public policies such as sexual harassment and identifying opinions on the Hill-Thomas controversy.

In applying this analysis to the Hill-Thomas controversy, the salient questions are: What is the attitude toward change in terms of the role of women? What is the attitude toward the status quo in terms of its treatment of women? Of African Americans? Of African American women? Of African American men? The Left tends to be pro change and, therefore, in favor of extending the rights of the status quo to oppressed groups, such as European American women, people of color, gays, and so on. The extremes (revolutionary, radical, reactionary, and counterrevolutionary) are, to varying degrees, opposed to the status quo and favor a forward or backward movement and goals. The revolutionary calls for a rapid progression toward complete and total change; the reactionary sees a return to the "good old days." Conversely, the Right is opposed to

Fig. A Political Tendencies

Attitudes toward change	LEFT			RIGHT		
	+++	++	+	–	– –	– – –
	R	R	L	C	R	C
	E	A	I	O	E	O
	V	D	B	N	A	U
	O	I	E	S	C	N
	L	C	R	E	T	T
	U	A	A	R	I	E
	T	L	L	V	O	R
	I			A	N	–
	O			T	A	R
	N			I	R	E
	A			V	Y	V
	R			E		O
	Y					L
						U
						T
						I
						O
						N
						A
						R
						Y

Attitudes toward status quo (public policy) ← –/+ + + +/– →

_____ MIDDLE _____

_____ EXTREMES _____ EXTREMES _____

change, and the middle supports the status quo (the existing or traditional order).

Historically, the genre of Black and feminist social and political thought, from revolutionary to counterrevolutionary, has generally been located well within the "Left" perspectives of the larger European American and nonfeminist society. When various forces are in motion in the whole society to change the direction of the country, this movement is most often stimulated by Black and feminist thought, as was true with Hill-Thomas. These societal forces, as a result, are generally more sensitive to issues around Blacks, students, women, and the aged in all racial and ethnic groups (Stewart, Smith, and Denton 1984). When society as a whole moves toward the Right, the range of tendencies for Black thinkers tends also to retreat backward toward the Right, which perhaps accounts for the diverse and often denigrating points of view that surfaced.

In the 1990s, a troublesome conservative African American force emerged ("Thomas Nomination" 1991; Phillips 1982; Carter 1991; Magner 1991). Conservatives see change occurring within the status quo and within the legitimate means of change. The Civil Rights Movement is often cited as the point at which the African American community, previously identified as a permanent underclass, including all Blacks, was split in two: a middle-class, which could benefit from the gains of affirmative action, and a ghettoized class. When all Blacks were lumped into one group by European American society, there tended to be greater unity of thought. Now there are two Black classes, and the gap between them is getting wider (Harrison 1992; Blonston 1991; Naison 1992). This accounts for the diversity in perspectives articulated from within the African American community.

Key, then, to understanding a person's perspective is understanding how he or she sees the whole picture. This requires an examination of the person's worldview, including not only where they are on particular issues and public policies within a given time period but also their understanding of the fundamental structures, values, and ideologies of the entire society. To understand the person's "big picture" in terms of how they see the world, what the problem is, how it got to be a problem, what the solutions are, and who will make the necessary changes helps to further the distinctions. Coupled with political tendencies, therefore, is Black ideology.

57

Black Ideologies

There are three basic perspectives or ideologies from which most African Americans operate.

Reformism, assimilation, accommodation, integration: Defines the "good life" as being achieved through moving into the existing order, the complete intermingling in the cultural, economic, social, and political life of the United States through acculturation or the "melting-pot" concept. Advocates the supremacy of western hegemony and ideology.

Nationalism, pan-Africanism, separatism, systematic nationalism: Defines the "good life" as being achieved through creating a separate society which may be within the geographic borders of the United States, within the minds of African Americans, or in Africa. Rejects European/ Western society in all forms. Identifies its enemies as "Uncle Toms" as well as European Americans and racist society. Makes a race analysis: Race is primary. Revolutionary nationalism can share some features of revolutionary ideology.

Revolution, radicalism, revolutionary womanism/feminism, Marxism/Leninism, revolutionary nationalism, African socialism: Defines the "good life" as being achieved through the destruction of the old, oppressive, and exploitive order and the creation of a "new order" and new wo/man. Problems cannot be solved within the existing societal structures and institutions. Utilizes any and all progressive ideologies. Identifies the enemy on the basis of analysis and on the intersection of race, class, and/or gender. Challenges African Americans to transform the external and internal through a cultural revolution, consciousness changing, and collective education. Addresses rhetoric toward various "social forces," including African Americans, other diasporic Africans, Latinos, Native Americans, women, gays and lesbians, Central and South Americans, Caribbean and other peoples of color, oppressed peoples, and so on.

Political ideologies become a useful tool in trying to understand refined differences among perspectives. What, for example, was the difference between a person who supported Anita Hill, made a gender-race analysis, and was critical of Clarence Thomas, and a person who supported Anita Hill, made a gender-race analysis, but was silent in support of Anita Hill and mute in criticism of Clarence Thomas? The latter's analysis would tend to be from the nationalist ideology.

Naming the Enemy

Recognizing that the concepts of gender, race, and class present the first level of analysis, the next level requires the identification and naming of the external enemy from the perspective of those who believed Hill and made a gender-only analysis, those who believed Hill and made a sex-and-race analysis, and those who supported Thomas and made a race-only analysis. Kenneth Burke provides a dramatistic framework for naming the enemy, identifying beliefs and attitudes toward the enemy, and understanding actions and behaviors by a collective body:

> We must name the friendly or unfriendly functions and
> relationships in such a way that we are able to do
> something about them. In naming them, we form our
> characters, since the names embody attitudes; and implicit
> in the attitudes there are the cues for behavior. . . .

> These names shape our relations with our fellows. They
> prepare us for some functions and against others, for or
> against the persons representing these functions. The names
> go further: they suggest *how* you shall be for or against.
> (1961, p. 4)

To give the external enemy a name such as "white people" or men or women, and to be even more specific by designating the enemy as "unfriendly" by attaching such labels as "sexism," "racism," or "classism" makes the struggle against the enemy very concrete. Naming the enemy helps mobilize a community, gives voice to its outrage, and provides a rallying point.

"I Believe Anita Hill!": Sexism

"I believe Anita Hill!" The words came swift and easy, with little, if any, hesitation as Hill's allegations of sexual harassment against Thomas in the eleventh hour of his confirmation hearings were revealed. From the very beginning in early October 1991, most European American feminists and European American middle-class and professional women quickly rallied around Hill (Leatherman 1991) and viewed her coming forward as a formidable blow by women, vis-à-vis the male patriarchy's "war against women."[1] Hill, according to this perspective, has done more to revitalize feminism than any event or person in the last decade (Sontag 1992). European American feminists in particular and European American women in general were truly grateful for her coming forth to focus the attention of the world on the struggles of women in the United States.

For those who believed Hill, who were European American, and who made a gender analysis, the enemy was patriarchal society. Men are the enemy. The sides are drawn along gender lines. Women are on one side, men on the other. The "maleness" of African American men is the determinant feature, not that they are oppressed as men of color. "All men are the enemy," as defined by an analysis based on gender and patriarchy.

59

"I Believe Anita Hill!": Sexism and Racism

During the Senate confirmation hearings, Black feminists and nonfeminists were reeling from the quickness with which white feminists and women's organizations mobilized and rallied around Hill. There was, as well, a component of the African-American community that supported Hill. Although this community supported Hill along with European American women, it was vigilant against having white women define the struggle of women of color or reduce their agenda to issues of gender only: "Some white feminists . . . myopically cling to the notion that sexism is the only issue, or the paramount issue. . . . No, sexual harassment in the workplace is not the burning issue for most black women. First you have to have a job" (Gillespie, 1992, p. 43). "We must protect the dignity of our women," Black women reasoned, and "the aggrieved party must always be taken seriously in questions of sexual harassment." But racism and sexism cannot be extricated from the issue.

For those who believed Hill but also believe that sexism, racism, and classism are inextricably linked (such as Black feminists, male and female, and some progressive nonfeminists), the enemy was sexism and racism. The face of the enemy was a lot more complex than naming "all men." The European American man was a major enemy. His racism and sexism were the features of this particular enemy. The names of this enemy were the "white right-wing misogynists" (Smith, 1992, p. 38), the "all-white justice" system (Norton, 1992, p. 43), represented by a "panel of white men" and the "white male ruling class" (Smith 1992, p. 39). Marcia Ann Gillespie produced a caricature of the white racist rhetoric around Hill: "Whoever heard of a hot-blooded Negress being sexually harassed, much less offended?" (1992, p. 41).

The European American woman was also an enemy. Her racism and classism were the particular species of the enemy. The names of this enemy were the "mainstream women's movement" (Smith 1992, p. 38), "white feminists," and "women who never spoke about the slick racism that set the entire debacle in motion" (Gillespie 1992, p. 43).

There were enemies in the African American community as well. The enemies were the sexism of the Black male, the internalized sexism of the Black female, and racism on the part of both genders. The naming of the enemy was quite descriptive: "African Americans who felt that she [Hill] had stepped out of line by accusing a black man chosen by white racists for high office [and] who decided that standing behind a Black man . . . is more important than supporting a Black woman's right not to be abused" and " 'our' male civil rights leaders" who challenged racism but not sexism (Smith 1992, p. 38). Gillespie, who admonishes the African American community for "speak[ing] in tongues," states:

> As for the African American community: it's way past time for women to call to account those leaders who put blinders on when it comes to sexism. Why were so many of "our" male civil rights leaders—who spoke eloquently about the racism of the Thomas nomination—so quiet when the issue of sexism arose? . . . Those sister presidents of all the myriad Black women's organizations, the preachers, and the African American sisters who supported Thomas and have internalized sexism were faces of a lesser enemy. (1992, p. 43)

Within the African American community was classism, which is key in understanding why a race-gender analysis could be made while simultaneously naming Thomas as the enemy. The face of the enemy was Black conservativism. The enemy was Thomas, who had a "career-long hostility to civil rights laws" (Norton 1992, p. 44) and an "utter contempt for the struggles of African Americans" (Smith 1992, p. 38), who was conservative, Ivy League, pro-Reagan, pro-Bush, and male. Thomas symbolized a new enemy within the African American community for those who made a gender-race-class analysis. Of the three perspectives analyzed here, this one represents the significant contribution the Hill-Thomas controversy brings to social and political thought.

In addition to the faces of the enemy identified above, which emerged as a result of the intersection of gender, race, and class, were those perspectives that emerged because one feature was primary over the others.

If sexism was the primary issue, then racism was important in examining the enemy from the perspective of the African American woman experiencing sexism. There were those who believed Hill, were women of color, and felt the enemy was equally racism and sexism. One was not more important than the other, and those who propagated that race was primary over gender, or vice versa, and pitted one enemy against the other were the enemy as well. Barbara Smith writes: "It's difficult to conceive how the hearings could be understood from anything other than a Black Feminist perspective: A perspective that doesn't require short-changing any aspect of Black women's reality or assume racial oppression is more important than sexual oppression or vice versa" (1992, p. 37). *Ms.* magazine understood that the integrity of its analysis of Hill required the inclusion of "these voices of rage, power, and hope" ("Refusing" 1992, p. 34) In its issue devoted to Hill, the editors acknowledged the centrality of this perspective, stating: "*Ms.* asked five African American feminist theorists activists to analyze what really happened—to U.S. women generically and the Black community particularly—and to address the question of where we all go from here" (p. 34).

All African American feminists were not so sure that there could be a smooth and equal uniting of the gender and race analysis. Joye Mercer, though never mentioning Hill or Thomas, captures the essence of concerns articulated by these darker feminist scholars when she warns that the unity between white and Black women has been full of difficulties and disharmonies. She says that there are differences between European and African American women and the way they see reality and set their separate agendas, mainly because historically "women of color . . . were largely excluded from the feminist movement" (1982, pp. 14–15). From this perspective, the "we" in "the question of where we all go from here" does not include African American women. The subject of this perspective's gender analysis is Black, not white, women. Therefore, this perspective makes a race-gender (a Black feminist) analysis which is anti-woman, that is, antiwhite woman.

For those who believed Hill and made a gender-race analysis but for whom race was primary, either by analysis or because it emerged as most salient, the role of racism was different from the question of whether African American women were included or excluded from the feminist movement. Eleanor Holmes Norton points out the primacy of race: "It is a mistake to read the outcome of the hearings as a comment on feminism; it is a comment on the continuing potency of race to push all else aside. Not surprisingly, with a nomination of a Black man to the Supreme Court at stake, race trumped sex" (1992, p. 44). Race was not just about European and African American women, it was also about institutionalized and internalized racism, historical and contemporary. From this perspective, feminism was the enemy, whether it was African or European American. Norton's challenge served to remind us that there were other perspectives on the Hill-Thomas controversy inside the African American community beyond that of feminists.

"Clarence Thomas Got a Bum Rap!": Race Is Primary

The complexity of this issue is best captured by the celebrity and clarity with which dissenting voices from the vast masses of African American men *and* women rose to defend and protect Thomas and to attack and chastise Hill for what many believed was her collusion in the castration of Thomas by European American males and feminists. From the perspective of many professional and "progressive" African American groups, Hill was not the undisputed heroine, nor was Thomas the mad-dog villain as he was characterized by many segments of the European American community. To the masses of African Americans, who was the hero or heroine and who was the villain were highly contested. The enemy was racism. The face of the enemy was European Americans, white feminists, and the race betrayers.

For those who believed and/or supported Thomas and made a race-only analysis, including grassroots women, the significance of race was the salient determinant for what they believed was a "progressive" analysis within the black community. Gillespie captures the rhetoric of this perspective which saw the controversy through race-colored glasses:

> She must be delusional, a.k.a. crazy! Or else she's just one
> of those jealous vindictive Black women—mad because she
> doesn't have a man; mad because the man she wanted
> didn't want her; mad because he married a white woman.
> No? Well, then she's an innocent dupe of sinister forces—
> those professional feminists, evil liberals—a dumb bitch!
> (1992, p. 41)

For those who believed Hill but were silent, or who believed and for whom the attack against Thomas was half-hearted and less adamant than the attack by European American women, race also had primacy over gender. This group didn't see Hill as the enemy, but there was a feeling that the African American male, not just Thomas, was on trial. Thomas and Black manhood had to be protected. It wasn't that the community supported Thomas but rather that "Blacks did not squarely veto" him, and "whites carried Thomas over" ("Refusing" 1992, p. 45). This third perspective was shaped by a history, experience, and a consciousness fashioned by the intersection of issues of race and class, with no commitment to the women's movement or gender issues. The Left was unclear about how to integrate the thinking of this third group into its analysis of the role of race, gender, and class. Those among the Left who made a race-only analysis tended to be of the middle and right tendencies; reformism and nationalism reflected their ideologies. Those who were antifeminist also tended to be counterrevolutionary. For all three cohorts, support of Thomas or Hill represents a kind of collective purging of the psyches within each of these groups, through focusing on a common external enemy and evading the struggle against an internal enemy.

The Scapegoat and the Sacrificial Lamb

Kenneth Burke's works on the struggle against the enemy within and the struggle for internal change is valuable in understanding (1) the differing perspectives on the Hill-Thomas case, (2) the assigning of blame for oppressed groups, (3) the internalized victimization of oppressed people in the United States, and (4) the need for transformation of people and institutions in the society. Specifically, Burke's concept of secular purification through scapegoating is instructive in explaining the resistance to change in our behavior and the thinking and the desire to keep things the way they are and have always been:

> If one can hand over his infirmities to a vessel, or "cause" outside the self, one can battle an external enemy instead of battling an enemy within. And the greater one's internal inadequacies, the greater the amount of evils one can load upon the back of "the enemy." (1973, pp. 202–3)

63

We are more comfortable placing the blame on something or someone outside ourselves. "By objectively attributing one's own vices or temptations to the delegated vessel, the scapegoat is taken to possess intrinsically the qualities we assign it," explains Burke (1973, p. 46). This dialectic of the enemy within and without is crucial in understanding the process of revolutionary transformation that must occur in each of the perspectives.

European American women were confused when African American women did not have the same response as they had to the Hill-Thomas conflict. White feminists expected Black males to justify the attack against Thomas as racist and to take a chauvinistic posture. However, they were shocked by the anger directed toward Hill and the defensiveness and protectionism of Thomas by the majority of grassroots women in the African American community. The European American feminists were also wrong about the several African American males who supported Hill and the many African American feminists who sympathized with the race analysis of the masses of African American women in the community. Why had European American women missed this?

White feminists identify all men as the enemy and lump the African American male with the European American men who run this country. When Black women refused to denounce Black men as the enemy, white women generally got upset. They accused Black women of once again putting a premium on the needs and interests of Black males at the expense of Black females. Most European American women argued that the desire of African American women to have educated and respectable Black men (as opposed to school dropouts, prison inmates, drug users, or otherwise undesirable) to marry was the most backward antiwoman idea they had ever heard. They looked at African-American women as if they were from an era when women as healers were burned at the stake as witches. Black women were holding the torch for Hill.

While European American feminists were focusing on an enemy outside themselves, they failed to see their own internal contradictions, and they generally failed to see the controversy from any other perspective than their own myopic one. They had dismissed the enraged response of the masses as simply the backward collective unconsciousness of grassroots African Americans. European American feminists believed they had failed to give leadership to Black feminists who, in turn, could have revolutionized the thinking of the masses of African American women around the manifestations and evils of sexism. When African American feminists were not compliant with the wishes of European American feminists, the Black woman became expendable. If the Black woman had to be sacrificed along with Thomas in order to advance the cause of white feminism, many of these feminists saw her demise as an unfortunate, but unavoidable, sacrifice. In fact, the Black woman's death was her own fault.

Feminists will hold up a principle crucial to dismantling sexism in the society. The principle will be applied to the Black male who becomes a vessel for the evils of society. It is as if all the burden of the sexist sins of the society are dumped on the Black male. Those who attack the Black male scapegoat are "purified through its suffering" (Burke 1969, p. 406). Instead of examining themselves, once European American feminists identified men as the enemy and Thomas as the specific vessel of evil, then the scapegoating of Black men became the process that led to the purification of a contaminated society defined as patriarchal by white women.

Gillespie challenges this arrogance: "Feminists who watched those hearings . . . assumed that at last Black women were going to 'get the message' and come into the fold" (1992, p. 43). White feminists failed to struggle against their own racism, classism, and sexual prejudices about Black males and females, and they ignored the significance of race in the United States. By attacking the African American male, European American society generally and European American women specifically evaded the struggle against the enemy within.

Women can attack the Clarence Thomases while not touching white male privilege or dismantling the white male power structure (for example, the sexual harassment of Hill by the white male senators). In each case, purification for the whole society comes through the offering of a sacrificial lamb (the Black female, Hill) that accompanies the scapegoat (the Black male, Thomas). Burke states: "In the sacrifice there is a kill; in the kill there is a sacrifice. But one or the other of this pair may be stressed as the 'essence' of the two" (1973, p. 46). The Black woman is symbolically thrown upon the raging death fire with the Black male. She complies in the drama because she sees a particular male, such as Thomas, as worthy of sacrifice for the evils he has committed against her.[2] She does not see this black man, as some may want her to see him, as every Black male. Black feminist ideology is consistently combating the stereotypes of the African American man as a "disreputable character" who must die so that the "slayer" (European American society, including European American women, or the old ways) may live (Burke, 1973: 47). "If Thomas had not been confirmed," Rebecca Walker states, every man in the United States would be at risk (1992, p. 39). Regardless, the effect is the unification of all European Americans and some African American women around a common enemy, the African American man.

Women and society then purge themselves of this evil through moral indignation, destroying the scapegoat as vessel of vicarious atonement. The sacrificial lamb is consumed as well. Their moral indignation, however, has the effect of diverting attention away from the need for European American women to struggle against their own complicity in a racist and sexist society and for European American men to engage in a comprehensive process of transformation.

Sexism is the oppression, objectification, and devaluation of a person on the basis of gender. It is difficult for white women to understand how in a male-dominated patriarchal society, a person can be objectified and devalued if he is of the male gender. If you are a male of African descent in a white-male-dominated society like the United States, you are also a victim of sexism and racism. Whites must be willing to discuss the contradictions of racism and sexism as they affect the race-gender code of white America.

Many leaders within the Black community advance the idea that the African American male is a victim of the racism of European Americans, particularly of European American feminism. Race consciousness garners strength with each attack against the Black male and subsequent evasion of (white) group self-criticism. Are Black men endangered? Haki R. Madhubuti noted that "the world has gotten worse for Black men [and their status was] beyond the endangered species category" (1990, p. v). European American feminists are suspicious. They see such talk as a backlash against the rising militancy of Black women in the African

American community. Many Black feminists question this sudden characterization of a shortage of eligible Black men and see it as a ploy on the part of bourgeois African American males to promote themselves as rare gems while propagating polygamy as an accepted lifestyle.

On the other hand, some African American feminists argue that the issue of the plight of young Black men is not some ego-boosting ploy of the few African American men who are educated, working, not in prison, and still alive. They believe that the desire to "save" the Black male is not some internalized oppression of Black women who define themselves through their relationships with men (even though many recognize that some Black women have not eradicated all vestiges of sexism). Rather, they argue that current "save the Black male" philosophies have evolved out of a sense of reality: the African American community is losing its fathers, sons, husbands, brothers, and uncles in unprecedented numbers.[3]

In any discussion of Black male victimization, however, one would be derelict without also discussing the African American male's objectification and devaluation of women, particularly Black womanhood. Male chauvinism is rampant in the Black community among both males and females. Barbara Smith identifies the enemy within the African-American community:

> The worst consequence of the Hill-Thomas hearings for me
> was in what they revealed about African Americans' level
> of consciousness regarding both sexual and racial politics. It
> has always taken courage for women of color to speak out
> about sexism within our communities. In this instance it
> was done more publicly and dramatically than at any time
> in history. (1992, p. 38)

Black men must struggle against their complicity in a racist, sexist society. Within the African American community, too many still see racism as primary. Gillespie asks: "[What about] the preachers who went about business as usual the Sunday of those hearings? . . . Acting as if racism was primarily, if not solely, about men" (1992, p. 43). However, to ignore the African American male's victimization in order to win a victory against male patriarchy is just as irresponsible.

The difficulty is in developing sensitivity to the gender issue without African Americans accusing Black feminists of simply following white women. To dismiss the gender issues that African American feminists were raising as brainwashing by European American women becomes a way for the African American community to evade the need to transcend its sexism and misogyny. Barbara Smith writes about this confusion in the African American community:

> It was demoralizing to see how the confrontation reinforced
> the perception that any woman who raises the issue of

sexual oppression in the Black community is somehow a
traitor to the race, which translates into being a traitor to
Black men. It is particularly disheartening knowing that
probably a lot of Black people took this stance despite
believing Anita Hill. (1992, p. 38)

Black women must struggle against their own complicity in a racist and
sexist society. They must not deny that racism and gender intersect to
create internalized oppression. Gillespie addresses this issue:

The night before Anita Hill walked into that Senate
chamber, a sister-friend said to me, "Time and again we are
called to be the conscience of this nation." So on Hill
came, having steeled herself for the ordeal, and quietly
purged herself by putting in words the memories swallowed.
Watching the blood spill on the hearing room floor,
overwhelmed by often conflicting emotions, I knew that the
consciences in need of raising were neither all male nor all
white. (1992, p. 42)

Those consciences were, Gillespie points out, "those sister presidents of
all the myriad Black women's organizations who seemed to disappear into
the woodwork when the chips were down" (1992, p. 43).

The internal weakness of African American women who made a
race-gender analysis was their failure to make a revolutionary analysis,
their lack of courage to challenge backward ideas in both the European
American women's and the African American communities, their evasion
of leadership and of the responsibility for creating an agenda, and their
alienation from forces within the African American community. The
struggle within is to have the courage to challenge backward ideas wher-
ever they come from. This includes not allowing white women or Black
men to decide the Black woman's agenda without her input and leadership. It means, however, setting a revolutionary agenda, total and complete change of the status quo. Vivian Gordon reflects this concern: "Black
women have not clearly defined their own agenda, and you can't form
coalitions with others when you don't have your own agenda" (Mercer
1992, p. 15).

Charshee C. Lawrence-McIntyre's viewpoint and, indeed, warning
perhaps best captures a feeling emerging within the African American
community, an impending boomerang reaction to the community's evasion of its own internal contradictions: "I think African Americans need
to look deeply into the political nature of the Anita Hill role. . . . We
need to shift toward and maintain an Afrocentric value system and to stop
reacting to other people's covert and overt agendas" (1992, p. 120). The
African American community did not name or identify an internal enemy

or enemies—such as racism, sexism, or classism—within the community. It was ineffective in making analyses of those perspectives that did not address the intersection of race, gender, and class. Therefore, the community's reaction to attacks on the community, individually and collectively, from those outside the community had the effect of placing the entire African American community on defense and having to respond to varying agendas. The community did not seize the opportunity to give leadership and direction to the whole society around the intersection of race, gender, and class. Thus, neither Thomas nor Hill was successfully defended by the African American community. An essentially Afrocentric perspective that calls for placing the needs and interests of the people at the center of any analysis was not served.

The struggle of the African American community, men and women, for their own transformation and self-determination must come from within. They must struggle against the internal enemies, alienation, classism, and sexism. African American females and males who understand the intersection of race and gender but who have alienated themselves from the indigenous masses, who have been lukewarm in speaking out against racism, who have participated in the miseducation of the native classes in the community, while simultaneously mobilizing with white feminists around women's issues, must look within themselves, as well as externally, in order to achieve total change.

Those who emphasized race, gender, and class drifted toward left political tendencies and represented either a reformist or a revolutionary tendency. Change for this perspective was desirable; the internal challenge was to be inclusive, rather than protective, of the competing victim statuses of oppressed groups. We must discuss the African American male and his plight in society, and the plight of the African American female, while challenging the African American male's chauvinism and that of the African American community. The African American male is not a species in and of himself. "Endangered species," in this case, therefore, could only refer to the African American family, which would include both male and female. "Black men are not the only ones endangered in the United States of America" (Gillespie 1992, p. 43). Black women are endangered as well; the struggle is just different.

Transformation: Rhetorical Strategies

Amilcar Cabral identifies the two-front revolutionary struggle of the people of Guinea-Bissau against Portuguese colonialists—the struggle against an external and internal enemy, the struggle without and within:

So at each moment of this great struggle we are waging, we must focus on two phases: one, against the colonialist capitalist ruling classes in Portugal and imperialism; the other, against all the internal forces, whether material or spiritual (meaning ideas from the mind), which might arise against our people's progress on the path of liberty, independence and justice. These demand courageous struggle against imperialist agents. But in addition permanent and determined struggle against those who, even if they are militants, responsible workers or leaders of the Party, do anything which could prejudice our people's march to total conquest of their dignity, their liberty and their progress. (1979, p. 79)

Similarly, in U.S. history, Malcolm X, for example, cajoled the African American community into struggling against a "slave mentality" while struggling against racism; to transform themselves and all human relationships, while changing the existing oppressive and racist institutions. The struggle against a slave mentality and self-victimization is one of the crucial lessons the community can learn as a result of the Hill-Thomas phenomenon.

Those who "believed in Anita Hill" and utilized a gender analysis to mitigate the tension between competing rhetorical strategies must recognize that the perspectives and reality of European American women are not the only ones; there are race and class issues. Necessarily at the core of any legitimate discussion of Hill-Thomas is the Black perspective. A close rhetorical analysis of *Ms.*'s explanation reveals the essence of the difference between a collective social consciousness that has one monolithic voice and one that has diverse voices speaking for the collective whole. First, *Ms.* uses the qualifier "African American" before the phrase "feminist theorists/activists," thus implicitly acknowledging that there is a unique genre of analysis separate from that of white feminists. Second, the emphasis on "all" in the phrase "where we all go from here" is a conscientious effort to legitimize the Black voice as essential for defining the collective feminist voice for all, and simultaneously recognizing the uniqueness of the Black perspective. Finally, *Ms.*'s identification of five different voices rather than *a* Black voice indicates an understanding of the diversity within the African American feminist perspective.

Black males do not have the privileges of white males. Until the Black Liberation Movement and Affirmative Action, contrary to what some European American women want to believe, African American men had few of the privileges of European American women in the middle and ruling classes in racist America (Giddings 1984). White women under the protection of white manhood, and therefore under the protection of every law of the land, are afforded all the privileges of white males in the society, economically, socially, and politically, albeit these privileges may only result from the European American woman's influence over or

69

association with husbands, fathers, or sons; that is, these privileges may well be limited to the status of males in the European American woman's family or attained through marriage to a European American male. Oppressed as the white woman may be by white male patriarchy, her state and that of her children in American society (with the exception of poor white women) are significantly different from that of either the African American male or the African American female. The objective conditions of the European-American woman's life improve in direct correlation to the status of the European American man and the economy of American society. Few European American women give up this privilege, even when they have dissociated themselves from European American males. The African American woman also benefits and/or suffers from her association with and attachment to the African American man. The African American woman's objective condition is directly correlated to that of the African American male.

The Hill-Thomas issue provides a fundamental conceptual base for discussing and understanding wide-sweeping revolutionary transformation in the values and beliefs of individual and collective groups of people within the United States. This base requires an open and honest examination of the intersection of race, gender, and class. Not making a clear analysis of the external and internal enemy has caused both feminist and African American communities to find themselves supporting all kinds of backward behavior.

70   Understanding institutionalized and internalized racism, historical and contemporary, helps to explain the internal enemy within the African American community and to separate out those aspects of the struggle against racism that are in the interests of the people. Norton, for example, explains how some Blacks such as Thomas use race in an opportunistic and exploitive way:

> That Anita Hill was also Black did not count for much; she declined to use her race (or her gender, for that matter) to enhance her charges, while Thomas made race his central, indeed his only, defense . . . though he had spent his entire career criticizing Blacks for ascribing their condition to race. (1992, p. 44)

Thomas fed upon Blacks' historic feeling of victimization. Rather than a race analysis leading to an Afrocentric and empowering perspective, such a race analysis underdeveloped the people.

> To many Blacks the Senate Judiciary Committee looked like nothing so much as an all-white jury. Thomas took no chance that this symbolism would be missed. Declining subtle racial allusions, he brought race front and center with

brazenly undiluted charges of racism—"high-tech lynching"
and the rest—sending the message, especially to Blacks,
that the leak and the public hearing had come because he
was Black. (Norton 1992, p. 44)

Race-only analysis limited many by restricting their view of Thomas
entirely through Black-tinted glasses. Hill brought the contradiction to the
forefront.

[She] unintentionally brought forward the race-sex tension
that is unavoidable when ethnicity is the mark of
oppression. Color, country, culture, and language define an
entire group; sex is only half of it. This is a country where
racism has been the longest standing national neurosis. Is it
any wonder that it sometimes has been difficult for the
black community to come to grips with its internal
complexity? Some believe that even a concession to gender
could threaten the solidarity necessary to resist and defeat
racism. (Norton 1992, p. 45)

The realization that one of the enemies has a face quite familiar to
you as a European American woman and/or an African American is quite
a revelation. To focus only on the enemy outside was to focus on institutionalized sexism and/or racism only and was a way of not addressing
the totality of enemies including sexism, racism, and classism within each
community. But with Hill, race had the possibility of leaping forward
toward this progressive Afrocentric perspective. The revolutionary position would be to have a complete struggle against the enemy without and
within. Barbara Smith believes in a comprehensive and revolutionary
analysis: "As a Black feminist, I've long believed that political analyses
and strategies that take into account how racism, sexism, homophobia,
and class oppression dovetail and interlock provide the clearest and most
revolutionary agendas for change" (1992, p. 37).

Revolutionary leadership, then, could in fact come from an African
American female who could, within the women's and African American
communities, identify with the struggles and interests of the whole community (including the "least" of the people) and provide models of moral
and ethical character, leadership, and direction to both communities (see
Karenga 1990; Robinson 1980). Perhaps an African American could indeed serve as the conscience and hope of both communities, helping them
to see up and climb out of the abyss of oppression, poverty, sexism,
classism, and racism. However, Black women have not provided that
leadership. We failed to counter the attack by white women against the
Black male and the Black family by bringing forward a race and gender
analysis. Julia Hare asserts:

> The entire women's movement was almost "anti" the Black
> family . . . because it attempted to tell black women how
> they should treat—and be treated by—Black men. It often
> has pitted Black women and men against each other. . . .
> The women's movement never understood that equality was
> not the same as sameness. (Mercer 1992, p. 15)

A race-gender analysis would provide for the naming of those African-American males (and females) and those European American feminists and perspectives that are enemies to progressive change, while identifying those that facilitate change. Conversely, analyses and strategies that propagate the mythology that one oppression is more important than another and pit one oppression against the other are exploitive. Such analyses accept the most base and dehumanizing aspects of western culture and do not provide for the creation of a new and more humane reality. What's required, then, is a revolutionary analysis, the courage to set an agenda and not compromise it on the basis of competing oppressions, to avoid alienation from the masses of people, and to provide leadership to all people:

> Anita Hill was everybody's daughter, every community's
> model student, every sister. At the same time, she was an
> enigma in the African American community, still struggling
> with racism, still searching for its rightful place in its own
> country, still sorting out race and sex and class. Anita was
> ahead of a time she has helped define—a time to be Black
> and a woman. ("Refusing" 1992, p. 45)

Life in these United States will never be the same as a result of the debate and discussion of the Hill-Thomas controversy that has been unleashed in the feminist and African American communities. As the African American woman takes her rightful place, issues of race, gender, and class and their intersection provide both a danger and an opportunity. The danger is that the African American woman will be the scapegoat for many perspectives. The opportunity is that she will help define fundamental change in our society and our humanity.

Notes

1. Representative Pat Schroeder, in a book review of *Backlash: The Undeclared War against American Women* by Susan Faludi (New York: Crown, 1991), summarily compares the "outpouring of women's anger over the Senate's handling of Anita Hill's sexual harassment complaint" with Faludi's observation of the "rages" that women have felt over "the erosion of rights and the lessening of respect . . . during the past decade" (p. 8b).

2. Burke describes this relationship: "When the attacker chooses the object of attack, it is usually his blood brother; the debunker is much closer to the debunked than others are" (1973, p. 406).
3. Kunjufu (1982, 1986) writes that society was conspiring against Black boys, and, unknowingly, Black teachers, principals, parents, and other adults in the community were complying.

References

Blonston, Gary. "Class Dilemma Fractures Black America: Some Consider Clarence Thomas a Troubling Symbol." *Detroit Free Press*, Aug. 4, 1991, p. 1F.

Burke, Kenneth. *Attitudes Toward History*. Boston: Beacon, 1961.

Burke, Kenneth. *The Philosophy of Literary Form*. Los Angeles: University of California Press, 1973.

Burke, Kenneth. *A Grammar of Motives*. Los Angeles: University of California Press, 1969.

Carter, Stephen L. *Reflections of an Affirmative Action Baby*. New York: Basic Books, 1991.

Cabral, Amilcar. *Unity and Struggle: Speeches and Writings of Amilcar Cabral*. New York: Monthly Review, 1979.

Coleman-Burns, Patricia. "Social and Political Thought of African Americans." Paper delivered at closing conference of National Council of Black Studies, June 1992.

Giddings, Paula. *When and Where I Enter: The Impact of Black Women on Race and Sex in America*. New York: Morrow, 1984.

Gillespie, Marcia Ann. "We Speak in Tongues." *Ms.* (Jan.–Feb. 1992): 41–43.

Harrison, Lawrence E. "Why Does America Ignore Black Success?" *Detroit News*, July 5, 1992, p. 3B.

Karenga, Maulana. "The African Intellectual and the Problem of Class Suicide: Ideological and Practical Dimensions." In M.K. Asante and K.W. Asante, eds., *African Culture: The Rhythm of Unity*. Trenton, N.J.: Africa World, 1990.

Kunjufu, Jawanza. *Countering the Conspiracy to Destroy Black Boys*. Chicago: African-American Images, 1982 (Vol. 1) and 1986 (Vol. 2).

Lawrence-McIntyre, Charshee C. "Anita Hill: Black Women and Sexual Harassment." *Upscale* 3 (1992):120.

Leatherman, Courtney. "Panel's Handling of Allegations Against Thomas Brings Angry Responses from Women in Academe." *Chronicle of Higher Education*, Oct. 16, 1991, p. A17.

Madhubuti, Haki R. *Black Men: Obsolete, Single, Dangerous? The African-American Family in Transition*. Chicago: Third World Press, 1990.

Magner, Denise K. "Black Intellectuals Broaden Debate on Effects of Affirmative Action." *Chronicle of Higher Education* Oct. 16, 1991, p. A17.

Mercer, Joye. "Black Women/White Women: Does Gender Unite More Than Race Divides." *Black Issues in Higher Education* 9 Jan. 2, 1992, pp. 14–15.

Naison, Mark. "Inner-city Teenagers Created Their Own Version of Corporate Raiding and Insider Tradings When Drug Dealers Figured Out a Way to Market Cocaine at $5 and $10 a Pop." *Chronicle of Higher Education* June 12, 1992, p. B5.

Norton, Eleanor Holmes. "And the Language Is Race." *Ms.* (Jan.–Feb. 1992):43–45.

Phillips, Kevin P. *Post-Conservative America: People, Politics, and Ideology in a Time of Crises*. New York: Random House, 1982.

"Refusing to Be Silenced," Editorial. *Ms.* 2:34. 1992.

Robinson, Cedric. "Domination and Imitation: Xala and the Emergence of the Black Language." *Race and Class* 22(1980):147–58.

Smith, Barbara. "Ain't Gonna Let Nobody Turn Me Around." *Ms.* (Jan.–Feb. 1992):37–39.

Sontag, Deborah. "Anita Hill and Her Role in Revitalizing Feminism." *New York Times* April 26, 1992, sec. 1, p. 21 (N). 31 (L).

Stewart, C., C. Smith, and R. Denton, Jr. *Persuasion and Social Movements*. Prospect Heights, Ill. Waveland, 1984.

"Thomas Nomination Highlights the Different Species of Black Conservatives." *Michigan Chronicle 54* July 24, 1991, p. 6A.

Whose "Boy" Is This?

MARGARET WALKER ALEXANDER

T he Anita Hill-Clarence Thomas episode on national television gives us a cosmic picture of race, gender, and class in the twentieth-century United States of America. Politics, education, and religion are reflected in the mirror of ever-changing sexual and monetary morality. Family, church, and school, in the whole spectrum, seem nastily exposed to our appalled viewing. Recovering from the shock of this subtle, and not so subtle, pornography, we struggle to analyze its meaning, its purpose, and its attendant phenomena now and in the future. If we begin with the premise that we have a fascist, sexist, and racist society, understanding this whole sorry spectacle should not be difficult. Fascism is forced government by the strong and powerful, big money, and big guns. The sexism of the society is evident in disregard for women's rights, the use of women's labor for male purposes, placing women on a lower salary scale than men for the same work; most of all, this sexism is evident in male chauvinists exploiting and using sex to dominate the lives of women. Racism is evident in the Anglo-Saxon/ white man's fight for power and control over all nonwhite people in the world. Anglo-Saxon strongholds are European, American, South African, and Israeli.

Let us ask ourselves a half-dozen questions in order to analyze, assess, and summarize this conundrum:

Who are these people?
From whence have they come?
Why are they doing this?
How did our country get to this point?
What can we do about it?
What is the lesson we are learning here today?

According to their testimony during the hearings, Anita Hill and Clarence Thomas had known each other a considerable length of time. He had been her boss on at least two jobs. Even though she was bringing the charge of sexual harassment against him, she had continued to have contact with him, to be recommended by him, and to telephone and congratulate him on his promotions and his sudden rise to very powerful positions. This would seem paradoxical if it were not for our basic premise regarding fascism, sexism, and racism.

Who are these people? They are admittedly Buppies—Black, upwardly mobile, conservative Republicans. They are the new breed of Black middle-class professionals who have turned their backs on the race. In spite of themselves, they are conservative in race, religion, and politics. He was educated in Roman Catholic schools and at prestigious Yale University; she was connected to a fundamentalist Protestant school. Both fit the bill for conservative Republicans—obviously against abortion, against women's right to control their own bodies, against affirmative action, and against the basic premises of the New Deal and the Civil Rights Movement: freedom, justice, and human dignity. Do not misconstrue their protestations. Their ambivalence merely reflects their confusion. They are both Buppies. Their combined success in our ultra-corrupt society is testament to this positive fact. How corrupt is our society? From whence did these people come? We live in a drug empire. This entire hemisphere is affected by an economy based on drugs and drug-related crime in a politically fascist police state. We are suffering from a world plague of AIDS. We have lived through a century of war and revolution over land, money, property, and race. Although neither Hill nor Thomas may claim to be a paragon of virtue (which they very well may be), they both certainly are victims or examples of this corrupt society. They are not outside the pale of this culture. They may believe they are. We know they cannot be. Sexual and monetary morality affects all our behavior. In biblical morality, lies are as big a sin as adultery—and as big a blasphemy against the Holy Spirit. Who is as pure as the driven snow in this case? Do they know what they are saying about each other and about themselves? Psychologically, is he really a sadist and she a masochist? Is he mad with the world because he is Black, and both white and black men have abused him because of his color? Does she look around and see herself mirrored in the dozens of Black women whom Black men have used before marrying white women? What's going on here? Whether they are telling the truth or lying, they have allowed themselves to be trashed on television before the nation, and the mark of Cain is on their heads. Family structure, religion, school, and education are no longer guided by ancient meaning. Yet Americans still give lip service to standards of biblical morality in the face of ever-changing fascist, sexist, and racist standards where the old ways do not matter anymore. The world is not the same place.

One decibel of credit goes to Thomas for realizing that this public manipulation of life, masked by confirmation hearings, is shameful and not worthy of the position. But the shoe was on his foot. He still got the job. What is the future for Hill? She is the woman, the victim in this sexist mess! Although she never intended it, she was the one trashed before our eyes. She may not have intended to dig a ditch, but she certainly did dig two. You can't hurt your brother without hurting yourself. But that is the old morality.

This brings me to the racist remark made by Thomas's white wife that Hill was in love with her husband and wanted to marry him. I have heard that infamous remark before this incident. Why would a woman like Hill—good-looking, well-educated, holding a substantial position—having accused a man of sexual harassment, want to marry that man? Is Virginia Lamp Thomas's snide remark Hill's punishment for having come forward? If she is telling the truth, she would have to be out of her cotton-picking, or wool-gathering, mind to marry any such creature, snail, worm, caterpillar, or crocodile. Perhaps you say it is all just the sexual and racial jealousy of a scorned woman. Maybe Thomas was interested in Hill, and if he made those pornographic remarks, he was trying to tittilate her to get into his bed. How does that sound for starters? This further elucidates the sexual ingredient in racism.

The remark by Thomas that he was the victim of racism was a red herring of false and mammoth proportions. He placed himself on the side of the racists, sexists, and fascists in the bosom of powerful Republicans. These are the enemies of all Black people regardless of gender, class, or color. I could not believe my ears when I heard his mixed metaphors, illusions, and innuendoes in the name of race. Going back to pre-desegregation days, this man qualified as a white man's "boy," bought, paid-for, and guaranteed to deliver to "the man." Most Black people view him this way.

I could understand his awkward and painful position as a candidate in the confirmation hearings, but I fail to see him as a victim of racism. Hill holds that unenviable position. She was and is the victim of racism, sexism, and fascism. But how sorry can we feel for her? She has willingly joined a system she knows to be fascist, sexist, and racist. I believe she does not want my pity, and I have none for her. She is not ignorant, unconscious, or naive. She knows about playing with fire and getting burned.

77

I save my contempt and pitiful scorn for Thomas. He has paid a fearful price. God help the poor soul who comes before him to be judged! He is the victim of the kind of abuse and misuse Black people cruelly show their own—within our own ranks, the kind of treatment uppity Blacks or Buppies show other Blacks because of color, class, and location. Here was a "nobody" who came from the misnamed lower class, a Black with no money, no position, and no prestige. Only whites befriended him, the nuns first of all. He owes his allegiance to whites, not to Blacks, certainly not to Black middle-class uppity Buppies. He is exactly where he belongs, with a white conservative Republican Court. Even in the choice of a mate, he reveals an insecurity in his Blackness—perhaps also in his maleness. Rumor has it that his first wife, who is black, said he was a wife beater. He has three strikes against him: He has been chosen by friends who are fascist, sexist, and racist.

How did we get to this place in America? Truly television seems to be the fourth arm of government. If we examine the headlines of the past three decades, the television stories and the printed news should answer all our questions. It is basically a Republican story—a Republican-planned revolution and success story. We could begin with personalities before movements, but these eventually will coalesce into our present fascist predicament. We could begin in 1963 with Richard Nixon's election to Congress and his defeat of Helen Gahagan Douglass. It really does not mean much, though, until Barry Goldwater in 1964, when the southwestern sun belt rebelled against such Republican northeastern liberals as Nelson Rockefeller and Jacob Javits, and their so-called authoritarian control of the Republican Party. The country has elected three presidents from that conservative Republican sun belt—two from California (Nixon and Reagan) and one from Texas (Bush). Kennebunkport, Maine, was Bush's summer home, but he voted in Texas. As early as 1968, extremist hate groups, such as the John Birch Society, the Ku Klux Klan, the neo-Nazis, Americans for the Preservation of the White Race, the military-paramilitary America First, and the skinheads began to rear their ugly racist and fascist heads in the Republican Party. In the minds of these extremist groups, *Black, liberal*, and *leftist Democrats* are dirty words. The Democratic revolt in the South began with Roosevelt and Truman when the solid white South and the white Democratic primary, which had scorned the Black and Tan Republicans, began to form the lily-white Republicans. Nixon had the "plan," Reagan had the "revolution," and Bush brought his operation as head of the CIA to form the bases of his foreign policy. The scandals of Watergate, the Iran-contra affair, the sale of American land and industry to Japan, the breaking of the back of American unionized labor with the aid of the Mafia, the stockpiling of armaments while downgrading education, health, welfare, and the domestic infrastructure—this is how we got to this place. This is why the country can put on a circus, such as Hill-Thomas, on television, with complete impunity.

This is what the society has been breeding for three decades. And the worst is yet to come. We have sown the wind. How can we escape reaping the whirlwind?

Does it matter that the 1992 presidential election gave us a Democrat? Will it end a fascist, sexist, and racist society? Will the global problems of our planet continue to remain outside the United States? Will a new political administration turn around the economy? In our present police state, is there such a thing as the difference between bourgeois democracy and a people's democracy? What is the lesson we are learning here today, and what can we do about it?

There are two critical lessons. One: If you play with a puppy, he will lick your mouth. Two: Based on the past, the future will take care of itself. We can do nothing to keep it from happening. As the Black Nationalists of the 1970s put it: "There's a shit storm coming!"

High-Tech Lynching on Capitol Hill: Oral Narratives from African American Women

The Senate hearings on Anita Hill's allegations of sexual harassment during Clarence Thomas's confirmation to the Supreme Court in the fall of 1991 sent shock waves through the general public. As Americans were choosing sides according to whether or not they believed Hill or Thomas, a more insidious process was taking place within the hallowed Senate. A young, well-educated, African American woman was being lynched symbolically for exercising a fundamental right of all Americans—freedom of speech. The complementary question of justice could not and would not be entertained, because Hill was speaking out against a customary male ritual that had long been the bedrock of institutional sexism. While the hearings ended without guilt being officially established, Hill was made an example for all women to consider.

Yet, in spite of the commonalities of women's oppression, has Hill's notoriety as a modern-day everywoman obscured the unique plight of African American women who belong to two oppressed groups simultaneously? Can their daily encounters with sexism and racism be conveniently separated into individual variables that do not necessarily overlap or interact? Does the language of telling or speaking out reflect their distinct position within American culture?

The following discussion provides some answers to these questions and is based on preliminary findings from a study of African American women's reactions to the Hill-Thomas hearings in the form of oral narratives. Six narratives elicited from women thirty-eight to fifty-four years of age were selected for analysis and discussion. Three of the women resided in the South and held high school diplomas in addition to vocational training. The other three women lived in the Midwest and had completed bachelor's degrees and various postgraduate programs. All of the women had been married at least once, had at least one child, and had been in the workforce for a minimum of fifteen years.[1] Between December 1991 and April 1992, each woman was interviewed for one hour. There was a set of questions asked of all women as well as several questions specific to each one's experience and profession. All audio tapes were transcribed and checked for accuracy.[2]

Networks and Closed Ranks

All of the women received information about the Hill-Thomas hearings primarily from television coverage. Initial impressions ranged from embarrassment to anger:

(1) Well, I think, I think the whole thing was exploited.
(Harriet)

(2) I couldn't stand to look at it. . . . I felt that Anita Hill
was being raked over the coals . . . it was painful . . .
it made me angry because, it was also, it seemed also
a racial thing to me. . . . Here they have this Black
guy who has become one of them, as part of the good
old boys network. And they all ganged up on this, this
Black female. . . . It made me sick. (Loretta)

(3) I had very conflicting emotions. I was angry, and I
felt embarrassed for Anita Hill. (Lynn)

(4) At first, I thought it was necessary, something that uh,
you know, like needed to be exposed, and as the
proceedings progressed I thought the manner in which
they were handled was um, biased, racially biased.
(Barbara)

As examples (2) and (4) suggest, some of the women detected racial overtones in the hearing. So the proceedings not only represented a timeworn, unresolved conflict between women's and men's interests but also were a signal of the discrimination still operative in the lives of African Americans. As for embarrassment, many narrators felt that since Hill and

81

Thomas were both African Americans, the hearing amounted to an un-necessary airing of "dirty laundry." Grace, a 42-year-old machine op-erator, best expressed this view: "It was to me just like what happens in black life all, you know the time. When one tries to get up, there's some-body down there trying to pull that leg, pull 'em back down." Thus, the hearing was perceived through a complex network of issues, all ultimately connected to race.

Four of the six women expressed unconditional belief in Hill; two felt certain that she was lying. There were no interviewees undecided about who was telling the truth.

(5) And I believed her entirely. Why should any woman put herself through that kind of public experience if it had been a lie? And, um, then to see the white male establishment running the hearing. Here they are again, you know, in charge of the whole damn world . . . the men sort of closed ranks around him [Thomas]. 'Cause they all know they do stuff like that. (Lynn)

(6) I believed Hill uh, for a number of reasons. One, she was not the one that uh, brought this, you know, like, into the public eye . . . Um, because of the fact that they [Thomas's comments] were made so long ago and she really had nothing to gain, uh, from lying about it. . . . Especially working in industry, you see it [sexual harassment] going on all of the time. You know, comments being made. (Barbara)

(7) The thing that really made me believe her was that during the period of time she was in Washington, I was in Washington. And some of the very phrases that she was using were phrases that I knew the guys used. So it just sounded familiar." (Loretta)

(8) I'm just sure that he did the things she said. But I'm sure she didn't see it as sexual harassment at the moment. I think someone told her it was sexual harassment. . . . I don't think she realized it because of black women's background. You know, they accept stuff so easily." (Harriet)

(9) Well, really I just feel like Miss Anita was a liar because I myself know I'm not in a position like she was. She was in a highly paid position, and if anybody had done me the way he did her . . . I would

have told him where to go, and it wouldn't have taken
me that many years to tell it. (Helen)

(10) I think she was lying to an extent. But then, he
could've been lying, too . . . if he had done all the
things she said and what she said, in my opinion, I
don't see why she followed him around, called him,
changed jobs to get with him, and all that. (Grace)

Since most of the women acknowledged that sexual harassment was
an intrinsic part of daily life, they found Hill's story believable. Also,
note the term "Miss Anita" in excerpt (9). Helen, a 38-year-old machine
operator, used this term as a false marker of respect. "Miss" singles out
Hill as one who has made it, as well as one who has exposed or betrayed
one of her own people. Such linguistic marking serves to identify the
"other" and, in this instance, carries social class overtones. In other words,
if Hill had been a poor, uneducated working woman, "Miss Anita" probably would not have been used.

Motivation: Keeping Silent and Being Cute

Speculation on the behavior of either Hill or Thomas was widespread throughout the narratives. In the absence of written documentation
and an official assignment of guilt, interviewees wrestled with the issue
of motive. As may be expected, the question of why Hill waited so long
to speak out was at the core of the matter. When directly asked why they
thought Hill waited so long, narrators provided the following responses:

83

(11) Because she accepted it. . . . It was kinda OK. . . .
Maybe she thought it was an attraction toward her,
you know . . . until she knew better. (Harriet)

(12) Well, what recourse did she have? I mean, who, you
know, could she have come forward even, you know,
when it happened? And there were things at stake for
her. (Lynn)

(13) [For women to wait to tell] it would have to be for
their security. If I was the only breadwinner, maybe I
would think about it. . . . No, I wouldn't take it.
(Helen)

(14) There's the possibility that she might not have spoken
up at all if she had not been approached. Ten years
ago it wouldn't have done her any good to say
anything. But uh, I think that she realized that she had

a duty to at least speak up because this man is going
to be deciding cases which just might be sexual
harassment cases. (Loretta)

(15) It was not a matter of her waiting, it was something
she was coerced into uh, bringing to the forefront.
(Barbara)

(16) I just don't think a black woman would really take the
stuff that she said happened. She wouldn't take it, you
know, for ten years, not say nothing for ten years if it
really happened. She would've said something then.
Regardless of the job or whatever. (Grace)

Helen was very adamant about her belief that Hill was lying. When first
asked why Hill waited so long, she said immediately and without hesitation, "Because it was a lie." Later, as example (13) indicates, Helen
allows for the possibility that one could wait for a long time to speak
out, especially if there is a job at stake. However, the more she thought
about it, the stronger Helen felt that she personally "wouldn't take it."
Other women cited the risk of losing a job and lack of recourse as key
factors that discouraged open disclosure of sexual harassment in the workplace.

84

The language women used to describe their opinions was equally
important. Words and phrases like "you know," "I mean," and "I think"
occurred frequently and in strategic positions. Specifically, "I think," "you
know," and "I mean" tended to precede or introduce propositions. While
these familiar expressions may on the surface appear to be harmless, they
actually dilute or limit the force of a proposition or idea. A similar pattern
was found in descriptions of sexual harassment in a narrator's workplace.

Although none of the women was asked why some men engage in
various forms of sexual harassment,[3] a few provided reasons in their responses to other questions. Men's behavior was explained primarily by
means of clichés:

(17) I mean, you know, men are gonna be men, and so
sometimes I think things get out of hand. . . . But I
think it goes as far as you let it go, too. (Grace)

(18) So maybe that was a habit with him. (Loretta)

(19) (a) I'm not saying he's a villain, though, you know,
because men like to have fun like that. You know,
and if he's used to doing it, and it was accepted,
really it was just no big deal between them until
the press made it a big deal.

(b) He's just a cut-up, acts silly all the time.

(c) He would, I think he just always did things like that for a reaction. I don't think he meant any harm because he dated a friend of mine, and he kissed her on the hand at night and treated her like a perfect lady." (Harriet)

(20) It was something that he thought was cute. (Barbara)

The most disturbing issue suggested in these segments is the "men will be men" phrase, in one form or another, that is used to characterize most typical male behavior, especially behavior involving women. Perhaps we have become so accustomed to this as an inevitable and permanent condition of manhood that Loretta's statement about "habit" in example (18) is not surprising. We fail to understand, however, that as long as we attribute inappropriate behavior to men's habits or fun or harmlessness, we not only promote such behavior by default but also conceal underlying problems whose resolution is fundamental to establishing successful human relations.

Returning to the question of language, there was a slight increase in the frequency of limiting phrases such as "I mean," "you know," "maybe," and "just" during the discussion of incidents of sexual harassment. It is interesting to note that in the context of explaining men's motives, these phases diminish the effect of their inappropriate behavior ("He's *just* a cut-up"). It is important for women to be aware of how certain words and patterns of phrases can restrict meaning and intent.

Personal Experiences

The most revealing segments of the interviews were those that focused on personal experiences. All interviewees admitted that they knew of women who had experienced sexual harassment on the job, and some spoke of their own personal encounters:

(21) Yes. I tried to talk to him. I'd be working, you know. He was my boss. He was kinda awkward, you know. You just, in a nice way, you know, 'Do you like that arm? Would you like to keep it?' Something like that. But he was still pretty persistent, you know, and I found me another job. But, you know, I got so I just ignored him or I just played it off. But I think if I was younger, I don't know what I would have done. You know, uh. He was real cordial in the way he liked to bother you or aggravate you or want you to come and

get close to him, you know. Or reach for a pencil and get close to your breasts, stuff like that. (Harriet, 43 yrs. old, beauty salon owner/operator)

(22) Yes. Uh, well, I guess, you know, like, the one that really sticks out most in my mind, there was an older gentleman that worked—gentleman, I use the term loosely—that worked in uh, the plant, you know, like at one time I'd had my hair braided and we were at the copier, and uh, he walked up to me and asked me if I had my other [pubic] hair done to match. You know, like, uh, and it just totally floored me when he said it. You know, like, and I told him that uh, I did not appreciate, you know, like, his making any reference to uh, you know, like, any private parts of my person, and he says, 'Well, I would've asked that of my wife.' And I told him, I says, 'I, I'm not married to you.' And I said, 'And I don't care, you know, like who it is,' I said. 'That is not the type of thing that you say to a woman.' Uh, but, you know, like, this was a guy who had harassed a lot of women as a matter of fact, women that worked with him uh, asked to be transferred and were taken, you know, like out of his, uh, you know, like from working with him because of the fact that he did make such sexual overtones all the time, but uh, you know, like, it was something that he thought was cute. Uh, you know, like, and you know like, there always, you know, like, the comments about your physical uh, appearance, you know, like, the um, I have had men come in for treatment and, you know, like, reach up and grab your breasts or, you know, like, grab your, your buttocks and, uh, so yeah, I've experienced it, yeah. And you have to, uh, you know, like, rebuff them. Uh, I've never had anything that I didn't feel that I couldn't handle. You know, like, so I it was uh never anything that I brought up to uh, management. (Barbara, 42 yrs. old, registered nurse)

(23) Oh, I can remember this sergeant said to me, 'Girl, what do you mean by taking a vacation?' Now, I was an officer. There's no way he would've ever said that to a man. That's the only person that I made, and this man was probably fifty years old, and I was about twenty-seven, the only person that I made stand at attention and told him that he that could call me Dr.

86

Smith, he could call me Mrs. Smith, or he could call me Captain Smith, but he didn't call me girl. So, that, that's, that was probably a bit of sexual and racial discrimination. (Loretta, 44 yrs. old, doctor)

(24) Yeah, I think so. . . . Maybe other things have happened and I just didn't pick 'em up. 'Cause I, you know, I'm slow at doing this. But this one. No, I hate talking about this. Um, I was superintendent of the Sunday school at church. And they have meetings from time to time. And so I went to one of these. It was, you know, at the, you know, at a campsite. And this was around Halloween, and um, they were talking to the kids. They were representatives from the various churches around. And so they were talking to the children about things, about Halloween. Well, I sat in on one of the sessions. And I was horrified to hear the ignorance being splashed around. And it upset me so much, I had to go outside. I talked with the people that I had come with who were in charge of Christian education at our church. So they said I should confront the minister who was doing this, running this thing, and tell him about my concerns. And so I did. And so in the midst of our discussion, the man turned to me and said that he was celibate, he hadn't slept with a woman in years and years and that the last woman he had slept with had been, I don't know, years ago. And, you know, it seemed not to fit what we had been talking about. And, I mean, the kind of intimacy, you know, that he was using to speak to me about this. So it was way over in the evening that I thought, 'Oh, dear, I think I've been hit on.' And so you know, I thought, 'Oh, no. That can't be.' But the more I thought about it, the more I thought, yeah, that must've been what it was. So I was anxious to get home and talk about this with my husband because I have to depend on his, his insight since my own are so faulty. Or I'm so slow on the take-up. So he agreed that, you know, that's what had happened. Oh, he [the minister] said to me that my understanding of these matters having to do with the history that he was spoiling were equal to a minister's understanding, and then he launched right into this, you know, celibacy and when he had last slept with a woman and stuff. (Lynn, 54 yrs. old, college professor)

87

Interestingly, most women began with experiences of sexual harassment that were physical and sometimes violent. For each episode of sexual harassment that was exclusively verbal, there was at least one other encounter with physical sexual harassment in which men would touch women intimately and without their permission. Harriet, a beauty salon owner, remarked that verbal sexual harassment was more tolerable than physical sexual harassment and chose to describe a confrontation with a former boss. As the excerpt indicates, she found it difficult to rebuff her boss in a "nice way." Ironically, her boss found a "nice way" to harass her since she noted that "He was real cordial in the way he liked to bother you." Nonetheless, polite or not, the "persistent" intentions of the boss eventually forced Harriet to transfer out of that section of the plant.

Verbal sexual harassment was more frequent than physical and more likely to occur on the job. Interviewees expressed shock and anger when they were presented with lewd comments and sexual innuendos by superiors and coworkers. Barbara, a registered nurse, moved from a description of verbal to physical sexual harassment in item (22). A common thread of all of these events in Barbara's narrative is that she did not tell authorities. Loretta, a real estate agent who had served in the military, immediately recognized the insult inherent in the sergeant's remarks: "There's no way he would've ever said that to a man." In contrast, Lynn, a college professor, was not sure that the minister she described was actually "hitting on" her until after she thought it over and discussed the situation with her husband.

Five out of the six women said that they knew of other women who had experienced sexual harassment. Some could recount specific events. However, in telling of others' experiences, most interviewees were sympathetic and offered judgment or analysis of the situation:

> (25) I ride with a lady who works for the city. And I don't
> even know how we got on this. I guess we were
> talking about the conference, and we were talking
> about discrimination and she was talking about um,
> when she first started working for the city her boss
> was horrible. She said he couldn't talk to you for more
> than three minutes before he was making a play and
> trying to get you in corners, and she said she started
> taking her lunch outside of the office because he
> would come into the um, lounge and just get totally
> crazy. And she was a supervisor at that time, she had
> one person that she supervised. This person was
> younger than she, and came to her with a complaint
> about the same man, but she said her hands were tied.
> And she said that, um, I'm trying to think, maybe this
> was seven years ago, she was so glad to get out of the

department. That's how she remedied it. She got an
opportunity and she left that department. So she said it
was just so, um, and there was nowhere for her to go.
She felt there was no one to tell, no one to complain
to, that she just had to endure. But she said he was
absolutely ridiculous. . . . She, she said she tried to
counsel the younger girl, you know, ignore him, but
she said he was so vulgar, he was just downright
vulgar, she said. He would say things that would just
have her almost in tears. (Loretta, 44 yrs. old, realtor)

(26) Yes, I do know of other women's experiences. And
the one that stands out in my mind is, you know, a
person whose services I call upon frequently. She
talked about how, you know, in her earlier life she
had worked as a maid and housekeeper and that she
had worked in the housekeeping section of a restaurant
or hotel or whatever. And she described the job that
she had to do. She was in charge of, you know, table
settings and stuff for big parties and stuff. And, um, I
guess the discussion came around her wanting to be
off for, you know, a religious holiday or something.
And the man who was her immediate boss said to her,
'Yes, you know, I know that you're a religious
person, otherwise I'd've had you over behind the
piano long before now.' I think I asked her what did
she do. It seems to me that she said pretty soon after
that she quit that job. But, you know, she'd had no
come-back to this person. He was white, she was
black, this was the South. And I guess she felt she had
no recourse. She didn't say if she told anyone about it.
(Lynn, 54 yrs. old, college professor)

(27) Like it was some guy, it was some guy at work one
time, and he was telling, like, little nasty jokes and
things back there in the back. Then this one woman
got real offended about it and turned him in. And they
disciplined him, though. They told him, you know, he
had to stop that talk, you know, because some people
didn't like it. And so, I guess that was some form of
harassment, sexual harassment, telling dirty jokes and
things. Some people's religion don't, you know, don't
want them, they can't, they don't want to listen to this
stuff. But she went to the, you know, the office on
him. And he about lost his job over it, though, too.
But the only thing I think that saved his job was that

89

he wasn't talking specific to her. He was just talking
in general. And she was there, you know. So, but
that's why I saying a lot of people, you know, be
playing with you. Like he was just a cut-up anyway.
And he just talked nasty all the time anyway. It's just
how you took it. You know, I had heard him before,
but I didn't pay no attention to him. 'Cause he
couldn't say no more than I could say. . . . I think he
might have got, like, maybe wrote up about it. He
eventually lost his job, come to think about it. I don't
think it was because of that one, but I think something
else happened on the same line, you know. But then,
see, that's why I'm saying it all depends. Because,
like he was saying all this stuff, but then, like one of
the bosses [female] at night winds up going [having an
affair] with him. So it just depends on what way you
take it. Like that woman was offended and the other
one wasn't. (Grace, 43 yrs. old, machine operator)

Loretta's precise depiction of a coworker's experience in excerpt
(25) highlighted the helplessness that some women often feel: "There was
no one to complain to, that she just had to endure." The coworker and
her assistant were stuck in a no-win situation. Eventually the coworker
transferred out of that department. In addition, it is interesting to note
that Loretta does not make explicit the man's remarks. Instead, she consistently refers to his remarks and his behavior as "horrible," "making a
play," "crazy," "ridiculous," and "downright vulgar." It may be that
Loretta herself did not know what the man had said, or, if she did, she
avoided being explicit. Silence about a man's specific words suggest that
keeping quiet on any level creates an untenable predicament. If we do
not know specifically what was said, how can the problem be corrected?
How can we establish standards of appropriate language in the workplace
when we all have diverse ideas about what is vulgar and unacceptable
language and what is not? Or, even more to the point, does women's use
of language, especially prohibition against use of vulgarities and profan-
ities ("talking like a lady"), put them at a disadvantage when coping with
and confronting verbal sexual harassment?

Other examples indicate that even though the interviewees agreed
that sexual harassment was common in the workplace, they did not con-
cur on how to define or react to it. In example (26), Lynn concluded that
variables like being in the South and that he was a European American
man left little choice for the African American maid. In comparison, Grace
felt that women had options since their perceptions of sexual harassment
were not fixed but varied from woman to woman: "It's just how you took
it"; "that's why I'm saying it all depends"; "it just depends on what way

you take it." She emphasized her position by pointing out that the very man who was guilty of sexually harassing female coworkers also had a "successful" affair with a female supervisor who Grace felt was not offended by the man's remarks. Furthermore, Grace's own reaction to the same man ("I had heard him before, but I didn't pay no attention to him. 'Cause he couldn't say no more than I could say") demonstrates that some women respond with a kind of verbal sparring or backtalk as a defense.

In general, the women's active strategies for defusing verbal sexual harassment included talking back, talking with, or ignoring the perpetrator. However, the most frequent solution was to change jobs or transfer out of a particular section or department. Interviewees felt that if they could "handle" the situation themselves, then there was no need to tell authorities.

Telling

Telling anyone, especially authorities, was a very sensitive issue for all interviewees. Even recounting the actual incident was difficult for some women, as can be seen in Lynn's remarks: "I hate talking about this." In most cases, not only is a job at stake but also human dignity and self-esteem. Many women never told anyone about their own personal experiences, but when they did choose to reveal the information, usually it was to a coworker, not a superior. Prior to this point, they had decided not to tell because they felt that it wouldn't make a difference: 91

(28) No, uh-huh. It wouldn't have done any good. Um, the dean was a man, um, and I knew other instructors who did the same thing to other female students, um, and it was just one of those things that you handled yourself. It wouldn't have done you any good. As a matter of fact, things would have probably gotten harder. (Loretta)

(29) Oh, no. I didn't tell anyone. Since I handled it kinda OK. I just passed it off like he was a bit crazy or whatever. (Harriet)

(30) I didn't, you know. How would you bring it up? I know I sure back away from any more contact with him. (Lynn)

(31) No, I've told coworkers. Uh, especially [about] those two, flagrant instances. You know, like, uh, because it's something that's so shocking. . . . I did mention [one] to the doctor who was, of course, my supervisor, and he more or less just, you know, like brushed it off

because of the individual that was involved. 'Well, you know, he's a gross individual.' (Barbara)

(32) She felt that there was no one to tell, that it wouldn't help. (Loretta)

The issue of telling evoked the highest frequency of limiting phrases or hedges—"just," "kinda," "you know," "maybe." All narrators used at least one hedge, with some using several in a single utterance. This may be evidence of speakers' reluctance to break the silence about a topic that traditionally has been suppressed. How does one find words to express something that should not be talked about?

Further, in these excerpts, the women point out the awkwardness and difficulty of reporting sexual harassment ("How would you bring it up?") as well as the futility of such action ("It wouldn't help"). Again, many stress the importance of "handling" the situation on their own. This not only protects them from the consequences of speaking out, but it also allows them to maintain a peaceful coexistence with the very problem that threatens their well-being: "We got along just fine."

The consequences of telling take many forms. In instances where authorities were told explicitly, typically little or nothing was done. So the message is clear and unmistakable, as can be seen in excerpt (31) as well as the following examples:

(33) Oh, it was brought to management's attention, they just never did anything about him. . . . He'd been around the company for better than thirty years, and no one ever did anything about him. (Barbara)

(34) Because society makes it . . . it's kinda of like being raped, you know. And nobody cares anyway, that's kinda how you feel, you know. Except maybe your husband, and you don't want him to make a scene. And, uh. Yeah, I do know, yeah, I do know of someone else that was sexually harassed on the job. And the man was fired. I was warned how he would be, you know. So, you know, we got along just fine. Things he came by and said, you know, I just knew how to fix him. But he happened to say something to the wrong person that hadn't been warned, and she got real upset and went home and told her husband. Her husband came and made a big scene, and they fired the guy. He had been there twenty-five to thirty years. (Harriet)

Embedded in excerpt (34) is a very important piece of information: "I was warned how he would be." On the surface, a warning may be a way of safeguarding the potential victim. However, focusing on the victim instead of the perpetrator ensures that sexual harassment will continue. Many interviewees reported that they were warned about various men in the workplace, and even though they found the information helpful, most eventually had to transfer or quit. If a warning is the only measure taken to address the issue, then administrators and others have merely created a safe environment for prolonging a serious problem.

Telling about or speaking out against sexual harassment on the job carries with it the natural expectation that those in charge will take some type of action as soon as possible. Yet, in those rare instances where authorities were told, women did not always receive a satisfactory solution:

> (35) These guys say this, that, and the other, and if they
> [women] do say something to management, they, you
> know, like, they're told up there, women basically
> [are] working in a male environment and they have to
> expect it or, you know, like, it's just shop talk.
> They're more or less told that they have to tolerate it.
> (Barbara)

In this case, action from management follows the familiar pattern: nothing is done. However, the fact that women do indeed come forward may be a first and necessary step toward honest resolution of the problem. Equally important is the repercussion of telling. What happens to women who speak out? Does the situation become more difficult? (As Loretta predicted, "Things would have probably gotten harder.") Do women and men go back to their jobs as if nothing has happened? Do working conditions improve? Are there certain penalties for telling, and is the risk worth the effort?

Finally, telling can be nonverbal. Loretta's "evil eye" gets the message across and sometimes may be more effective than words:

> (36) Um, the sexist jokes, I think that's the biggest thing.
> Uh, that hits you in the face. It's very subtle. . . .
> Some of the older employees are still into the little
> sexist jokes. And we've got this one guy in the office
> that, you know, I'm always giving him the evil eye.
> (Loretta)

Loretta's decision to use body language instead of words signals the joke teller that something is wrong. Her response leaves open the possibility for more action later if this subtle hint is ignored. It temporarily allows the speaker to save face and simultaneously puts him on notice. While it should be obvious that being the object of a sexist joke is embarrassing

93

and degrading, the practice is alive and well in the workplace. It puts women at a clear disadvantage because they can neither censor the act of telling nor control the impact on an audience. Chris Kramarae suggests that some forms of humor are successful because they exaggerate popular stereotypes (1986, p. 227). So a sexist joke, regardless of a narrator's intention, is damaging to both the speaker and the listener because it promotes inaccurate information and harmful attitudes.

In sum, telling others and speaking out about sexual harassment goes beyond personal well-being. In all those instances where women (and men) did not tell authorities, there remained a situation detrimental to the next woman, as was the predicament of the younger female employee described in example (25). So, while not telling may preserve some people, it sacrifices others.

Language and Sex

Language plays a special role in female/male interactions. (For more on this point, see Coates and Cameron 1988; also the essay by Troutman-Robinson in this volume.) Not only is it a primary mode of communication, but it also is an instrument of power and status. In the event of sexual harassment, language is used in violation of social codes for respectful behavior. When men in the presence of women tell dirty or sexist jokes, make sexual innuendos, and use vulgar language, the act of speaking or telling becomes an exercise of power and control. Yet it would be erroneous to assume that women are always objects and that they play no part in shaping linguistic aspects of their own social roles. Women are also subjects, and, as the following discussion indicates, they produce distinct patterns of language use.

One of the most striking features in the narratives of the African-American women interviewed is their use of hedges. According to Coates, these linguistic markers are "epistemic modals" whose semantic function is to "indicate the speaker's confidence or lack of confidence in the truth of the proposition expressed in the utterance," and to protect or save face (1986, pp. 113–14). Words and phrases such as "you know," "sort of," "perhaps," and "just" make propositions or ideas seem undecided or tentative, while others such as "I think," "in my opinion," and "I believe" suggest doubtfulness or hesitancy ("I think that some people feel this way" vs. "Some people feel this way"). Research indicates that women tend to use these kinds of responses more frequently than men (Coates 1986, p. 102).

Although hedges are natural components of spontaneous language, their function intensifies in the context of sensitive and/or highly emotional topics. Therefore, it was not surprising that all of the women used hedges throughout their narratives. Specific items varied from single words[4] to phrases and clauses:

phrases/clauses	*words*
It seemed	sorta
I think	mighta
I thought	kinda
	so
I believe	
My belief is	
In my opinion	
Now this is just my opinion	
I formed my opinion prior	
I just was already prejudiced	
Maybe I'm narrow minded	
I felt that I was so opinionated	
You know	
You know what I mean?	
You know like	
I mean	
I guess	
I felt	
That's how I felt.	
I just feel	
I might be wrong.	
I myself know	
Me personally	
It's just me.	

Recurring phrases such as "I know," "I feel," and "I believe" dilute the authoritative force of the propositions they precede. Such phrasing is not as potent as the unmarked form: "A lot of black people said that" vs. "I think that a lot of black people said that." In addition, such overt marking has face-saving potential since the self in phrases such as "I think," "My belief is," and "In my opinion" speaks only for one person who can be proved wrong or incorrect.

Sexism versus Racism

Does the generalization of Anita Hill's experiences to all women obscure the unique circumstances of African American women? Can the sexism and racism that they have encountered for a lifetime be separated into discrete variables? Undoubtedly, the complexity of African American women's lives suggests that answers to these questions are neither easily discovered nor readily available. Furthermore, since it is not possible physically to separate one's sex from one's race, although these qualities can be disguised, then it follows that these variables are permanently intertwined. Loretta observed in several instances: "That was probably a bit of sexual and racial discrimination." She continued:

(37) But um, I did have a woman once who sat down in
my chair and told me what her problem was, and I
told her what I was gonna do, and when I proceeded,
got ready to do it, she stopped me and said, 'Oh, I
want a doctor to do this.' And I said, 'OK, go out
there and have a seat in the waiting room and a doctor
will be with you.' And when I have finished seeing
everybody who was on emergency that day, I was the
emergency doctor, she came back and said, 'Ah, I
didn't know you were the doctor.' I had my name tag
on, my captain's bars, and I had talked to her. So I
told her, 'One of the doctors will see you, just have a
seat.' One of the guys, they [the other doctors] were
mad at me, but I had to prove a point. I had to prove
a point. And once again, part of that was sex and part
of it was race, you know. When you're, when you're
a minority female, it's almost a double whammy. It's
almost a double whammy. And you, I was always
proving myself. Both to the other doctors and the
patients. So, it wasn't, there wasn't a lot said, but uh,
it was subtle. (Loretta)

Loretta senses that others' reactions to her may be influenced by the fact that she is female *and* African American. The above example is especially important because the antagonist in this instance is a woman. Although it is tempting to argue that this is a clear case of racial discrimination, it is important to note that a good number of women do not necessarily gravitate to or empathize with other women. So in Loretta's situation, doubt is evident in the female patient's reaction, seeming to say, "Can a woman be a doctor, especially if she is black?"

When applied to the Hill-Thomas hearings, the issue of sexism versus racism assumes additional significance for observers. As was previously mentioned, not only do we find male-female relations at odds here, but many women felt that the entire African American community was on trial. Therefore, in order to uncover feelings about the issue of sex versus race, the following question was posed: If Hill had been white, how would the hearing and the outcome have been different? This was the only response that was unanimous:

(38) Um, Thomas would not have made it. He would not, I'm sure that he would not have been sworn in as a Supreme Court justice at this point . . . if she had been white. Here was this black man, and he had harassed her sexually. I don't think Thomas would have been, and I don't think she would have been raked through the coals like that, either. I think they would have taken it easy on her." (Loretta)

(39) Because automatically, you know, they would have tried to hang him really. 'Course you know you aren't supposed to mess with white women. And if they had done that, and it was a white woman, they would've hung him." (Grace)

(40) I think that they would have found in Hill's favor in that instance. Simply because it's an allegation made about, from a white woman against a black male. Uh, and more credibility is put on that than it had been, you know, like, than the situation as it was, a black-on-black thing. So I, I think the outcome would have been different had it been a white woman." (Barbara)

(41) If she was white, oh my. I don't think they would have waited to have a hearing really. (Helen)

(42) She probably would have been believed. I think, I think there's a myth that Black men want white women. And that, you know, any accusation that a white woman would make would probably be given more credibility than anything a Black woman would have said. Um, you know, Black men are seen as sort of slathering beasts who, you know, desire white women. And I think, you know, that would've happened there, too. (Lynn)

All the women agreed that if Hill had been white, the dynamics of race would have taken precedence over the issue of sex, and Thomas would have been found guilty without any lingering doubts. Most women cited taboos and racial stereotypes generated during enslavement as a main reason for the predictable shift in priorities. Furthermore, they cited incidents in American history (such as the murder of Emmett Till)[4] as evidence that the combination of African American man and European

American woman would have guaranteed Thomas's guilt and the hypothetical white female's truthfulness.

These interviewees perceived race as an integral component of the hearing rather than a neutral by-product. It was not simply a matter of a woman and a man who happened to be African Americans, but a specific situation in which two prominent African Americans were embroiled in a controversy not necessarily of their own making. Narrators felt certain that the distorted public images of Hill and Thomas as well as publicity about their heretofore "private conflict" had a direct, negative impact on the African American community.

Conclusion

While these preliminary findings cannot be generalized, they indicate that race and sex are complex variables that cannot be separated neatly into discrete entities. As for African American women, their history, dual status, and daily experiences suggest a unique state of being and believing that has a profound impact on American life. Accordingly, the fact that Hill is an African-American woman should not be lost in a cultural perspective that on the one hand regards all women as the same and on the other hand regards all African Americans as the same. Hill's distinct voice opened up the possibilities for other voices, especially those of African-American women.

Notes

1. The women worked in the following occupations:
   Barbara: registered nurse in industry.
   Grace: machine operator.
   Lynn: college professor.
   Loretta: doctor.
   Harriet: beauty salon owner-operator.
   Helen: machine operator.
2. Fictional names of persons and places are used to protect the identities of the informants.
3. All of the women were asked and agreed that women can indeed sexually harass men on the job. However, they did not regard it as a problem, since most of the women they knew were of status equal or subordinate to the men they approached.
4. Emmett Till was a fourteen-year-old Black man from Chicago visiting relatives in Mississippi when he allegedly made sexually suggestive remarks to a white woman shopper in a Money, Mississippi, general store. According to details given by Stephen Whitfield in *A Death in the Delta*, Emmett Till was taken from the home of his uncle, Moses Wright, on August 28, 1955. He was severely beaten, shot, and thrown into the Tallahatchie River. His murderers were arrested, tried, and convicted.

References

Coates, Jennifer. *Women, Men and Language: A Sociolinguistic Account of Sex Differences in Language*. New York: Longman, 1986.

Coates, Jennifer, and Deborah Cameron, eds. *Women in Their Speech Communities*. New York: Longman, 1988.

Kramarae, Chris. "Folk Linguistics: Wishy-washy Mommy Talk." In Gary Goshgarian, ed., *Exploring Language*. Boston: Little Brown, 1986.

Imaging Lynching:
African American Women,
Communities of Struggle,
and Collective Memory

ELSA BARKLEY BROWN

I t has been several years now since
I found under the couch at my parents' home a scrapbook of my father's
political cartoons published in the *Louisville Defender*, my hometown's
Black newspaper, in the 1930s and 1940s. At the time, I was struck prin-
cipally by seeing a political side of my father with which I was previously
unfamiliar. I was most impressed with his depictions of lynchings.

Several years later, I bundled up this scrapbook to take to my home,
hoping to sort through, catalogue, and one day exhibit and write about
the materials contained therein. I shared these cartoons with a number of
friends and colleagues at a meeting and particularly pointed out the depictions of lynchings, emphasizing my pleasure at the depictions but also
my sense of their uniqueness. I commented that I could not recall any
photographs, drawings, or other visual images of lynching that showed
women, although I was fully aware of the record on the lynching of women.
Both when I first saw the scrapbook and when I was showing the illustrations to my colleagues, I felt a sense of connection that was, as I think
about it now, in some senses a yes. For the first time, I had seen a depiction that fit what I knew, and it was a kind of connection or confirmation not only intellectually but also someplace much deeper. When I
showed the pictures to my colleagues, I was most struck by the casualness
with which people moved past the particular ones to which I was most
connected. This, I am sure, reflected many things, including their interest

in other issues (international and community issues, issues of segregation, etc.) with which my father dealt. At the time, I wondered why what I felt was important clearly did not ring the same for others. I tried to see if somehow the lynching cartoons were not as well drawn or if there were some other reason for their being so much more easily passed over than I had anticipated. But I remained puzzled. Mulling over these images, I wondered if I was making too much of them.

Fall 1991. These thoughts come back to me. Like many African American women across the country, I am glued to a television set and a telephone the weekend of October 11. Clarence Thomas:

> From my standpoint, as a Black American, as far as I'm concerned, it's a high-tech lynching for uppity blacks who in any way deign to think for themselves, to do for themselves, to have different ideas. . . . You will be lynched, destroyed, caricatured by a committee of the U.S. Senate, rather than hung from a tree.

I am struck by many things this weekend, but for me, and perhaps many other people, this is the cruelest moment, the most ironic moment, the moment of greatest outrage, the moment of greatest isolation. Through the rest of the weekend, I listen, my ears begging for someone—some caller to C-Span or BET's "Our Voices," some commentator, some interviewee, lawyer, whoever—to question that image. I do not hear a challenge this weekend on television. I do, however, hear it in my telephone conversations with friends. I hear it in the Petition of African-American Professors of Social Science and Law, which circulates over telephone, computer message, and fax lines all weekend, and in my conversations with the women who helped draft and then signed onto the Official Statement to All Members of the United States Senate from African American Academic and Professional Women: A Petition to Reject the Clarence Thomas Nomination.[1] And I hear it from hundreds of women with whom I speak over the next several weeks, as we organize the African American Women in Defense of Ourselves campaign (see Ransby, this volume). But even then, I realize that what I hear is people questioning Thomas's use of the lynching image. No Black man was ever lynched for attacking a Black woman; Thomas, a man who had previously disconnected himself from racial imagery, was now painting himself as a victim of racial discrimination. But I still do not hear people question the notion that lynching itself is a masculine experience.

During the weeks following the hearings, in the numerous conversations I have with different people, I continue to listen for this insight. In one conversation, about two weeks after the hearings, a friend and colleague tells me that the real problem is that "Black women have no image, no symbol that they can call up so readily, so graphically in just

101

a word as Black men do with lynching." He says this, and my mouth flies open; the protest wells up from the pit of my stomach, but these protests do not come out. They have no voice. At the moment, I reflect back to my father's cartoons, and how much they don't represent what we now think we know and the images we now hold regarding lynching. And so I slump back, accepting the notion that we have no image. Nonetheless, I wonder why it is that people don't remember the lynching of Black women and the brutality of that experience. Why it is that the other experiences of violence that have so permeated the history of Black women in the United States—the rape, the sexual and other forms of physical abuse as employees in white homes, the contemporary domestic and public sexual and other physical violence—are not as vividly and importantly retained in our memory. Why it is that lynching (and the notion of it as a masculine experience) is not just remembered but is in fact central to how we understand the history of African American men, and indeed the African American experience in general. But violence against women— lynching, rape, and other forms of violence—is not.

I write this not only in the aftermath of the Thomas-Hill hearings but, months later, in the aftermath of the 1992 Los Angeles rebellion as well. And here, too, I see and hear a story, a history that wipes out, ignores, disremembers violence against Black women. And once again I strain to understand. I hear a speaker—a well-known, progressive, even feminist African American male—at a public gathering in May 1992, and he says urban violence and police brutality are directed against Black men and that explains why the L.A. rebellion is male. This time I open my mouth, and the sounds do come out; I object to the ideas themselves, and I try to formulate a theory of why people have these images. I stumble, but it is a step. I take many steps this year, some more hesitantly than others. Perhaps they take me/us closer to understanding why the women in my father's cartoons are no longer in our history, our memory. And why their daughters and granddaughters, walking in our midst now, are often invisible as well.

Clarence Thomas, October 12, 1991:

In the 1970s, I became very interested in the issue of lynching. And if you want to track through this country in the nineteenth and twentieth century the lynching of black men, you will see that there is invariably, or in many instances, a relationship with sex and an accusation that that person cannot shake off. That is the point that I'm trying to make, and that is the point that I was making last night, that this is high-tech lynching. I cannot shake off these accusations, because they play to the worst stereotypes we have about black men in this country.

Eleanor Holmes Norton, October 13, 1991:

This is about sex and not about race. A black woman raised
these questions, not a white woman or white men. (1991,
p. 25)

Thomas has constructed a racial history for himself. In many arenas,
his version of African American history stands. Norton does not challenge
Thomas's construction of history—she says African American history is
irrelevant here. But many African American people know that it is never
irrelevant. Claiming or imposing a particular historical memory is a central means of imposing political ideologies. Forgetting or omitting particular histories underlies the exclusion, marginalization, and subordination of certain peoples in political struggles.

Columbus, Mississippi, December 17, 1915:

Thursday a week ago Cordella Stevenson was found early in
the morning hanging to the limb of a tree, without any
clothing, dead. . . . The body was found about fifty yards
north of the Mobile & Ohio R.R. and the thousands and
thousands of passengers that came in and out of this city
last Thursday morning were horrified at the sight. She was
hung there from the night before by a bloodthirsty mob who
had gone to her home, snatched her from slumber, and
dragged her through the streets without any resistance. They
carried her to a far-off spot, did their dirt and then strung
her up. (*Chicago Defender*, Dec. 18, 1915)

Valdosta, Georgia, 1918:

Mary Turner, pregnant Black woman, is hanged to a tree,
doused with gasoline and motor oil and burned. As she
dangled from the rope, a man stepped forward with a
pocket knife and ripped open her abdomen in a crude
Caesarean operation. Out tumbled the prematurely born
child. . . . Two feeble cries it gave—and received for the
answer the heel of a stalwart man, as life was ground out of
the tiny form. (Bennett 1982, p. 352)

Does Thomas's reconstruction of African American history include Cordella Stevenson and Mary Turner? Would he recognize my father's cartoons? Cordella Stevenson's and Mary Turner's families and communities
would. My father's cartoons would be inappropriate illustrations not only
for Thomas's history but for Norton's as well.

Harriet Hernandes, Spartanburg, South Carolina, July 10, 1871:

Mighty near everyone in my neighborhood has been
whipped. . . . Ben Phillips and his wife and daughter . . . I
could not begin to tell all—Ann Bonner and her daughter,
Manza Surratt and his wife and whole family, even the least
child in the family, they took it out of bed and whipped it.
They told them if they did that they would remember it.[2]

Essic Harris, a Black man, North Carolina, July 1, 1871:

The rape of Black women by the Ku Klux Klan is so
common in my community that it has got to be an old
saying.[3]

We need only listen to our parents and grandparents to realize that black
women have a specific history of violence, of sexual abuse, of sexual
harassment. But our parents and grandparents aren't the voices we hear
in the media this weekend.

November 1991.[4] When Hill testified, a number of women—African and European American, individually and collectively—rallied to
support her and to advance awareness on the issue of sexual harassment.
Many of Hill's most visible supporters, or at least those on whom the
media focused, however, ignored the fact that she is a Black woman, the
thirteenth child of Oklahoma farmers, or treated these as merely descriptive or incidental matters.[5] Like Eleanor Holmes Norton, European-
American women, such as feminist legal scholar Catharine MacKinnon
and leaders of the National Organization for Women, spoke forcefully
and eloquently about the reality of sexual harassment in women's lives,
but in doing so they perpetuated a deracialized notion of women's experiences.[6] One wonders if many European American Feminists, especially, were not elated to have found an issue and an African American
woman who could become a universal symbol, evidence of the common
bonds of womanhood. Elevating Hill to such a status, however, required
ignoring the racialized and class-specific histories of women's sexuality
and stereotypes, and our different histories of sexual harassment and sexual violence.[7]

Hill experienced sexual harassment, not as a woman who had been
harassed by a man but as an *African American* woman harassed by an
African American man. Race is a factor in all cases of sexual abuse—
inter- or intraracial—although it is usually only explored in the former.
When European American middle- and upper-class men harass and abuse
European American women, they are generally protected by white male
privilege; when African American men harass and abuse European American women, they may be protected by male privilege, but they are as

likely to be subjected to racial hysteria; when African American men harass and abuse African American women, they are often supported by racist stereotypes that assume different sexual norms and different female value among African Americans.[8]

Hill's supporters, however, left it to Thomas and his supporters to construct the race and class analysis that would permeate the media. The result was that instead of a grand-scale lesson in sexual harassment, false notions of universal women's experiences and false notions of race were disseminated. In the end, ignoring racialized and class-specific histories became a political liability. Having constructed Hill as a generic or universal woman with no race or class (or with race or class being unimportant to her experience) and having developed an analysis of sexual harassment in which race and class were not central issues, many of Hill's supporters were unable to deal with the racialized and class-specific discussion when it emerged.[9] Thus, once Thomas played the race card and a string of his female supporters raised the class issue, they had much of the public discussion to themselves.[10] Thomas and his supporters did not create a race and class context; they exploited it. When many of Hill's supporters refused to address race as well as class—which both Black and white people throughout the United States knew to be issues—they forced the public to rely on the analysis of Thomas's supporters.

Thomas constructed himself as a black man confronting a generic ("white" or "whitened") woman assisted by white men. By "manipulating the legacy of lynching," Thomas sought "to deflect attention away from the reality of sexual abuse in African American women's lives" ("African American Women in Defense of Ourselves").[11] Such a strategy could have been countered effectively only by putting the experience of sexual harassment for Hill in the context of her being a Black woman in the United States.[12]

Eleven years earlier, Hill embarked on her legal career. This was a woman who began her formal education before the Morris, Oklahoma, schools were integrated and who had gone on to graduate from one of the country's most elite law schools:

> When she confronted the sexual harassment, so painfully
> described in her testimony, the weight of how to handle
> these advances lay on Anita Hill not merely as [a woman or
> a Yale Law School graduate], but as a young Black
> woman, the daughter of Oklahoma farmers, whose family
> and community expected her to do well. It is essential to
> understand how this may have shaped both her experiences
> and her responses. (official statement)

Hill's friend Ellen Wells, herself the victim of sexual harassment on the job, explained in her succinct statement before the committee: "You don't walk around carrying your burdens so that everyone can see them. You're supposed to carry that burden and try to make the best of it."[13]

Few Black women of Hill's age or older grew up unaware of the frequency of sexual abuse as part of African American women's employment history. Many of us were painfully aware that one reason our families worked so hard to shield us from domestic and factory work was to shield us from sexual abuse. And we were aware that the choices many of our mothers made (or our fathers insisted upon) to forgo employment were, in fact, efforts to avoid abusive employment situations. Sexual harassment as a legal theory and a public discussion in European American middle-class communities may be a late-1970s phenomenon, but sexual harassment not only has been a long-standing and widespread phenomenon of Black women's labor history, it also has been the subject of widespread public and private discussion within African American communities. From the late nineteenth century, Black women and men spoke out about the frequency of sexual abuse of Black women laborers, the majority of whom were employed in domestic service.

Maggie Lena Walker, Bethel A.M.E. Church, Richmond, Virginia, March 15, 1925:

> Poverty is a trap for *women*, and especially for our women.
> . . . When I walk along the avenue of our city and I see
> our own girls employed in the households of the whites, my
> heart aches with pain. Not that I cast a slur, or say one
> word against any kind of honest employment, yet when I
> see the good, pure, honest colored girl who is compelled to
> be a domestic in a white man's family—while I applaud the
> girl for her willingness to do honest work in order to be
> self-supporting, and to help the mother and father who have
> toiled for her, yet I tremble lest she should slip and fall a
> victim to some white man's lust.

It is hard to read the politics of Black communities, especially Black women's organizations, in the late nineteenth and early twentieth centuries without recognizing the awareness of the reality of sexual harassment.[14] By the mid-twentieth century, this was no longer as public a discussion in our communities, but it was still a significant part of the private discussion and necessary socialization of an African American female living in a racial and racist society.[15] A collective memory of sexual harassment runs deep in African American communities, and many Black women, especially those born before the 1960s Civil Rights Movement, would likely recognize sexual harassment not as a singular experience but as part of a collective and common history.

Given the economic and racial circumstances, African American women understand from an early age that figuring out how to endure, survive, and move forward is an essential responsibility. As a newly minted young Black professional, the pride of one's family and community, one would find the responsibility to do so even greater. One thinks, "They endured and so should I." One thinks one is expected to represent success.

How can you dash your family's and community's joy at your achievements and their hopes that education, mobility, and a good job would protect you?

Analyses that offered as explanation of Hill's long silence only that it was representative of the common tendency of women to individualize the experience, to feel isolated, and therefore not to report such incidents assume, in fact, a lack of socialization around these issues or a socialization that leads women to see themselves as alone and unique in these experiences: thus, such analyses miss the complexity of these experiences for different women (e.g., MacKinnon 1991). By enlarging the discussion beyond individual explanations, or in ways that truly explored the differential dimensions and expressions of power, one might have expanded the base of support—support not based on a commonality of experience but on a mobilization that precisely spoke to particularities and differences.

Recognizing the different experiences of African and European American women requires us particularly to consider the consequences of the sexual history and sexual stereotypes of African Americans, especially African American women. "Throughout U.S. history Black women have been sexually stereotyped as immoral, insatiable, perverse; the initiators in all sexual contacts—abusive or otherwise." Political, economic, and social privileges of European Americans (especially men but also women), as well as the stereotyping from which these privileges stem, inevitably resulted in "the common assumption in legal proceedings as well as in the larger society . . . that Black women cannot be raped or otherwise sexually abused" ("In Defense of Ourselves").[16] This assumption has several effects.

One consequence is that an African American women is most likely not to be believed if she speaks of unwarranted sexual advances, or will be believed to have been either the initiator or a willing participant. Both African and European American women have struggled throughout the nineteenth and twentieth centuries to gain control of their sexual selves. While elite European American women's sexual history has included the long effort to break down Victorian assumptions of sexuality and respectability in order to gain this control, Black women's sexual history has been just the opposite, requiring a struggle to be accepted as respectable in an effort to gain this same control of their sexual selves (Crenshaw 1992, p. 29). Importantly, this has resulted in what Darlene Clark Hine (1989) has described as a culture of dissemblance—Black women's sexuality is often concealed, that is, African American women have had to learn to cover up all public suggestions of sexuality, even of sexual abuse. Black women, especially those of the middle class, have learned to present a public image that never reveals their sexuality.

Another effect of the mythical assumption that African American women cannot be sexually abused is that, given the sexual stereotyping of black men, a young Hill also may have recognized that speaking of the particularities of Thomas's harassment had the potential to restigmatize the whole Black community—male and female. This is not merely, as some have suggested, about protecting Black men or being "dutiful daughters." Black women sought their own as well as the larger community's protection through the development of a politics of respectability. When Black colleges insisted on rigid dress requirements for female students, they were, in part, hoping to offset the hostility toward Black higher education by presenting students as respectable. When Spelman College students were required always to wear gloves and hats in downtown Atlanta, officials hoped to set them off, to have them be seen as "respectable" and less subject to harassment. During the 1906 Atlanta race riot, when the only places protected by city police were the campuses of the Black colleges which then encouraged Black residents to seek shelter within their walls, the idea that respectability could protect you gained even greater credence. As with all efforts to establish a uniform community standard and require everyone to live by it, the struggle to present Black women and the Black community as "respectable" eventually led to repression within the community, as when the Neighborhood Union, led by Lugenia Burns Hope, used the power of its organization to remove what it considered unsavory elements, prostitutes, alcoholics, and Sanctified churches, the latter judged to have too unrespectable a worship service (Brown 1988; Rouse 1989).

The struggle over respectability is an important and complex dimension in the development of African American communities, as many Black women and men sought to establish their own behavioral norms and still exercise basic educational and political rights. The popularity of female blues singers, many of whose recordings would not have received a "respectable" label, suggests that people within their own communities found their own ways of negotiating the protective elements of this emphasis on behavior, dress, and so on. Nevertheless, it is instructive to realize the degree to which Black women's sexual and political history has been shaped by a widespread belief that while respectable behavior would not guarantee one protection from sexual assault, the absence of such was certain to reinforce racist notions of Black women's greater sexuality, availability, or immorality, as well as the racist notions of Black men's bestiality which were linked to that.[17]

October 11, 1991. Clarence Thomas: "I will not provide the rope for my own lynching." But by exploiting the issue, Thomas provided for another's lynching—not only Hill's but also that of other women of color and poor and working-class women throughout history. Only a discussion of the differences and linkages in Black and white women's and working-class and middle-class women's struggles for control of their sexual selves could have effectively addressed Thomas's manipulation of race and class and the fears that many Black people, especially women, had about the public discussion of what they perceived as an intraracial sexual issue. Dismissing or ignoring these concerns, or imposing a universal Feminist standard that ignores the differential consequences of public discourse, will not help us build a political community around these issues. The political liability here and the threat to creating a community of struggle came from *not* focusing on differences among women and *not* seriously addressing the race and class dimensions of power and sexual harassment. Uncomplicated discussions of universal women's experiences cannot address these realities. Race (and, yes, gender) is at once too simple an answer and a more complex answer than we have yet begun to make it.

October 17, 1991

My students tell me they have seen on Black Entertainment Television a talk show that focused on Black women's history of betrayal of the race, as traitors, dating back to slavery and their collaboration with white masters, continuing through contemporary struggles. My students are shocked, angry, and curious. How have such ideas developed, and what keeps them alive?

Nathan and Julia Hare: *109*

We had seen Anita Hill before . . . during the 1984
Democratic campaign in the form of Congressman Maxine
Waters, who following the script of the white pro-choice
feminists, boasted in *Ms.* that she persuaded Jesse Jackson
. . . to switch his position [on abortion] in a futile quest for
the white feminist vote he should have known he wouldn't
get . . . in the firestorm of white-promoted fiction that
flashed across two decades (the 1970s and 1980s) exorcising
the Black male (whose pen was by contrast put on ice by
the mainstream publishing industry . . . Michelle Wallace
. . . *Black Macho: The Myth of the Superblack Woman* . . .
Alice Walker . . . *The Color Purple* . . . Ntozake Shange
. . . *For Cullud Girls Who Commit Suicide When the
Rainbow Is Enuf* . . . in the form of black female
representatives of the ACLU and National Organization for
Women Legal Defense Fund, when these bodies determined
[that] . . . the all-black male school movement [was] invalid
and wouldn't be allowed to fly . . . in the form of Faye
Wattleton, Planned Parenthood's puppet black mannequin
. . . appeared with the first squad of white feminists that
initially stormed the Senate in an effort to shoot down the

Black man's Supreme Court nomination. . . . In the years
ahead . . . we will never have to look very hard for Anita
Faye; if you yourself should ever decide to embrace some
white feminist scheme . . . Anita Faye will appear in the
form of you; and we will be watching you. (1991,
pp. 24, 29)

Jacquelyne Johnson Jackson:

My lasting impression of Hill, formed when I first saw her
very first televised press conference, was she's "them
against US." Among Hill's major faults, perhaps her two
most crucial ones were her apparent belief that slavery's
legacy of the highly peculiar triangle of black male, black
female, and white male relationships meant that white males
were more partial to black females than to Black males.
. . . The "them against us" hearings undoubtedly showed
that most Blacks—female and male alike—objected to
Hill's witting or unwitting acquiescence to white male
superiority, improper use of black females against black
males, and the extension of that peculiar triangle into a
rectangle of conniving white females. . . . So Hill was, for
whatever reasons, "them against us." (1992, p. 49)

Beverly Guy-Sheftall, quoting Evelyn Hammonds:

Black women too often become suspect and discredited in
our communities when we raise issues of sexism, such as
sexual harassment, rape, incest, battering, date rape, or
what we have experienced as women under patriarchy, a
structure of domination which exists in the larger society
and also within the Black community. . . . Historically, we
have been accused of being traitors to the race when we
align ourselves with women's liberation struggles. . . . As
we prepare ourselves for the most difficult time of our
sojourn in America since slavery, it is imperative that black
men and women rid ourselves of all ideas and behaviors
that will result in our individual and collective
underdevelopment and debasement. . . . Black men do not
need subservient women who remain silent about the abuse
and suffering they experience, no matter who is the
victimizer. We must reject antiquated and counterproductive
notions of manhood which dictate that men maintain power
over women and prevent them from speaking, even in their
own behalf. (1992, p. 36)

April 1992. Just as we need to complicate our discussion of women's issues, we need to complicate our definition of "Blackness." The present masculine construct of collective memory and African American identity—that which allows us to forget the female fruit hanging from Southern trees, fending off unwanted advances, and organizing to "uplift the race"—carries powerful implications for our contemporary politics and struggle. Maggie Lena Walker, an early-twentieth-century activist, always contended that the most difficult part of any political struggle is the struggle to "catch the vision." I think for persons attempting to build communities and political struggle within these United States, it is especially important—and especially difficult—to understand the ways in which political struggles that are designed to create a new society and new sets of relationships between peoples within this society are most often framed by and grounded in the very notions, assumptions, and practices that they are ostensibly—and consciously—intended to subvert. Learning to *think* in new ways is, in fact, the hardest and most necessary step in any political struggle.

An integral goal of the struggles in which many of us within African American communities have engaged over the past several decades has been continuing efforts to learn how to envision the world different and differently. I, along with many other committed people around the country, spent the first five years of the 1980s working to organize a National Black Independent Political Party. In NBIPP, we tried to build a political party that would be integrally based in the day-to-day life of African-American communities. We tried to create new models of leadership, new models of male-female relations within a political struggle, new models of mass participation. One of the principles we started with was a commitment to equal leadership of men and women. And one of the things I continue to believe about NBIPP was the genuineness of that commitment on the part of men and women. And yet on questions of political development and leadership style, masculine constructions pervaded our organizing efforts.

We began with an assumption of coequal leadership so that all positions had to be held by two individuals, one female, one male. Yet throughout the party's history, we continued to have conversations about who were more politically developed, men or women. It is not merely the fact of these conversations that is important, but rather the assumptions about what political development was. Thus, one of the questions was who had a history of radical political struggle and who did not. And a history of radical political struggle generally meant people who had been involved in national, overt, formal activity, whereas people who had spent their lives working in their local communities, committed to the institutions and the relationships that make this struggle possible, were considered less politically developed. In questions of leadership style, while we, in fact, had and were committed to coequal leadership, it also

111

often was premised upon a notion of masculine leadership style, an assumption of particular kinds of leadership; a fairly charismatic, ministerial kind of leadership was appropriate, more developed, and more important. And so in NBIPP, which I consider an important example of people committed to creating new kinds of relationships and a new kind of struggle, we were continuously held back by the inability to see something different, to envision, as Walker said, something different, and therefore to create something different.

Our inability to move forward was tied, I am convinced, at least in part to the pervasive effects of a masculine construction of our history, of "Blackness," and of racial interests. Such a construction has dominated post-1960s historical memory, popular culture, and political struggle, although it can be seen most clearly in the degree to which black liberation groups of the late 1960s and 1970s—the Black Panther Party, for instance—defined the liberation struggle as a quest for black manhood.[18] Huey Newton:

> The historical relationship between Black and white here in America has been the relationship between the slave and the master. . . . The master took the manhood from the slave because he stripped him of a mind. . . . The slave-master [became] very envious of the slave because he pictured the slave as being more of a man, being superior sexually, because the penis is part of the body. . . . He attempted to bind the penis of the slave . . . he psychologically wants to castrate the black man. (1968, p. 502)

112

With this historical interpretation, Newton then characterized the black liberation movement as the struggle for the Black man to "recapture his mind, recapture his balls, then he will lose all fear and will be free to determine his destiny . . . the Black Panther Party, along with all revolutionary black groups, has regained our mind and our manhood" (p. 498).

The liberation of African Americans was thus linked to the physical, intellectual, political, and sexual position of African American men, not that of African American men *and* women. Black women were defined out of historical memory and out of an active, positive role in the liberation struggle. In this scenario, they could be passive observers; the only active role allowed them was that of coconspirators with the enemy, the white masters. It was the condition of men that was the determinant of the condition of the race, and it was men who were the primary actors and agents of change. Importantly, this was merely a partial reconstruction of African American history and of the actual operations of the Black Panther Party itself. The actual circumstances within the Party were far more complex, and the role of women was central to much of the Party's work—self-defense, liberation schools, breakfast programs, health clinics. However, equally important is the fact that the rhetoric, the imagery, and the collective historical memory of the Black Panther Party, for almost twenty-five years, have been masculine, emphasizing the centrality of men to the liberation of Black people and rendering virtually invisible women's condition and women's struggle as the preconditions and components of that liberation.

The equation of the masculine condition and struggle with that of the entire race was, in part, a reflection of the vast and justifiable outcry against Daniel Patrick Moynihan's *The Negro Family: The Case for National Action* (1965), which emphasized a Black matriarchy and, by extension, the inability of Black males to be "real men." A focus on the masculine condition was also foreshadowed in the acceptance of Richard Wright's *Native Son* (1940) as the ultimate protest novel, one that addressed boldly and graphically the oppression of African American males and exposed the political and economic underpinnings of African American oppression. Forgotten in this process of affirmation of Wright's presentation of our history and condition was Bessie, the African American woman whom Bigger Thomas rapes and murders, first smashing her head with a brick and then tossing her down an airshaft where she freezes to death (Harris 1990; Painter 1991; Fischer 1992). If Bigger Thomas came to stand for the oppression of African Americans and *Native Son* for the ultimate protest novel, what does it mean for our collective memory and our definition of blackness that Bessie, her life, and her death were lost in that process? Can we claim Bigger without claiming Bessie, and how would claiming both revise our historical memory and our definition of Blackness?

In a similar vein, consider African American historians' reconstruction of our history in the 1970s. It was a reconstruction that very importantly moved away from the race relations integrationist/assimilationist paradigm that had shaped so much historical writing. This reconstruction began to argue for a history that respected African Americans as actors, not merely as passive victims or reactors. However, it also ushered in a masculine idea of community. One of the most important books in that reclamation was John Blassingame's *The Slave Community: Plantation Life in the Antebellum South* (1982), a book that significantly overturned the way the history of slavery and of African Americans is written. Blassingame insisted on looking at slavery from the point of view of the slave and brilliantly demonstrated that this could be done despite the dearth of written records left by slaves themselves, by using music, folklore, WPA interviews. It was (and is) a brilliant reclamation, a "re-remembering" of our history. Yet it was at the same time a partial memory, one that rescued slaves from charges of pathology by asserting their normalcy in terms of two-parent households with patriarchal authority. Writing in the post-Moynihan age, Blassingame re-remembered slavery and the slave community as masculine; group identity, community even, hinged on men.

This masculine focus is evident contemporarily in the widespread equation of the crisis in the Black community with identifying black men as "endangered." Appropriately, we should focus our attention and energies on the homicide and imprisonment rates for Black men; their life span, educational opportunities, drug and alcohol usage, unemployment and underemployment; and the violence—physical, economic, and social—that surrounds and engulfs many Black men in the late-twentieth—century United States. Yet we must recognize that this is only a partial reading of our current state, one that cannot and should not be abstracted from focusing on the violence of many Black women's lives—as victims of rape and other forms of sexual abuse, murder, drugs, alcohol, poverty, and the devastation of AIDS.

My point is not to argue that women are more endangered but to assert that the life chances of African Americans in the United States are equally decimated for women *and* for men. However, one would never know this from the talk both within the Black community and within the larger society. Prevailing assumptions seem to equate the condition of the Black community with the status of Black males. It is a continuation of an ideology of Blackness, of group identity, that equates the status, condition, and progress of the race—the good of the race—with men. It is a masculinization of Blackness and race progress. Often, therefore, it is an ideology that looks to ways to improve the lot of men while not just omitting women from the picture but often even accepting the violence against them. By what standards would Mike Tyson, even before he was charged with the rape of an eighteen-year-old African American woman, have stood as a role model for young African American men? By what standards would a man who has often acknowledged that he enjoys brutalizing women be someone we would put forward as a role model—unless rescuing African American men from poverty and inner-city death at any price, including violence against women, is how we define the good of the race?

The erasure of women from contemporary assessments of the Black condition and from Black political struggle is found in the reconstruction of the entire political history of African Americans—by scholars and by activists—and it is found in our definitions of what constitutes political struggle and whom we remember as our political leadership. Our collective memory of historical struggle ignores the fact that the National Association of Colored Women was, in the late nineteenth and early twentieth centuries, the country's leading national race organization—predating the creation of the NAACP by fifteen years. Even after the founding of the NAACP, the NACW remained for some time the leading Black national organization working for the individual and collective advancement of African Americans and particularly for self-determination and community development. The NAACP, by contrast, was not only integrationist in perspective but also for many years white-controlled. In fact, W. E. B. Du Bois in 1912 called the women of the NACW the "intellectual leadership of the race."

The club women themselves were clear that they stood in leadership positions along with men. These women put forward a different ideology of Blackness and political struggle. In defining themselves as race women, they also redefined the roles and notions of African American manhood. A strong "race man" traditionally meant one who stood up fearlessly in defense of the race. But women like Maggie Lena Walker argued that the development of the Black community could not be achieved by men alone, or by men on behalf of women. Only a strong and unified community of *both* women and men could wield the power necessary to allow Black people to shape their own lives. Therefore, only when women were able to exercise their full strength would the community be at its full strength. Only when the community was at its full strength would it be able to create its own conditions, conditions that would allow men as well as women to move out of structural isolation at the bottom of the labor market and to overcome political impotence in the larger society. They, therefore argued that it was in the self-interest of Black men and the community as a whole to support expanded opportunities for women and to define the race's progress as much by the status of women as by that of men. Only by aiding and defending women's assaults on the social, political, and economic barriers generally imposed on women could Black men really defend the race. Race men therefore, were defined not just by their actions on behalf of Black rights but also by their actions on behalf of women's rights. The two were inseparable.[19] Du Bois endorsed this view of the connection between race struggle and women's struggle when he wrote: "The present mincing horror of a free womanhood must pass if we are ever to be rid of the bestiality of a free manhood; not by guarding the weak in weakness do we gain strength, but by making weakness free and strong" (1920, p. 165).

Few histories of African American political struggle incorporate the NACW. For many people in our communities, Frederick Douglass, Booker T. Washington, and Du Bois stand as the sole symbols of Black political activism. Our understanding of Black politics and even of Blackness itself is often centered around these three men. Meanwhile, a large national association of women with numerous state and local chapters developed and sustained hundreds of community institutions that were the basis for African American life in the era of segregation and at the height of racial violence (Shaw, 1990).

Frederick Douglass:

Our history has been but a track of blood. . . . The
question forced upon us at every moment of our generation

115

has not been, as with other races . . . how shall we adorn, beautify, exalt, and ennoble life, but how shall we retain life itself. The struggle with us was not to do, but to be. (1865, quoted in Gutman 1987, p. 296)

Audre Lorde:

My political obligations? I am a black woman . . . in a world that defines human as white and male for starters. Everything I do including survival is political. (1989, p. 27)

Helen Lee Jackson, writing about growing up in Richmond, Virginia, in the early twentieth century, remembered that her grandmother, Mumma Lou,

always dressed in a long black skirt which swept the ground, with three white petticoats underneath, a black shirtwaist and hose, all of cotton. . . . In her skirts, which she sewed herself, she made deep wide pockets which . . . were used to cart away food from white people's houses where Mumma Lou did day work. These pockets could hold a good-sized ham bone, with some meat clinging to it, chicken legs and breasts, and even a Mason jar filled with beef stew. From the food she carried away from her employers, Mumma Lou fed not only her own family, but other poor people in the neighborhood. (quoted in Brown, 1991; see note 20)

116

If Black elite women, such as Josephine St. Pierre Ruffin and Maggie Lena Walker, and their well-developed, formalized, institutionalized, political struggles have been lost to our collective historical memory, the Mumma Lous have fared even worse.[20] Their actions are often seen as apolitical forms of survival; they are viewed as politically underdeveloped as we privilege presumably more sophisticated ideologies and tactics.

Bernice Johnson Reagon counters such notions when she contends that her participation in the 1960s Civil Rights Movement was at base "simply a continuance or more complexly a continuance" of the resistance efforts of many women who preceded her in her community—women who sewed clothes for school plays, sang in church, taught school, raised the community's children—sustaining community and culture, enlarging the space in which the community operated, creating the logic and grounding on which, in fact, the Civil Rights Movement was based. This suggests the problems with the dichotomous manner in which we often posit survival and resistance as separate entities, as well as the problems with unilinear theories of political struggle that assume progression from survival to everyday forms of political resistance to presumably more sophisticated ideologies and tactics. Differentiating what precisely is political struggle, however, should require us to examine closely the realities of race, class, and gender in a given time and place and to invest meaning not in specific acts themselves but in the social relations in which those acts are embedded. Feeding one's family or one's neighbors, teaching school, and building a stage for the school play are not inherently political acts. Yet we understand them as such in African American history if we take seriously Frederick Douglass and Audre Lorde: at no point in the history of these United States have African American people lived in a society in which their right to life was a given.

In our reconsideration of our history, we also may begin to remember the realities of lynching—not just that Black women were subjected to violence but also that they were in the forefront of the struggle to eliminate this horror. How is it we forgot what Ida B. Wells-Barnett in her struggle against lynching fought so hard to show us and the world— that no discussion of lynching could be disconnected from the reality of the sexual stereotyping and sexual abuse of Black women? How is it that Black women were remembered as betrayers of the race and Black men as victims when it was Wells-Barnett and later the Black women's group the Anti-Lynching Crusaders who were foremost in the struggle against lynching? While not achieving a federal antilynching bill or completely eliminating lynching, they were successful in altering public opinion sufficiently to seriously decrease societal acceptance of lynching and thus to lead to a decline in lynching in our society.

1991–1992. This has been an amazing year for "we who believe in freedom." A year in which we have witnessed the death of fifteen-year-old Latasha Harlins, shot in the back of the head in a dispute over a $1.79 bottle of orange juice; the subsequent release without imprisonment of her murderer and the reelection to the bench of the judge who decided the case; George Bush's announcement of Clarence Thomas's nomination to the Supreme Court; the Thomas confirmation hearings, complete with Thomas's misrepresentation and maligning of his sister, Emma Mae Martin, in order to present the "politically correct" image and ensure conservative support and a seat on the bench; the Anita Hill-Clarence Thomas phase of the Thomas nomination hearings; the Simi Valley verdict, acquitting the four policemen who brutally beat Rodney King, followed by the televised police, armed forces, government, and media assault on the men, women, and children of south-central Los Angeles. This has been an amazing year for "we who believe in freedom." But, as Sweet Honey 'n' the Rock's song continues, "We who believe in freedom/Cannot rest until it's won/Until the killing of Black men/ Black mother's sons/Is as important as the killing of white men/White mother's sons/We who believe in freedom/Cannot rest until it's won."

Naomi Wolf:

It is those professional women on the "inside"—with the most to lose—who express the greatest fear of what they describe as the professional suicide of speaking up for one's own rights or beliefs as a woman. This silence is neither apathy nor selfishness nor cowardice. It is silencing by economic pressure in a male-dominated workplace during a worldwide recession. Clearly, the best way to stop a revolution is by giving people something to lose. (1991)

Rosemary Bray:

The parallel pursuits of equality for African Americans and for women have trapped black women between often conflicting agendas for more than a century. We are asked in a thousand ways, large and small, to take sides against ourselves, postponing a confrontation in one arena to address an equally urgent task in another. . . . Despite the bind, more often than not we choose loyalty to the race rather than the uncertain allegiance of gender. (1991, p. 56)

Late May 1992. I reflect on the voices of those many African American women who opposed Anita Hill. I am here particularly interested in what became—and I think in some ways remains—the common refrain, succinctly put by Rosemary Bray, of "taking sides against ourselves." According to Bray, this often results in the privileging of race over gender; or, as others would argue, of an antifeminist strand among Black women. What I am particularly concerned with here is the way in which many of the conversations about African American women's opposition to Hill are conversations about false consciousness, problematic identities, and the problem that African American women have in choosing among different identities.

I think it might be useful to start from a different premise, one that assumes that people generally do act in their own best interests, as they understand them, and, therefore, that perhaps the place to start is with the discourse on sexual harassment before, during, and after these hearings—to presume just for a moment that the problem may lie there. Start not with the discourse created by the senators, Thomas, or Bush but with that created by feminist activists on sexual harassment issues. It is clear that the discourse would have been different if we had started building a history and theory of sexual harassment from the experiences of African-American domestic workers. What would the discourse on sexual harassment have been like if we had begun with women on welfare? What are our differing basic assumptions about what sexual harassment is?

If, in fact, sexual harassment in the workplace is about unwelcome sexual advances, suggestive or derogatory gestures, or remarks being imposed upon one as a condition of ensuring one's livelihood and that of one's family, what might our theory be like if we had listened to welfare rights activists in the 1960s, '70s, and '80s who raised the constant surveillance of welfare mothers as, in fact, a form of sexual harassment? Why have we created a discussion of sexual harassment that takes us back to private/public distinctions? Why have we constructed an entire feminist argument about what work is and where the workplace is? Isn't the struggle of people to take care of their families and homes "work"? How did that get written out of the kind of workplace in which sexual harassment might, in fact, occur? I suggest that having created a discourse and theory of sexual harassment that omitted the experiences of domestic workers, women on welfare, and others, and which often privileged professional women, it was difficult if not impossible to make a connection to the many women who understood their exclusion. And it was much easier for Thomas's supporters, emphasizing class distinctions, to portray Hill's charges of sexual harassment as about maintaining degrees of privilege and power on the part of elite women.

I also reflect on questions of violence. I wonder where in the last month, and where even before, is the organized Feminist outrage over south-central Los Angeles? Where is the same kind of organizing around south-central Los Angeles, around the women there, around the people there, that we saw around Hill? Or is that somehow not a feminist issue? *119* If so, how did we get to that definition of feminism particularly if feminism and feminists are concerned about violence against women? To what degree do we think of the systematic surveillance of people on welfare, the systematic surveillance of people in public housing, the police brutality in the streets of our cities as issues of violence against women?

In the African American community, the discourse of Black-on-Black crime and on violence often excludes rape and other sex crimes. Many feminists have created a discourse around violence that has excluded state repression and police brutality as a central part of the violence many women face. Can we build a radical political struggle if we, in African America, do not take the necessity of organizing as strongly around the sexual harassment of one woman as we do around the obtaining of political positions? Can we build a radical political struggle if we, in feminist communities, do not take the necessity of organizing as strongly around what is happening in south-central Los Angeles (and elsewhere) as we took organizing around sexual harassment?

July 1992. Our efforts at constructing communities of identity have been grounded in our constructions of history. When we construct universal notions of women or masculine notions of Blackness, when we impose rigid distinctions between the workplaces in which people of different races and classes establish the means to maintain themselves and their families, when we claim only some forms of violence as central or important to our struggles, we are claiming or remembering particular histories. What holds communities of struggle together are the collective memories. We give life and validity to our constructions of race, gender, class, community, and politics by giving those constructions a history.

As we have struggled to build communities of struggle over the last several decades, however, as Toni Morrison said, "somebody forgot to tell somebody something."[21] And in the process, our collective memory became partial, distorted, dismembered. The group identities, definitions, and issues of political struggle that came from that partial memory were limited. Central to constructing more radical political struggles is the reclamation and reconstruction of fuller, more complex histories. My father's political cartoons remind me of the differences between our histories and our historical memory. They remind me that we have some powerful lot of re-remembering to do.

Notes

My appreciation to Jamie Hart and Nataki H. Goodall for research assistance. For thinking through the ideas with me, I thank Nataki H. Goodall, Jacquelyn Dowd Hall, Tera Hunter, Jerma Jackson, Robin D. G. Kelley, Deborah K. King, Tracye Matthews, Zoharah Simmons, the numbers of people who shared their analyses along with their energies to African-American Women in Defense of Ourselves, and the students in my Black Women in America class, fall 1991 and spring 1992, and my graduate Historiography of Black Women in America class, fall 1991, University of Michigan.

1. "Official Statement to All Members of the United States Senate—A Petition of African-American Professors of Social Science and Law," 12 October 1991; Letter to The Honorable Senators of the United States from African American Academic and Professional Women Who Oppose the Clarence Thomas Nomination, 15 October 1991; "Official Statement to All Members of the United States Senate from African American Academic and Professional Women: A Petition to Reject the Clarence Thomas Nomination," 15 October 1991; all in my possession.
2. Harriet Hernandes testimony taken at Spartanburg, South Carolina, July 10, 1871, in U.S. Congress, *Testimony Taken by the Joint Select Committee to Inquire into the Condition of Affairs in the Late Insurrectionary States, South Carolina*, p. 586 (hereafter cited as *Ku Klux Klan Testimony*). The thirteen volumes of this testimony are filled with reports of whipping and/or raping of black women—for their refusal to work in the fields or in white people's homes, for their own and their husbands' political activities, or for their and their families' efforts to acquire land.
3. Essic Harris testimony, ibid., *North Carolina* volume, p. 100.
4. Much of this November 1991 section is taken from Elsa Barkley Brown, " 'What Has Happened Here': The Politics of Difference in Women's History and Feminist Politics," *Feminist Studies* (Summer 1992):295–312.
5. The discussion that follows should be read as a critique not of Hill's testimony but rather of those who set themselves out as political and intellectual experts able to speak with authority. It is concerned with public discussion in mainstream media. I am not naive enough to think the conclusion of the Thomas confirmation process would have been different if these issues had been effectively addressed. I do believe public discussion and political mobilization then and in the future could have been shaped differently by these discussions. Given that for two decades black women, according to almost all polls, have supported feminist objectives in larger numbers than white women, I think we have to look to something other than black women's reported antifeminism

or privileging race over gender for the answer to why an effective cross-race, cross-class political mobilization and discussion did not develop.

6. This is not to say that they did not acknowledge that Hill was black or even, in McKinnon's case, that "most of the women who have brought forward claims that have advanced the laws of sexual harassment have been black. Because racism is often sexualized, black women have been particularly clear in identifying this behavior as a violation of their civil rights" (*People*, October 28, 1991, p. 49). It is to say that having acknowledged this, race is not a significant factor in the analysis of women's experience of sexual harassment.

7. For an analysis fully attuned to questions of race and class, see Crenshaw 1991 and Crenshaw 1992. It is useful to compare Crenshaw's analysis in the former with Catharine MacKinnon's and in the latter with Ellen Willis's.

8. One of the most egregious examples of the latter as related to this particular case can be seen in Orlando Patterson's argument that if Thomas said the things Hill charged, he was merely engaging in a "down-home style of courting" which would have been "immediately recognizable" to Hill "and most women of Southern working-class backgrounds, white or black, especially the latter," but which would have been "completely out of the cultural frame of [the] white upper-middle-class work world" of the senators who would vote on his confirmation. See Patterson 1991, and the even more obnoxious defense of his position in Patterson, 1992. See also Kochman, 1991 and 1992. While Staples discounts Patterson's analysis, he does so on the grounds that Hill, being "upwardly mobile, quasi-Southern, religious," would not have adopted those cultural patterns. At the same time, relying in part on nineteenth-century constructions of black women's sexuality, he contends that the black community's "historical sexual liberality mitigates against current definitions of sexual harassment."

9. Race has been methodologically and theoretically written out of many analyses of sexual harassment. See, for example, the pioneering historical work of Mary Bularzik and the pioneering legal theory of Catharine MacKinnon. Bularzik is, quite appropriately, writing on white women and developing a discussion of the class dimensions of sexual harassment; in the process, however, she offhandedly dismisses many black women's understandings as false consciousness since they "often interpreted sexual harassment as racism, not sexism." See Bularzik 1978. McKinnon acknowledges race as a factor only in cases involving persons of different races. See, for example, MacKinnon 1979, pp. 30–31. More importantly, her legal theory is built upon a notion of universal women and generic men which assumes that "men" are white and heterosexual.

121

> Over time, women have been economically exploited, relegated to domestic slavery, used in denigrating entertainment, deprived of a voice and authentic culture, and disenfranchised and excluded from public life. Women, by contrast with comparable men, have systematically been subjected to physical insecurity; targeted for sexual denigration and violation; depersonalized and denigrated; deprived of respect, credibility, and resources; and silenced—and denied public presence, voice, and representation of their interests. Men as men have generally not had these things done to them; that is, men have had to be Black or gay (for instance) to have these things done to them as men. (MacKinnon 1989, p. 160)

10. The class issue was most notably raised in J. C. Alvarez's venomous references to Hill as a black female Yale Law School graduate who, by Alvarez's account, could have gotten any job anywhere that she wanted. Throughout the hearings, Thomas's supporters effectively inserted references to Hill's "aloofness," law degree, and career as a college professor as evidence of not only her elite status within the African American community but also concern for self before all others (personal advance at the expense of the black community). Alvarez portrayed herself as tough, streetwise, able to stop a mugging singlehandedly (working-class having to deal with the realities of life) versus Hill, who thought she was above the others and who expected not to have to deal with the mundane matters of regular people's lives (working-class women take lots of stuff and handle it; Hill thought she should not have to). The effectiveness of

this portrayal can be seen in part in many working-class women's attitude that they faced sexual harassment on a regular basis all their work lives and had to learn to be tough enough to handle it—tell the guy off, keep on working and ignore it, etc. In effect, Hill's raising a charge of sexual harassment was turned into a middle-class/ elite/professional privilege. The fact that some Hill supporters argued that sexual harassment was worse for professional women (they had more to lose) only played into Alvarez's and others' scenario.

11. "African-American Women in Defense of Ourselves," guest editorial in *New York Amsterdam News*, Oct. 26, 1991, and advertisement in *New York Times*, Nov. 17, 1991; San Francisco *Sun Reporter*, Nov. 20, 1991; *Capitol Spotlight*, Nov. 21, 1991; *Los Angeles Sentinel*, Nov. 21, 1991; *Chicago Defender*, Nov. 23, 1991; *Atlanta Inquirer*, Nov. 23, 1991; *Carolinian*, Nov. 28, 1991.

12. The following discussion is not meant to speak for or analyze specifically Hill's personal experience but to suggest why complicating the issues was essential.

13. Testimony before Senate Judiciary Committee, Oct. 13, 1991.

14. Black female domestic workers' own public accounts, e.g., "I lost my place because I refused to let the madam's husband kiss me. . . . I believe nearly all white men take, and expect to take, undue liberties with their colored female servants—not only the fathers, but in many cases the sons also. Those servants who rebel against such familiarity must either leave or expect a mighty hard time, if they stay." A Negro Nurse, "More Slavery at the South," *Independent* LXXII, 3295 (Jan. 25, 1912): 197–98. Black club women such as Fannie Barrier Williams talked publicly of the letters they received from black parents urging them to work to secure employment opportunities that would save their daughters from "going into the [white] homes of the South as servants." "A Northern Negro's Autobiography," *Independent* LVII, 2902 (July 14, 1904): 96.

15. The primary persons continuing these discussions were, of course, domestic workers themselves e.g., "When maids would get together, they'd talk of it. . . . They always had to fight off the woman's husband"; or "nobody was sent out before you was told to be careful of the white man or his sons." Florence Rice interview in Gerda Lerner, ed., *Black Women in White America: A Documentary History* (New York: Vintage Books, 1972): 275; Elizabeth Clark-Lewis, "This Work Had a End: The Transition from Live-in to Day Work," Southern women: The Intersection of Race, Class, and Gender, working paper no. 2, Center for Research on Women, Memphis State University, 15. It was common practice for domestic workers to gather together to socialize and/or to provide support and advice regarding working conditions and survival strategies. Since many of these gatherings occurred in the workers' homes, they were often overheard, if not participated in, by the young people in the homes. See, e.g., Bonnie Thornton Dill, " 'Making Your Job Good Yourself': Domestic Service and the Construction of Personal Dignity," in Ann Bookman and Sandra Morgen, *Women and the Politics of Empowerment* (Philadelphia: Temple University Press, 1988), 33–52; Paule Marshall, "From the Poets in the Kitchen," *New York Times Book Review*, Jan. 9, 1983. As the majority of black women in the labor force up to 1960 were employed as domestic workers, a substantial number of African-American women grew up with one or more family members who did domestic work and therefore in frequent earshot of such conversations. In my own family, a majority of my aunts and great-aunts were employed in either domestic or factory work; my mother, even though she had a college degree, when she took on paid employment to supplement the family income worked as a domestic or in a factory. For discussions of sexual abuse among black female factory workers, see, e.g., Beverly Jones, "Race, Sex, and Class: Black Female Tobacco Workers in Durham, North Carolina, 1920–1940 and the Development of Female Consciousness," *Feminist Studies* 10, 3 (Fall 1984): 443–50. Robin D. G. Kelley suggests that the strategies adopted by black female factory operatives to resist sexual harassment may have been passed down and developed out of domestic workers' experiences. " 'We Are Not What We Seem': Towards a Black Working-Class Infrapolitics in the Twentieth Century South," unpublished paper.

16. For a good discussion of the sexual stereotypes of African-American women in the late nineteenth and early twentieth centuries, see Beverly Guy-Sheftall, *Daughters of Sorrow: Attitudes Toward Black Women, 1880–1920* (Brooklyn, N.Y.: Carlson Publishing, 1990), esp. chapters 3 and 4. See also Patricia Morton, *Disfigured Images: The Historical Assault on Afro-American Women* (New York: Praeger, 1991).

17. This is not to ignore the implications of such emphasis on respectability over time. Some black women's conscious adoption of a Victorian desexualized persona was in opposition to dominant notions of black female sexuality. Their experience proves that race shapes patriarchal authority, which in turn determines forms of resistance to that authority. But, as the Neighborhood Union demonstrates, forms of opposition create their own limitations, in this instance leading to the effort to limit black women's own expressions of their sexuality, one potential result of which was the reinforcing black male patriarchal authority. A history that deals with respectability, sexuality, and politics in all its complexity in black women's lives has yet to be written.

18. My analysis here relies heavily on Tracye Matthews, " 'No One Ever Asks What a Man's Role in the Revolution Is': A Preliminary Examination of Gender Role Construction in the Black Panther Party, 1965–1971," paper delivered at 76th Annual Meeting of the Association for the Study of Afro-American Life and History, Nov. 2, 1991.

19. For a more detailed discussion, see Brown 1989.

20. This discussion is based on Elsa Barkley Brown, "Many Ways of Being Political," *Truth: Newsletter of the Association of Black Women Historians*; Elsa Barkley Brown, "We Always Talked Back: African-American Communities and the Political Realities of the Jim Crow Era," paper delivered at "Behind the Veil: African-American Life in the Jim Crow South" conference, Durham, North Carolina, March 1991.

21. Toni Morrison interviewed by Ntozake Shange on "It's Magic," WBAI radio show, New York, in 1978, quoted in Barbara Christian, " 'Somebody Forgot to Tell Somebody Something: African-American Women's Historical Novels," in Joanne M. Braxton and Andreé Nicola McLaughlin, eds., *Wild Women in the Whirlwind: Afra-American Culture and the Contemporary Literary Renaissance* (New Brunswick, N.J.: Rutgers University Press, 1990).

References

Bennett, Lerone, Jr. *Before the Mayflower: A History of Black America*, 5th ed. Chicago: Johnson, 1982.

Blassingame, John. *The Slave Community*. New Haven: Yale University Press, 1982.

Bray, Rosemary. "Taking Sides Against Ourselves." *New York Times Magazine*, Nov. 17, 1991, p. 56.

Brown, Elsa Barkley. "Educating Southern Black Women: Hartshorn Memorial and Spelman Colleges, 1881–1930." Paper presented at the Conference on Women in the Progressive Era, Smithsonian Institution, Washington, D.C., March 11, 1988.

Brown, Elsa Barkely. "Womanist Consciousness: Maggie Lena Walker and the Independent Order of Saint Luke." *Signs: Journal of Women in Culture and Society* 14, 3 (1989): 610–34.

Bularzik, Mary. "Sexual Harassment at the Workplace: Historical Notes." *Radical America* 12 (July-August 1978).

Crenshaw, Kimberle. "Roundtable: Sexuality after Thomas/Hill. *Tikkun* (Jan.-Feb. 1992): 25–30.

Crenshaw, Kimberle. "Roundtable: Doubting Thomas." *Tikkun* (Sept.-Oct. 1991): 23–30.

Du Bois, W. E. B. *The Negro American Artisan*. Atlanta: Atlanta University Press, 1912.

Du Bois, W. E. B. "The Damnation of Women." *Darkwater, Voices from Within the Veil*. New York: Harcourt, Brace and Howe, 1920.

Fischer, Elise. Letter to the Editor. *The Nation*, Feb. 3, 1992, p. 110.

Gutman, Herbert G. "Schools for Freedom: The Post-Emancipation Origins of Afro-American Education." In Ira Berlin, ed., *Power and Culture: Essays on the American Working Class*. 1987, pp. 260–98. New York: Monthly Review.

Guy-Sheftall, Beverly. "Breaking the Silence: A Black Feminist Response to the Thomas/Hill Hearings." *Black Scholar* 22, 1 (1992): 49–52.

Hare, Nathan, and Julia Hare. "The Many Faces of Anita Faye Hill." *Final Call*, Nov. 18, 1991, pp. 24, 29.

Harris, Trudier. "Native Sons and Foreign Daughters." *New Essays on 'Native Son.'* New York: Cambridge University Press, 1990.

Hine, Darlene Clark. "Rape and the Inner Lives of Black Midwestern Women." *Signs: Journal of Women in Culture and Society* 14, 4 (1989): 912–20.

Jackson, Jacquelyne Johnson. "Them Against Us: Anita Hill v. Clarence Thomas." *Black Scholar* 22, 1 (1992): 49–52.

Kochman, Thomas. *Black and White Styles in Conflict*. Chicago: University of Chicago Press, 1981.

Lorde, Audre. (1989). What I do when I Write. *The women's review of books 6* (10): 27.

MacKinnon, Catharine. "Hill's Accusations Ring True to a Legal Trailblazer." *Detroit Free Press*, Oct. 13, 1991, p. 6F.

MacKinnon, Catharine. *Sexual Harassment of Working Women*. New Haven: Yale University Press, 1979.

MacKinnon, Catharine. *Toward a Feminist Theory of the State*. Cambridge: Harvard University Press, 1989.

Newton, Huey. In August Meier, "Huey Newton Talks to the Movement." *Black Protest Thought in the Twentieth Century*. New York: Macmillan, 196 8. Pg. 495–515.

Norton, Eleanor Holmes. "No Immunity." *Washington Post* (October 11, 1991): A25.

Painter, Nell Irvin. "Who Was Lynched." *The Nation*, Nov. 11, 1991, p. 577.

Patterson, Orlando. "Race, Gender and Liberal Fallacies." *New York Times* (Oct. 20, 1991).

Patterson, Orlando. *Reconstruction*, 4 (1992): 68–71, 75–77.

Reagon, Bernice Johnson. (1982). My black mothers and sisters: Or, on beginning a cultural autobiography. *Feminist Studies 8* (1): 81–96.

Rouse, Jacqueline-Anne. *Lugenia Burns Hope: Black Southern Reformer*. Athens: University of Georgia Press, 1989.

Shaw, Stephanie J. "Black Women and the Creation of the National Association of Colored Women." *Journal of Women's History* 3, 2 (1990): 10–25.

Staples, Robert. "Hand Me the Rope—I will Hang Myself." *Black Scholar* 22, 1 and 2 (Winter 1991, Spring 1992): 95–98.

Walker, Maggie Lena. "Traps for Women." Sermon given at Bethel A.M.E. Church, Richmond, Virginia, March 15, 1925. Maggie Lena Walker papers, Maggie Lena Walker National Historic Site, Richmond Virginia.

Wolf, Naomi. "Feminism and Intimidation on the Job: Have the Hearings Liberated the Movement?" *Washington Post*, Oct. 13, 1991, p. C1.

The Circling of the Wagons: The Odyssey of Anita Hill

HARRIETTE PIPES McADOO

$$T$$he circling of the wagons is an   *125*
allusion to the manner in which wagon trains, on the way through Southern Africa to the Shona land of Zimbabwe, and in northern America on
the way west, circled upon themselves whenever there was strong evidence of danger. They circled to defend themselves and to fight off intruders. This internal arrangement allowed them to protect themselves and
to fight off outsiders. In a circle, fighters could move from one crisis to
another with ease. They also would be able to tell exactly who the enemies were in the heat of the battle. All of those inside the wagon circle
were friends, and all of those outside were the enemies. The white male
members of the U.S. Senate Judiciary Committee could be seen as returning to the tactic of circling the wagons against intruders. Those intruders, women and men of varying colors, may have been handling a
little truth, but, never mind, they had to be fought off with every possible
effort.

From the European perspective, the enemy in the old days was
Southern African and Native American tribal groups. Yet these groups
were fighting the European intruders for their very survival. They were
able to win many of the struggles; in some, they ran right over the new
settlers. In other battles, they were able to prolong the fighting until the
newcomers ran out of ammunition and food. Although they fought with
great skill and fortitude, they eventually lost. There were too many wa-

gons that kept on coming. The Europeans had guns and ammunition that were superior to the weapons the Shona and the native Americans possessed. They also had the mighty force of knowing they were correct in moving on into the natives' lands, for God was on their side. In similar fashion, the white male members of the Senate Judiciary Committee felt the righteousness of their convictions; they felt that right and might were on their side. Little did they know.

Anita Hill ultimately lost the battle, as did the Shona and the native Americans. She was an outsider, an intruder upon the very rights of the power establishment. There was no way the outcome could have been different. Women were shafted, and the men on the committee did not even appear to understand what was going on. She may have lost the battle, but she won the war, because she forced onto the national scene the seething rage of potential and actual victims of race and/or gender harassment.

Why Thomas?

The Hill-Thomas confrontation may have appeared initially to be one woman against one man. In reality, the issue was not one of race and gender but one of control over the judiciary system of this country. This event brought out the coalitions that represented all three areas of the government (Kaplan et al., 1991). That control is epitomized by the political orientations of the persons who sit on the U.S. Supreme Court.

The powers-that-be had decided that a colored person would be placed as an associate justice on the Supreme Court. They needed to prove their lack of racial prejudice. Another person of color would not do. They needed a "colored man" whom they could control. A woman would be too unpredictable, and they might not be able to control her; so a man was selected. The best means of control was to use a person who had been well trained in the ways of the master. This procedure had worked with enslaved persons in the past (Litwack 1979). There was no reason for it not to work in the present. An ultra-conservative was desired to ensure the votes needed for the issues that were to come before the Court. Those in power needed someone who would do their bidding without being told. Clarence Thomas was such a person, an extreme conservative, who had demonstrated that he could be trusted (Phelps and Winternitz 1992). He had been selected, and the Senate committee was to follow along and simply confirm him, with only a token questioning period.

Thomas's credentials could not be questioned, although the depth of his legal experience could be challenged. He was from a background of poverty. He was championed as a person who had worked against great odds to go forth and succeed in the big world, on the white man's terms. The help he had from his extended family, especially his grandparents, was downplayed. The help provided by parochial schools and nuns was only briefly mentioned. The fact that white colleges needed to have a few token blacks was not mentioned in detail and was passed over very quickly. The social support and kin help systems that are all too common in the South functioned in Thomas's behalf. The kin help system still works effectively for many other Blacks all over the country (McAdoo 1982; Staples 1991). In fact, Thomas had lived a life of ease with help being provided on all sides.

Although he did not have much money, Thomas moved right through the educational systems. He went to one of the finest law schools in the country. Despite all of the evidence of persons in his background who had struggled to help him, the images presented during the hearings were of a man who had worked against great odds to make it with no help from anyone, not even from affirmative action.

When Thomas completed law school, he wanted to enter the mainstream of governmental legal practice. However, he immediately hit the glass ceiling that all of us Blacks are all too familiar with (McAdoo 1989). The main job he was offered by those in power was one related to his race. He bristled, but he took it, for he wanted to stay where the action was.

Once at the Education Department and the Equal Employment Opportunity Commission, he acted as many men have in a position of authority. Hill reported that he used the power of his position to make sexual innuendos and propositions to women in his employment. We may never know the full story of what went on between Thomas and Hill, but the details are not that important. What is important is that if, indeed, Thomas made repeated sexual demands, then the law was broken. Harassment of a sexual nature has been defined as a form of sex discrimination under Title VII of the Civil Rights Act of 1964. The Supreme Court had expressed itself in reference to the act and had supported it. Demands for sexual favors are hidden threats if made between an employer and an employee. Actions of employers can range from denial of promotions, blatant verbal exchanges, or denial of pay raises based on the employee's response to requests for sexual favors (Kantrowitz et al. 1991; Priest 1992).

127

Racial and Gender Issues Evoked

The negative consequences of the Thomas confirmation hearings were unanticipated. The hearings brought forth the age-old issues of gender and race that went beyond the individuals and put these issues before the entire world. Instead of simply placing a person of African American descent on the Court, they galvanized women in ways that have not yet been completely revealed. The entire process exposed a vulnerability in males that even now is still being felt in the areas of official elections, employment practices, race relations, and gender harassment guidelines.

The analogy of circling the wagons can be seen in the very process used when the original charges against Thomas were so inertly handled. When these allegations were made in confidence to the staff of the committee by Hill, it was decided that they were not significant enough to stop the process of moving Thomas to the bench (Kaplan et al. 1991). Testimony in the files of the committee clearly suggested that the charges should be addressed before a vote could be taken. Yet the charges were all submerged. The elements of sexism were working overtime.

As happens all too frequently, Hill's charges were simply dismissed as not important. It is possible that the charges were felt to be so explosive that they needed to be kept hidden. We may never know the thinking of the persons who made the decision to use some information and data but to ignore others. However, racism and sexism were clearly at play when these decisions were made. It is a safe guess that the thinking was male-dominated.

Only through the hard efforts of Nina Totenberg of National Public Radio, Timothy M. Phelps of *Newsday*, and others was the information allowed to be released (Reed and McElwaine 1991; Thomas 1992). Unlike the way other data were handled, the members of the Senate committee decided to hold an open hearing. This was clear evidence that the wagons had already been drawn into a tight circle. The senator had been caught up short, and they were then responsible for carrying the process forward.

128   The committee was forced to address the information. There was a feeling that there was no way the committee could carry it off if sexual charges were aired in a nationwide, open hearing. But the way they decided, against an African-American woman, seemed to many to be a case of blatant racism and sexism. The outcome could have been determined well in advance.

Charges of Gender Discrimination

No real weight was put on Hill's charges, for, after all, everybody does it. Sexual harassment happens every day in Washington. No real thought was given to the possible derailment of the Republicans' candidate. Furthermore, both Hill and Thomas were unmarried at the time of the alleged incidents. So there was no real reason to pay that much attention to some simple woman who may have been motivated by many reasons. She may have been a spurned lover or a jealous former worker. Of course, if the senators had taken time to investigate the charges, they may have found some evidence that would have indicated that Hill's case should be handled differently. The important point was that the charges had been made by a woman, and women really did not matter in the real world of the male-dominated Senate.

But women do matter, as the senators certainly found out. Women were galvanized. Seven House members, who were female, stormed the room where the Democratic senators were in caucus. A Bush aide was quoted as saying that they had miscalculated the "reaction of the women, the girls' vote" (Kaplan et al. 1991; Cliff 1991). And well they did. The men were beginning to get the glimmer that something was being disturbed. The entire country was fixated around their radios and televisions sets. Malls emptied out, work went undone, and the entire population was given a sight that had never been presented before in the United States.

Charges of Racial Discrimination

The most important point in the prehearing thinking was that both the charger and the chargee were African Americans. A person of color has little power in our society, especially in the power-insulated environment of Washington, D.C. Little relevance is given to what a Person of Color says. The question that places the racial component in clear focus is whether or not Hill would have been exposed to this level of scrutiny if she had not been an African-American woman (Aldridge 1992). All that Hill had to say could be devalued. The process of devaluation is too common for all persons of color (McAdoo 1983). The elements of our society that are important to people of color are devalued every day. The devaluation is an insidious element that is as powerful as direct overt discrimination. If one simply lowers the value of what a person of color has to say, then one does not have to be overt with one's exclusionary activities. A person of African descent is considered less than a man anyway, as has been the case since the Constitution was first put on paper, and so it has continued from the radical reconstruction to the present day (Litwack 1979; Pipes 1992).

129

Initially, the committee did not feel that the hearings were an opening of age-old racial issues. It may have been considered unfortunate that Hill would have to handle the charges in public and on television. There apparently was no thought given to African-American reactions to having two very articulate Africans Americans confront sensitive issues in public. After all, who really listens to what African Americans have to say? Their words have had little significance in the past, and there was no reason to believe that it should matter now.

If the committee was wrong, why did the major Civil Rights organizations and political leaders not cry out? Persons or organizations who should have spoken out were surprisingly silent. Our Black "leaders" fell in line with the program of accepting Thomas that the power brokers had set out.

Many African Americans, especially women, questioned what was happening. Those who may have been independent of governmental funds and could have spoken out were silent. African-American leaders were all quiet, for too many of them had experienced the enjoyment, sexual and otherwise, that comes from being in powerful positions. We later found out that, indeed, the leaders of the major civil rights organizations had been kept quiet by those in power (Phelps and Winternitz 1992). These "leaders" had to go along with the game plan. Their overdependence on the Republican government for funds to carry out their programs made them ineffectual. They were unable to provide help at crucial points in the process of devaluing Hill and exalting Thomas.

The Public Debate: Hill versus Thomas?

Strong voices were heard on all sides. Voices were found in the African American community that defended Thomas and others that denigrated Hill. Never had an issue more galvanized the attention of African Americans. The entire situation highlighted the fact that African American women are doubly victimized. These women suffer from both racism and sexism at the same time. They were doubly offended by the entire process.

Many women felt that Hill was telling the truth. Too many of them had faced similar obstacles of sexual harassment as they attempted to maintain employment (Marton 1991; Balamaci et al. 1991). They strongly identified with her history. They argued that for her to publicly bring charges as painful as hers must have meant that there was some reality to them. They, too, had been victims and had found little support.

Men of all races tended to be ambivalent. Some supported Hill; others did not. But many of them ignored the statements of sexual innuendos. It was often remarked, "What was a little sexual dalliance between friends? We must get on with important things." Black men seemed to care even less. Many of them were on Thomas's side, for, after all, he was a brother. Many men did not realize the importance to women of sexual harassment on the job since most of them had never been victimized in this manner.

A few conservative and a number of middle-class and working-class African Americans rallied to Thomas's side. They were able, with the help of European American Republicans, to mount an effective campaign of support. There were articles written in key magazines in defense of Thomas. Niara Sudarkasa, an African American female anthropologist and president of Lincoln University, gave a well-thought-out and impassioned plea in support of Thomas (Sudarkasa 1991). She spoke eloquently of their shared backgrounds and of the fact that they both prided themselves on having gone to college before affirmative action. She stated that Thomas may not speak for the majority of African Americans, or for Black America's liberal leadership, but he should be allowed to serve

130

anyway. Her main points were that he had overcome great adversity and poverty and should be allowed to serve, for he would have "a moderating influence and [would be] a distinctive voice among his conservative peers."

Other Blacks joined in defending the appointment of Thomas. It was felt that it was more important to get an African American on board than to address his personal qualities or the extreme conservativism of his activities and positions. The fact was ignored that there were many more better-prepared and better-experienced legal minds, even conservative ones, who were also African American. Many other Blacks could have amply filled the position if race was an important criterion.

What the supporters of Thomas did not understand about the entire process was that sex and race were not the important, compelling elements. To those in power, the important, crucial ingredient for the appointment to the Supreme Court was conservative orientation. A happy convergence of orientation, gender, and background had been found in Thomas, a "colored" man. Hill was simply an impediment to the process. We had been disenfranchised on all sides.

The Assertions of Both Sides

The strongest statement of all was the demeanor, appearance, and control that Hill maintained throughout the hearings. She was under extreme pressure, yet she performed extraordinarily well. She was articulate, attractive, and, most important, calm. Hill was level-headed and precise as she handled the probing questions of the Judiciary Committee. She was probably more than the committee had counted on.

131

She handled herself as effectively as if she had been preparing for this moment her entire life. She exhibited the hard work, integrity, and intelligence that come from a strong family beginning (Hewitt and Austin 1991). Hill was a representative of all of us. All over the world, Women of Color, and those not of color, rejoiced in her performance.

In countering the testimony of Hill, Thomas pulled out his race card. This was out of context for a man who had run away from being Black for much of his adult life. He was a person who was against race-based remedies or decisions. Yet he pulled out all stops and used the ultimate race-based illustration. Thomas astutely changed the attention of the committee when he took the stand and charged that he was the victim of a "high-tech lynching." He effectively changed the direction of the hearings from a focus on sexually explicit language, innuendos, and action to a focus on the historical issue of attacks on African American men. Further, Thomas went on to state that "uppity men" were the targets of lynchings. John Fitch, in defense of Thomas, further said that many other African American men had been derailed because of accusations of sexual misconduct (Fenalson 1991).

The incompleteness of the picture of lynching that Thomas presented to the committee was ably analyzed by Estelle Freedman (1992). In a well-thought-out presentation of the different arguments made during the hearings, Freedman detailed Thomas's incomplete historical presentation of lynching. Lynching had been historically used when a Black man was accused, rightly or wrongly, of assaulting a white woman. Yet Freedman stated that to her knowledge no man had been lynched for assaulting a Woman of Color. Lynchings were used to help maintain the racial and gender hierarchies of the South. Both African American women and men were forced to be quiet in the face of adversity. African American women were expected to be available sexually to men of all colors. For an African American woman to speak up about sexual harassment and attacks from a European American man would put the men in her life at great risk. Often, the woman herself was lynched if she spoke out against a white man. African Americans were made to internalize the hurt, pain, and humiliation of a sexual attack. Women were forced to bear the brunt, and sometimes the children of the man, when attacks occurred.

Thomas's lynching image was effective with the Judiciary Committee. No one questioned him. Lynching is part of the terrible American heritage of which European American men are the perpetrators. They remained silent.

132

Positive Aspects of The Hill Testimony

From every bad thing some good must come. Positive fallouts are still raining down. Women are running for public office at a phenomenal rate. Many are in positions that will move them into Congress and into state and local offices at an unprecedented rate. Women all across the country are organizing in more powerful ways than ever before (Manegold 1992). The response has been more muted in African American communities. But gradually things are happening. People are reflecting and talking. Women are writing books such as this one. We are becoming more aware of the imbalances of power within our society.

One very positive benefit of the Hill-Thomas episode has been increased attention and sensitivity to the issue of sexual harassment. Sexual harassment complaints have risen sharply (Gross 1992). Following Hill's congressional testimony, there were significant increases in complaints against corporate employers. In the first half of the 1992 fiscal year, complaints had increased by more than 50 percent, totaling 4,754 compared to 3,135 the year before (Gross 1992).

After Hill's testimony, many government and corporate employers distributed notes and policies to their personnel (Priest 1992). Sets of sanctions are being developed by the Labor Department that extend from reprimands to dismissal for sexual harassment. The military has had to respond to allegations of sexual impropriety and has changed rules and procedures. Many managers and employers have been sent to sensitivity training sessions. Discussion sessions have been held across the country. Many persons have faced the reality that harassment is no longer to be viewed as a joke and must be taken seriously. Strong political decisions are being made in support of women (Gross 1992).

Another benefit of the hearing was the diversity of African Americans publicly presented. Many people of color of all political orientations were able to speak out. A variety of persons who have long been a part of the African American community were brought to the attention of wider America. Fitch stated that acknowledgment of the political and philosophical differences in African America is a positive step toward blacks' fuller cultural and political participation (Fenalson 1991). It is unfortunate that it took an event like this to present to the wider American public the many diverse attitudes and lifestyles of African Americans.

Into the Future

The hearings have evoked a greater reaction in the European-American women's community than in the African-American male or female community. The progress has been slower to come to fruition among Blacks because the interaction of gender and race is very complicated (Mercer 1992). It is an issue that unites and divides and will take time to meld. The interaction of race and gender has a long history. Women of all races have been exploited by European American men. Moreover, African American women *and* men have been oppressed by systems established by European American men. These systems have been utilized and enjoyed by European American women, to the detriment of women of color. On the one hand, Black women are connected with white women, but we are often offended by their very being, that is, by their cultural "whiteness." We have commonalities around which we can join together, yet these will go only so far. On the other hand, there are issues that divide us from African American men, based on past oppression. African-American women are neither fish nor fowl. It is a difficult place to be.

The Senate Judiciary Committee may have won the battle, but it truly did lose the war. The senators' actions unleashed a tidal wave that will not be stopped. Positive things are happening as a result of the stress of the hearings. There was no telling what impact the hearings would have on various segments of society. Women are running for office in record numbers. Men are slowly waking up to the realities of the world around them. For this we have Anita Hill to thank.

Small but very definite cracks are being seen in the circle of wagons. May they get even wider with the new faces of women being added

133

to the political scene. May they eventually stretch out into a strong line. Let there be race and gender war no more.

References

Aldridge, Daniel. "Beyond the Thomas-Hill Affair." *The Grapevine* (1992): 1–2.

Balamaci, Marilyn, Gail Wescott, Nina Burleigh, and Linda Marx. "The Price of Saying No." *People*, Oct. 28, 1991, pp. 44–50.

Cliff, Eleanor. "Congress: The Ultimate Men's Club." *Newsweek*, Oct. 21, 1991, p. 32.

Fenalson, Laurie. "A Testimony to U.S. History: Alumni Was Center Stage at the Thomas Hearings." *Michigan Today* 23, 4 (1991): 15.

Freedman, Estelle. "The Manipulation of History at the Clarence Thomas Hearings." *Chronicle of Higher Education*, Jan. 8, 1992, p. B2.

Gross, Jane. "Suffering in Silence No More: Fighting Sexual Harassment." *New York Times*, July 13, 1992, pp. A1, A16.

Hewitt, Bill, and Beth Austin. "She Could Not Keep Silent." *People*, Oct. 28, 1991, pp. 40–43.

Kantrowitz, Barbara, et al. "Striking a Nerve: Sexual Harassment Is a Fact of Life for Millions of American Women." *Newsweek*, Oct. 21, 1991, pp. 34–40.

Kaplan, David, Bob Cohn, Ann McDaniel, and Peter Annin. "A Moment of Truth: Anatomy of a Debacle." *Newsweek*, Oct. 21, 1991, pp. 24–32.

Litwack, Leon. "The Faithful Slave." In *Been in the Storm So Long: The Aftermath of Slavery*. New York: Vintage, 1979, pp. 545–56.

McAdoo, Harriette. "Stress Absorbing Systems in Black Families." *Family Relations* 31 (1982): 479–88.

McAdoo, Harriette. "Societal Stress: The Black Family." In H. McCubbin and C. Figley, eds., *Stress and the Family: Coping with Normative Transitions*. New York: Brunner/Mazel, 1983.

McAdoo, Harriette. "Work and Families: Climbing Up the Crystal Stairs." Paper presented at Research and Policy Agenda for Women in the 20th Century Conference at Radcliff College, 1989.

Manegold, Catherine. "No More Nice Girls: Radical Feminists Just Want to Have Impact." *New York Times*, July 12, 1992, p. 20.

Marton, Kati. "An All Too Common Story." *Newsweek*, Oct. 21, 1991, p. 88.

Mercer, Joyce. "Black Women, White Women: Does Gender Unite More Than Race Divides?" *Black Issues in Higher Education*, Jan. 2, 1992, pp. 14–15.

Phelps, Timothy M., and Helen Winternitz. *Capital Games: Clarence Thomas, Anita Hill and the Story of a Supreme Court Nomination*. New York: Hyperion, 1992.

Pipes, William. *Say Amen, Brother!* 2nd ed. Detroit: Wayne State University Press, 1992.

Priest, Dana. "Hill-Thomas Legacy May Be Challenges to Old Workplace Patterns." *Washington Post*, March 12, 1992, p. A8.

Reed, Susan, and Sandra McElwaine. "Full-court Presser." *People*, Oct. 28, 1991, pp. 55–56.

Staples, Robert. *The Black Family*, 4th ed. Belmont, Calif.: Wadsworth, 1991.

Sudarkasa, Niara. "Don't Write Off Thomas." *Newsweek*, Aug. 19, 1991, p. 10.

Thomas, Jacqueline. "Court Disorder: Clarence Thomas' Nomination Displayed Political Games." *Detroit Free Press*, June 21, 1992, p. 7P.

Faults in the Movement: The End of One Era and the Beginning of Another

DIANNE M. PINDERHUGHES

$\mathbf{T}$he request from Professor Ge-   *135*
neva Smitherman came in late fall when the immediate furor from what
have come to be known popularly as the Clarence Thomas-Anita Hill
hearings (actually Thomas's Senate confirmation hearing for the Supreme
Court) had passed somewhat. I resisted initially, not really knowing what
to say or how to translate the complex feelings I had, or the feelings that
rippled throughout my network of friends, into the kind of remote, rational, analytic discourse with which I am most comfortable. Nothing
about these events permitted such distance. Nothing was simple or insig-
nificant—from the moment Thomas unfolded his notes scrawled on yel-
low legal paper to speak to the press at Kennebunkport when he was
nominated, and had difficulty expressing himself without breaking down,
to his two swearing-in ceremonies, one in the White House almost immediately after the confirmation (as if he and the president feared some
·new revelation would preclude it) and a second at the Supreme Court.
African Americans saw ourselves as we never had before, and it was not
pleasant, nor was there reason for future optimism. Thomas, the man,
his presentation of self, and his policies of racial reform for the last generation became profoundly vulnerable and the subject of intense debate.

Why? How could one event touch on so many aspects of life, have
so much power, engender so much debate, and pervade seemingly every
dimension of society? Was it merely symbolic politics? According to Murray

Edelman, "condensation symbols evoke the emotions associated with the situation. They condense into one symbolic event, sign, or act, patriotic pride, anxieties, remembrances of past glories or humiliations, promises of future greatness: some one of these or all of them" (1964:6).

This battle over access to the Court seemed to have the power to condense great importance into a single event. Why? Certainly the Court itself has had great power. It became the center, the template, at least in theory, on which civil rights strategists wrote. They used it to rewrite the laws, to create leverage for moving the other branches at the national level, and to attack local and state politics.

The appointment of a justice to replace Thurgood Marshall, one of the finest warrior-attorneys ever to practice law in America, certainly deserved the focused attention it attracted. John Hope Franklin said, "For black people he holds special significance because it was Thurgood, Charles Houston [Marshall's law professor], and a few others who told us we could get justice through interpretation of the law" (quoted in Williams 1990:14). In its most serious error, the civil rights community framed the issues about replacing Marshall inappropriately. It sounded a theme that has come to be repeated all too often in an effort to address inequality: "descriptive representation." For example, Ben Hooks, president of the NAACP, called for the nomination of a Black person to the court, without any effort to address the substantive content of the person's policy interests, the nature of the individual's role on the Court, and his—or her, especially given federal judge Constance Baker Motley's availability— political positions. That strategic error invited, even welcomed, the nominee Bush offered, which was doubly ironic since it was the NAACP that had originally placed the issue of a Black Court nominee on the public agenda but which chose eventually to oppose Bush's candidate. Thus, when Thomas stepped to the microphone, the conflict that was to arise should have been expected, given the civil rights community's growing emphasis on race, majority Black districts, and descriptive representation, without a concomitant focus on the strategies and policies represented by "descriptively Black" entities.

The posturing of any one person or organization probably could not have prevented the divisive battle that ensued, but the NAACP clearly articulated the position of those who focused primarily on the value of having a Black man on the Court. This, of course, is not a new position, since an emphasis on ethnic and gender representation has been apparent in Supreme Court appointments for some time. Undoubtedly, it was the conjunction of the issue of racial representation with opposition to affirmative action by Republican presidents Reagan and Bush that gave the issue its special power. Both presidents were willing to exploit, in the basest possible manner, race and racism, and to nominate a man who was, to use Stephen Carter's words, an "affirmative action baby" (1990) but one who was unwilling to acknowledge that ancestry. Thomas also seemed to reflect a leadership style and politics eerily reminiscent of that Black leader of a century ago, Booker T. Washington, as he talked about being "up from Pin Point" at every opportunity.

All of this tells us something about why we responded so strongly to the political issues and why the politics of the confirmation battle were so strong. However, the intensity generated went far beyond a public political conflict. Once the battle moved into its second phase, with the revelation of a charge of sexual harassment by Anita Hill, all three of the powerful dimensions that receive so much attention in contemporary American society—race, gender, and class—were joined in a single policy event in perhaps an unprecedented way. There was certainly already internal debate about the nomination, which also crossed racial lines, but with the charges brought by Hall, an enormously complicated conflict increased in intensity, power, and impact on the American public. Further, the second phase of the Thomas hearings touched the issue of gender in all of its attendant complexities—affirmative action along racial *and* gender lines, sexual harassment and sexuality, sexual power struggles in the workplace, and the existing but unexpressed tension over the fact of Thomas's marriage to a white woman. Basically, all hell broke loose.

That all of these complex issues traversed the short distance between Thomas and Hill, and that they could so transfix most of the American media, political institutions, the African American community, the most senior career politicians of both major parties, political observers, and the general public across racial lines suggests the depth of meaning attributable to the civil rights-Horatio Alger-turned-Clarence-Thomas parable. Black Americans were already divided over whether they liked the "up from Pin Point" success story. When questions of Thomas's sexual preferences, sexual practices, and sexuality were raised by an African-American woman, the link to earlier times was so acute that it aroused the most basic defensive impulses among African Americans (Davis 1991).

When it seemed that Thomas's opportunity to attain the seat on the Court might be eluding his grasp, he did not refrain from responding. Some argued that the White House wrote the script he used, others that Thomas alone composed his statement. Whoever the author, Thomas delivered his lines with an intensity and authority that suggested that he owned them and embraced them, that he was willing to use them in order to achieve his ends, and that those ends were his alone to the exclusion of the rest of the Black community. Thomas was willing to use his race and class status against the empowerment of others like him, and he had no difficulty simply rejecting any accusation of sexually inappropriate action on his part if it stood in his way.

Hill was more difficult for people to understand. Most assumed she had acted in order to further her career, make money, or in some way increase her visibility in the new fast-forward media world. Some months after the event and her return to the world of academia without having

137

done the usual round of television talk-show appearances, signed a book contract, or entered into a movie deal, others began to ask, "What was the point?" Hill seemed to have acted because she thought she had some understanding of Thomas's fitness for the Court. Difficult as it was to talk about or to address in a public forum, she thought her understanding too important not to raise. While people are complex mixes of emotions, impulses, and goals, she seemed to have acted on behalf of a set of interests that made sense.

Hill's quiet demeanor struck a chord with a network of Black women, some of them academics, across the country. They organized and published the statement "African American Women in Defense of Ourselves" on November 17, 1991, in the *New York Times* and several African American newspapers. The academic and institutional leadership role, a new one for Hill as well as for many of the Black women who observed her, provided African American women such as Hill with a new visibility and a different responsibility from that of their mothers. However, the role she assumed, of challenging and questioning Thomas's fitness to serve, based on his violation of demeanor in office, was an act many Black women rejected as battling in public. They felt she should have settled the conflict in private. (See essays by Etter-Lewis and Grier in this volume for explanations of this reaction.) Many African American women felt that Hill pushed the hearings to the dimension that Thomas raised, that of lynching. Yet this was a century after lynching was used with frequency to control and regulate Black men and, though to a lesser extent, Black women. African American men, however, were *not* lynched on the word of Black women. As Nell Irvin Painter said, "Lynch victims have not been the protégés of presidents and senators" (1991:577). This was, in short, a very different context from that of earlier times.

Within the African American community, the debate raged. Was Thomas the courageous "bad nigger" (Henry 1991), putting on the mask of the Tom/coon to disarm the Man until he got over? Or was he the class Uncle Tom, ambitious and willing to act in whatever way was appropriate in order to move upward? Countless discussions speculated about this latter possibility. It was best depicted by television's comedy show "In Living Color," in the skit about Thomas's early days on the Court. He bows and scrapes, asking what he can do to please the other justices who have greater seniority. When he realizes he can serve for life, he stops asking what he can do to serve the other members, sits back, puts his feet up on the table, and begins to tell the other members of the Court what to do as he exults in his newfound power. That, of course, is not what Thomas's first term has demonstrated so far, from the voting rights case of *Presley* v. *Etowah County Commission* to his decision on the rights of prisoners. In all but one case, Thomas has chosen the most conservative of positions, positions least likely to enhance the political and economic rights of the Black community.

The complex issues in the Hill-Thomas conflict were so intense as to make the week after the second phase of the hearings difficult to absorb. Thomas's marriage to a white woman had been known about but not highlighted before the leak of Hill's charges. Justice and Mrs. Clarence Thomas's cover portrait on *People* magazine and Mrs. Thomas's statements in *People* made it clear that by the end of the twentieth century, sexual competition over males had crossed the color line. We had moved a very long way from Maggie Lena Walker's charge to Black men and women in early-twentieth-century Richmond. In her "Address for Men," Walker argued that one could not defend the race unless one defended Black women. Appealing to Black men's notions of themselves as the protectors of Black womanhood, she asked on behalf of all her sisters for their

> FRIENDSHIP . . . LOVE . . . SYMPATHY . . . PROTECTION, and
> . . . ADVICE. . . . I am asking you, men of Richmond . . .
> to record [yourselves] as . . . the strong race men of our
> city. . . . I am asking each man in this audience to go forth
> from this building, determined to do valiant deeds for the
> Negro women of Richmond . . . by let[ting] woman choose
> her own vocation, just as man does his. (quoted in Brown
> 1990, p. 192)

Emphasis on race detached from any other context can negate the very purpose of raising it. It can be used just as easily to subordinate, as to enhance, the Black population, the Black female, and the Black poor. Several centuries of such attention to racial categories should have alerted Black political leaders to the powerful and complex legacy of domination. Failure to be attentive to the multiple jeopardies (King 1990) associated with discrimination invite powerful repression. The battle over the Thomas nomination touched us so deeply because it resonated across racial, class, and gender dimensions.

References

Brown, Elsa Barkley. "Womanist Consciousness: Maggie Lena Walker and the Independent Order of Saint Luke." In Malson et al., eds., *Black Women in America: Social Science Perspectives*. Chicago: University of Chicago Press, 1990, pp. 159–72.

Carter, Stephen L. *Reflections of an Affirmative Action Baby*. New York: Basic Books, 1990.

Davis, Angela. "The Legacy of Columbus and the Future of South Africa." Address at the University of Illinois, Urbana, Oct. 16, 1991.

Edelman, Murray. *The Symbolic Uses of Politics*. Urbana: University of Illinois Press, 1964.

Henry, Charles. *Culture and African American Politics*. Bloomington: Indiana University Press, 1991.

King, Deborah K. "Multiple Jeopardy, Multiple Consciousness: The Context of a Black Feminist Ideology." In Malson et al., eds., *Black Women in America: Social Science Perspectives*. Chicago: University of Chicago Press, 1990, pp. 265–96.

Painter, Nell Irvin. "Who Was Lynched?" *The Nation*, Nov. 11, 1991, p. 577.

Williams, Juan. "Marshall's Law." *Washington Post Magazine*, 1990, March 21 pp. 12–29.

Anita at the Battle of the Bush: Thomas on the Hill: Dark Town Strutters Ball

NETTIE JONES

One day, what now seems a very, *141* very long time ago, I was requested by Dr. G. to give up a piece of my mind one more time in the name of truth-seeking. This time, I was honorably beseeched to speak on a then most recent American dilemma: Act IV of the Clarence Thomas Senate confirmation hearings, starring Anita Hill, produced by President George Bush, directed by the Senate Judiciary Committee, costumes by Brooks Brothers and Donna Karan, Miss Hill's hair by Ultra Sheen. I was excited. I said yes without even asking Dr. G. about my fee. I began the preliminary investigation and found that the issues at hand were far more complicated than expected at the time; so much was at play, key, relevant, baffling. It was not until approximately nine months after I accepted the challenge that my mind at long last began to decode the materials it at times was force-fed. Once I decided to use the entire absurd title that came to me over my long period of shuffling with the "how to do it" and to speak without reservation to you, the reader, without shame as only I can do, the dice stopped clicking 7–11 (craps). It is August in Detroit, and I am "do'n it"! Listen to my mind as it wanders through a thick, dark, lush forest of whizzing thoughts that I am about to unleash upon you. The entire sound and the entire fury of it all.

I want you to know up front, now, that in my way of thinking (which as I am older I find is more pedestrian than I would like to admit), both star attractions fulfilled their parts; both were believable; both are liars if the concept, the word, is interpreted traditionally. Each has proven without a doubt that *wizardry, magic, courage, charisma, cunning* are terms that could be appropriately applied to their character descriptions. There these two (rather) young, near perfect, specimens of African America sit in front of the absolute civilized world unfolding intimate aspects of their inner selves for uninterrupted hours, 127 years after the Emancipation, just as composed as one would expect a Vanderbilt, a Mellon, a Carnegie, or a Phipps to be under the circumstances. Barely out of the lush woods of Georgia and the dry plains of Oklahoma, articulate, multi-degreed, coiffured, and card-carrying American Express, approved, bona fide buppies. Neither one of them under that extreme pressure visibly surrendered until the end of his or her interrogation was near. Hill's hair never kinked, her lips never parched; Thomas's eyes never bulged, and not one "ya sa" did he ever give up to the distinguished panel of white, male senator-lawyers.

Try as each of them might to pretend that his or hers was a fact-finding mission, not a trial, both Thomas and Hill knew differently, as did we who sat hidden behind those intensely disrobing lights in the comfort of our media rooms eating our low-fat dinners. Each of them deserves applause for *forever* messing with the majority image of who and what is an African American today. Sexual conduct was the issue, not drugs, unemployment, welfare fraud, or criminal behavior. Thomas and Hill are for the most part squeaky-clean Harvard and Yale graduates probably earning well more than seventy-five thousand dollars apiece on that clear autumn day they appeared. Each truly dramatized what the eminent scholar W. Julius Wilson labels the "declining significance of race." Neither appeared to be what Wilson describes as "the truly disadvantaged." Gone are the days now when the majority can point its finger assuredly at a spiritually broken, physically starving, intellectually damaged person of color on the "ABC Nightly News" and say, "That's all there is to them." We owe Thomas and Hill applause and gratitude for having led exemplary lives *for the most part*. The pile of dirty linen in their closets could be washed easily in a miniature pullman porter sink.

As we travel into the depths of my mind, remember that, overall, I applaud both of these scholarly, disciplined, distinguished "credits to the race" (by this I mean "human"). All aboard. Let's journey back in time now as I reconstruct some of the events that led me to render this impression at long last. Listen.

On that October morning in 1991 when the confirmation hearings resumed, I, at fifty years of age, was a second-year graduate student attending the University of Chicago Divinity School, majoring in the art of ministry, as it is called there, seeking a graduate divinity degree and ordination in the Christian ministry. I was on that day headed for my class, walking down Fifty-third Street from my residence, an efficiency

142

apartment at Catholic Theological Union. Everyone housed there was involved in professional training in the public church. My housemates were, in other words, nuns, priests, ministers, or divinity scholars. It was a crisp Chicago corner that I crossed after staring down several blocks at a rather calm lake.

The door to the beauty shop was open, and the television was blaring. I could hear this clear voice saying something; the people in the shop were looking at someone whose voice I heard with great interest. I, who was ignorant of everything but my need to get down there to the quadrangle for a three-hour seminar, walked right on by, ignorant of, as Marvin Gaye says, "what's goin' on." I was thinking about some text or other—I believe, *The Evolving Self: Problems and Principles in Human Development*. Wondering how I could ever have thought my aging mind could endure the rigorous intellectual stimulation of a joint like Chicago Divinity. I was also missing the pristine environmental conditions of Michigan's Upper Peninsula, where I had resided as an adult, not a professional student.

Entering the Hyde Park Stationery Store, owned by Cheryl, a young African American woman, I found her listening intently to this same voice that now had a name, Clarence Thomas, the Black candidate for the Supreme Court who had for months been under Senate investigation. Cheryl clearly was fascinated, much more interested in that proceeding than in my need for more disposable ink pens in purple. So I did my do quickly and left, now speeding for the campus.

143

Thomas's resonant voice remained in my ear for the rest of the day. Every so often, I heard new mutterings about "the hearings," but it wasn't until I returned much later to my cell at the Union that I could listen undisturbed by the theories, proofs, concerns of faculty and students forging ahead in their pursuit of academic formation. I am not clear about whether it was Anita on my radio that night or Clarence. I do know that I heard it, rather than saw it, because I refused to join the throng of nuns gathered in the television room to witness the "truth." Somewhere between that Friday night and early Saturday afternoon, the flow of the hearings began to formulate thought upon my psyche. "Long Dong Silver," something about hair on a Coke bottle or a Coke can, he said. I felt embarrassment; charges of conduct unbefitting a candidate for the position were repeated over and over by America's most distinguished radio commentators, who acted as if the American public needed them to translate the events into English—and into reality.

At some point, dear listeners, I remembered that earlier in the struggle, I had arrogantly, and, I now feel, mistakenly, chastised an old friend by long-distance telephone for refusing to support the nominee. This prestigious gentleman, who is politically and socially powerful, had stated that in his estimation, Thomas was simply a pawn in a powerful, strategic effort by our Republican president to stack the Court deck with a man who was black in skin tone only. Thomas was not only unqualified to represent minority interests, he was not even interested in doing so. We ended our conversation with me saying I hated to see a prominent Black leader such as he help to feed a Black man, who had climbed Jacob's ladder, into a machinery that, it appeared, aimed to make fine strawdust of yet another Black man. So it seems that at some point I had done battle for Thomas before the electronic curtain rose.

At the front of the stage stood Professor Anita Hill. Initially, as a Person of Color who is much more a Womanist than a Feminist (this means I am suspicious of my white sisters' sexual politics, my leaning much more toward racial issues than is possible for them), I took Hill's side. I could empathize with her. After all, had I, too, not experienced sexual harassment on the job? Once, when I was fifteen, I worked for a man at his record shop who fired me because I asked him to cease squeezing his fat, old, smelly body up against mine behind the counter. I had also been sexually used on numerous occasions, but private sexual misuse is not the issue here, is it? The issue is sexual harassment on the job, in the public sector. It involves the right of a woman to exist as a worker alongside, beneath, above other workers in psychological and physical security.

Hill, as did Thomas, elicited a reaction when I first saw them on television that I am ashamed of confessing. I knew who they were, I was proud of their accomplishments, I was in her army, as I have explained. But, on a subliminal level, I would have preferred that he look more like Thurgood Marshall than Spike Lee. I would have more readily accepted her had she looked more like Lena Horne or Vanessa Williams than Cicely Tyson. Hollywood-ingrained sick notions of the superiority of color gnawed at my conscious power. I could not help but focus on her prominent lips, colored purple; his hair clipped down to the scalp; his broad, flat nose; her appeared-to-be-straightened hair. They did not look the part. I checked myself by bringing to the surface this bit of racial bull snot that somehow was causing me irritation. I was rooting for her but wishing she looked more like me, light, bright, blue-eyed. At first, I did not even see her as sexually desirable.

I deprogrammed myself by looking at ancient pictures of my brown grandmothers and aunts. I thought of that African woman, my great-great-grandmother, who was desirable and sexy to the ol' captain or one of his sons. She was the reason I had successfully survived this American racist system, was she not? Her strength of character rested in my genealogical system as assuredly as her dark mahogany color. Her spirituality had generated a line of fighting, cussing, strong women who dared to produce descendants who qualified for white conservative, capitalistic universities, academic training, and literary honors. Out of the red mud of rural central Georgia, I, too, rose, out of shame and out of scorn. Anita and, for that matter, Clarence were clearly not *physically* in the white image.

I asked God to forgive me for even momentarily falling into this pit of racist thought.

Late in the afternoon, I jumped into my 4X Jimmy Gypsy and headed for the United Church of Rogers Park, way up on the north side of Chicago. There I served an internship as one of two student pastors, each of us older women, one of us white from Garret Evangelical Seminary. This late Saturday, my charge was to teach the rudiments of creative writing to a small group of racially mixed, economically disadvantaged youth who cling to this church for spiritual survival. I listen to Soul Sister Number One, Aretha, as I glide past Lake Shore. "Everyday People" and "Mary, Mary," she chants for me in her greatness as only Aretha, my home girl, can do.

My mood is pensive as I travel the seventeen miles, park, and enter by the sanctuary door. I am a tad irritated at myself. For I have allowed the outside world to penetrate the cloistered one I had entered when I committed myself to preparation for ordination. Not that world affairs were nonpermissible; in fact, one of my duties at the United Church was to help coordinate the affairs of the Sunday afternoon soup kitchen. There I experienced a great deal of the injustice of American society at play. But by "outside," I mean the one created by the tensions between our fascist government and its far-reaching media arm. The "Thomas-Hill Show" was, for the most part, a cleverly designed, rehearsed skit created to cajole the American public into believing that some kind of democratic process was at work. Brer Bush pulled Tar Baby Thomas out of the briar patch for his administration's Republican purposes. And the good ol' Democratic boys reached into the patch and found Lil Liza recoiled there, asleep but not dead.

None of these producer-director-actors controlled the dialogue or the action after those two Black and beautiful *and brilliant* performers entered stage left and right. Why? Because the American public became mesmerized by the dialogue, setting, themes, characters, and action. Get back "Roots," come on "Clarence and Anita." Explicit language: Long Dong Silver, bestiality, rape scenes. Setting: Washington, D.C., conference room, complete with lifted dais for the clandestine panel of truth-seekers without their white robes and hoods. Themes: sexual harassment, sexual secrets of Kingfish and Sapphire, Bill and Beulah, Uncle Tom and Aunt Jemima action. Thomas passionately accusing his adversaries of a "high-tech lynching" (by the way bringing a new concept into the American language). His young white lawyer wife loving him in plain view of Strom Thurmond, the old and new South. A bevy of bureaucratic witnesses, African and European American, foaming at the bit. You could smell tons of microwave popcorn and taste the Diet Pepsi being consumed all over this land of liberty.

The sanctuary was darkened with only a streak of natural light filtering through the hundred-year-old stained-glass windows. I sat in a middle wooden pew, staring up at the dome ceiling that features pale white

145

angels in blue robes with fluffy wings. One of them looked like she was winking down at me, the other seemed to be smiling.

> Yes, Lord, I believe Clarence boy bragged about his prowess to Anita girl. He forgot she was more than the bureau's paid civil servant, he forgot he was on a GS level higher than she, not on a higher plane than she. Poor Clarence eyed her Coca-Cola fine brown frame and forgot that in 1981, Anita was his peer, his competition, not his piece. Anita was a powerhouse, not a power pouch. Anita was Miss Thing, not Miss Poon Tang, to him and everybody else, *in her mind* and in the minds of the *Other*.

I closed my eyes and thanked God for throwing into the game of humans once more the golden flying hammer that occasionally the Divine Other uses to beat sense into human folly. God used Brother Thomas and Sister Anita to force this nation to look deeply at the festering sores and bleeding scabs that mark our decaying moral fiber. The two great Judeo-Christian commandments are still "Love thy God" and "Love thy neighbor." Love of anything but power was surely missing at that truth-seeking circus that was taking place as I sat in this dark, sacred chamber.

I took the New Revised Standard Version of the Hebrew Bible out of its holder and turned to the book of Hosea. This prophet of Israel is a prime example of biblical misogynist thought. Hosea, the prophet, has been utilized for centuries by editors, priests, ministers, writers, and anybody else who cares to use the Bible as a source of support for discrediting women. Hosea defiled the image of his own wife, Gomer, successfully claiming that his utterances were divinely inspired by God. The language is explicit, powerful, and damaging subliminally, even when read for other purposes. Gomer is sometimes interpreted metaphorically, not as woman, not as wife, but as the nation of Israel, for example. Yet it is difficult not to associate the words with woman more readily than with the nation. Hosea, chapter 2, verses 1–3, dramatically demonstrates the power of this literature, which, be mindful, is, and has been considered for centuries by thousands of influential men (and women) as the very word of God. The words are what we deem divinely inspired:

> Say to your brother, Ammi, and to your sister, Ruhamah. Plead with your mother, plead—for she is not my wife, and I am not her husband—that she put away her whining from her face and her adultery from between her breasts, or I will strip her naked and expose her as in the day she was born, and make her like a wilderness, and turn her into a parched land, and kill her with thirst.

Both the Old and New Testaments are loaded with mysogynist language like that of Hosea. In fact, one task pertinent to Feminist theology is the problem this presents in interpreting biblical texts from a Feminist perspective. When the Bible is quoted as authority, the effect is often the formation of ingrained thought patterns that can result in the antiwoman behavior America was witnessing as I took a little time with Jesus.

> Lord, Lord, Lord, I do believe that there is some
> possibility that each and every one of those honorable white
> gentlemen and their honorable black candidate truly does
> not know that this Judeo-Christian text I hold, right here in
> my hands, has in some way influenced their behavior. It
> certainly is in the Judeo-Christian tradition to abuse women.
> Male superiority in America is supported by the public
> church. To sit there, the committee members had to
> undergo the process of church formation; each and every
> member is somewhere a trustee, a deacon, or a tithes-
> paying member of some church where women are
> underrepresented in the leadership. Lord, I continue to pray,
> I truly wish you had made one of those Marys a designated
> disciple. This could have truly changed the history of Jews
> and Christians.

With this, I ended my little talk with Jesus and headed for my young charges. Today, we were going to read Hosea in preparation for writing creatively. "How do I know the Lord loves me? The Bible tells me so." Or does it?

Late Saturday night, I returned to my cell on South Cornell Street at fifty-third Avenue. All was very quiet, as usual, by this time. A lone Irish sister watched the late-evening news. I guessed she was looking for more of the confessions of Thomas and Hill. As usual, I decided to make a few calls, as had become my habit, to some of my fellow "clergy." Most of us spoke to each other very late or very early, as these were times usually reserved for interfaith dialogues. The rest of our time was spent in study, classes, pastoral counseling, sermon preparation, or some such grace-seeking activities. Father C.C., an Episcopalian (as I shall call him here), was first on my list; he was tussling with the next morning's tight schedule, trying to figure out how to impose the Hearings onto the diocese's prescribed liturgy. I told him that I was lacing my prescribed United Methodist scriptural readings with a few mysogynistic lines from Hosea. I gave him the quote.

> Plead with your mother, plead—for she is not my wife, and
> I am not her husband—that she put away her whoring from
> her face and her adultery from between her breasts, or I

will strip her naked and expose her as in the day she was born, and make her like a wilderness, and turn her into a parched land, and kill her with thirst.

I paused and waited for Father C.C.'s response.

"Whew! Girl! Maybe I should pull out my Hosea commentary, too. Use that macho, mother fudge." He laughed.

"Who is lying, brother? The judge or the professor? That's my question."

"My question," he retorted, "is which one is more *believable*, not which one is telling the truth?" C.C., I could tell, was not going to attempt to answer either one of our questions.

"He scares me, regardless of the answer. That legal mind, that legal scholar, that candidate for one of the highest offices in America, the U.S. Supreme Court, said in front of all of the civilized world that he never discussed, never heard of *Roe* v. *Wade*! Do you hear me, Sister Jones?" His words came forth in a loud whisper. "*Roe* v. *Wade* is one of the most compelling issues of the century, as you know! Let me go, girl, I still have not recited my prayers—yet." He then hung up, as was our customary method of ending a conversation.

I placed my second call, this one to an A.M.E. Zion minister.

"Hi!" Reverend Love Smith responded as usual. "Speak, child, we got about a minute to run over the coals. I'm about to curl up with Zacharia and his picturesque visions."

"Who is lying? Clarence or Anita?"

"Child. This entire case would never have arisen if poor Clarence looked like Denzel Washington. That little woman would have been running out for some Eve mint before he finished his narrative description. Anita should have taken all of that bragging in its cultural context. She knows that some of the chocolate brothers talk like that to blow up a girl's dress. So do some of the vanilla ones, as a matter of fact. That was all just yin-yang, he was simply acting like a natural l-i-t-t-l-e man. Those luscious lips of hers all greased up in that purple lipstick was probably what inspired him. He simply forgot that it was 1982, not '62, and that he was not addressing a broad but an esquire-ette." He paused for breath. "They are both in denial, I would say, my dear. I must go now. So. Go on. Speak!"

"It was a 'Black Thang,' you are saying?"

"It was a man thang, Sister. See ya," he said, ending our conversation.

I dialed the African nun from across the hall. She was just finishing her rosary.

"Nettie, they both are liars, if you want my opinion. Yet neither one of them is a liar if we examine this word in light of contemporary practices. 'Lying' as a concept, like 'Truth' and 'Beauty' and 'Love,' is not infallible, universal, or timeless, invincible, permanent—a stable concept. Its definition depends on the facts surrounding it, the circumstances. For example, who is speaking? The President of the United States? The *Chicago Tribune*? The Bishop? What does the speaker believe he or she is doing at the time? Nettie, the power of the subconscious, particularly when it is protecting the fragile psyche of the human mind, is tremendous." She stopped and waited upon me. I loved her Southern African accent.

"No one was lying?" I waited. "No one was lying? No one was lying?" I repeated and waited.

"Not under these circumstances. Each party was forced by the stakes to believe totally in his or her own version of the events that led to that public confrontation." She waited for me.

"Good night, Sister," we both said in unison.

149

Making Sense of Our Differences: African American Women on Anita Hill

BEVERLY GRIER

The testimony of Professor Anita Hill before the Senate Judiciary Committee in October 1991 had a profound effect on most African American women. I was particularly struck by their diversity of views about Hill's charge of sexual harassment. In the beginning, I assumed that most African American women felt as I and my closest friends and associates did: painful and dangerous though it may be to air our linen before white America, African American women had been silent for too long about sexist oppression by African-American men. However, as the circle of women with whom I discussed Hill's charges widened, I began to realize that most of my sisters saw the issue differently from me. Some of the African-American women with whom I talked did not believe Hill was telling the truth. Many others felt that her experience of being sexually harassed by Clarence Thomas was a trivial matter. It certainly was not serious enough to keep a Black man off the Supreme Court. Most were very angry, and many were ashamed that Hill had made her charges public. There was some bitterness about the possibility that the charges might prevent the upward climb of an African American male (and, by extension somehow, the upward climb of the race). As it turned out, only a minority of African American women I encountered warmly embraced and defended Hill, heralding her testimony as the beginning of a new era in African American women's struggle against oppression from within the race.

What accounts for the diversity of views expressed by African American women on Hill's charges? How do we explain the absence of solidarity in our support of Hill? Can our disparate and contradictory views be connected in some way? What does our reaction to the Hill-Thomas controversy say about how we value ourselves and how we struggle as women in a racist, sexist, and classist society?

I will explore these questions using formal and informal discussions among groups of African American women in the Boston area. The women come from a variety of educational backgrounds, from those with high school diplomas to those with law and doctorate degrees. Most of the women are middle- and lower-middle-class, and their ages range from eighteen to eighty. Many are not native to the Boston area but, like me, were born and educated in other parts of the United States. Some are my college students. Though not a cross-section of African American women, these women can tell us a great deal about the anger and confusion generated by the double or even triple oppression of race, class, and gender of African American women. In discussions so heated at times that friendships and civility were strained, the ambiguous and divided identities and loyalties that have marked our outlook and forms of struggle since slavery were painfully apparent.

Unlike African American men and European American women, we have yet to articulate and act upon an identity that is ours in particular. This is because of the complexity of our multiple oppression. Most African American women believe that though we are women, we are Blacks first. We believe that racism is and always has been a more powerful force in our lives than sexism. In the current period in which many European Americans no longer hide their racism and in which African American men are under threat of extinction, this perspective is reinforced. Racial solidarity and struggle along racial lines, the argument goes, must take precedence over "in-house" or "family matters" such as the sexism of our men. We can deal with sexism quite easily, on our own, at a later time. I am sympathetic with this view and have held it for most of my life. However, I am becoming increasingly convinced that our situation as an oppressed people and as oppressed women is far more complex than the "race first" line allows. Just as we tell European American feminists that they must acknowledge race and class privilege as well as gender oppression as forces shaping their lives, African American women must acknowledge gender oppression along with race and class oppression as integral forces shaping our lives.

If Kimberly Rae Harbor were alive today, she would testify to this. She was the young African American woman who was repeatedly raped, stabbed, and bludgeoned to death in a park in Boston on Halloween night in 1991. Her attackers were several teenage African American and Hispanic males. The racial line would have us attribute her murder to the pressures of racism, primarily or even solely. It would have us deny the importance of the widespread anger, hostility, and emotional, physical, and sexual abuse that younger African American males, in particular, direct toward their mothers, sisters, girlfriends, and other females in their lives. Is it merely a coincidence that as racism has become more intense, so has sexism? Is it a coincidence that the 1980s and early 1990s have witnessed an increase in racist attacks and in the incidence of violence against women in all communities? We cannot deny the anger and frustration of young men who have been consigned to the permanent reserve army of the unemployed and who are despised, feared, and imprisoned by European American society. But sexism within our community only serves the larger dominant interests. It deflects anger and energy away from the real sources of oppression toward more accessible and acceptable targets, African American women. We will not be able to overturn race and class oppression until we see that it is intimately connected to gender oppression.

Bell hooks put it well when she wrote about the "devaluation" of African American womanhood by white men, white women, African American men, *and* African American women. Socialized by racism and sexism, African American women have been conditioned to "devalue our femaleness and to regard race as the only relevant label of identification" (1984:1). As a consequence, we identify more readily with the aspirations and frustrations of Clarence Thomas than with the humiliation and pain of Anita Hill. Cynically, Thomas knew he could play on African American racial sensibilities by calling the hearings a "high-tech lynching" when, in fact, the person who was degraded and "lynched" by the process was Hill. As could have been predicted, African American male and female support for Thomas increased after his speech. In spite of the personal experiences most African American women have had with sexual harassment, exploitation, battering, incest, or rape by African American men, we have been so conditioned to devalue our femaleness that we keep silent and label as traitors to the race women like Hill who dare to speak out.

152

"She's Lying. I Just Don't Believe Her"

Unfortunately, like the privileged white males who sat on the Senate Judiciary Committee, many African American women simply did not believe Hill's story. So deep was the distrust that some African American women, like the fourteen white men, resorted to elaboration and fabrication. Hill had to have had an ulterior motive.

(1) She's lying. She was probably in love with Clarence
    Thomas and was angry he did not return her affections.
    And then he turned around and married a white woman?
    I think Hill was trying to pay him back.

(2) She's envious. You know Black women have a history of bringing down Black men in this country. We never support our men.

(3) Hill allowed herself to be used by the leadership of the Democratic Party and the Civil Rights establishment, yes. But she was working out her own personal agenda with Thomas at the same time.

The actual sequence of events—the refusal of Hill to discuss publicly what had happened to her until she was compelled to do so by the FBI in early September 1991, followed by the leakage of the contents of the interviews—suggests to me that for a number of years, Hill was engaged in protecting the reputation and career of Thomas at the expense of her own self-esteem and that she would have continued to do so had it been her choice. However, knowledge of this sequence of events made no difference to the women who expressed disbelief.

What explains this level of distrust? As already suggested, in a society that is profoundly sexist and racist, African American women too often internalize sexist and racist views of themselves. In patriarchal societies, women and men are taught that women are not to be trusted; they are the source of evil, they always have hidden agendas, they are devious and manipulative, and they will lie to get what they want. Most men buy this, and, unfortunately, so do many women. Racism intensifies the mistrust of African American women. We belong not only to a gender that cannot be trusted but to a race that cannot be trusted as well. As a consequence, we become the least trustworthy of all human beings. With our origins in enslavement, the myths surrounding us are numerous: we are disloyal and unfaithful to our men, devious, opportunistic ("golddiggers" in the current lingo); we are sexually insatiable and promiscuous. These myths were and continue to be functional to our sexual and economic exploitation by both European and African American men and by European American women. At some level, Thomas and every other man who has sexually harassed, raped, and otherwise abused an African American woman have been aware of the double burden on African American women. Since we are not to be trusted, we are not to be believed. Anything can be done to us, and the perpetrator will not be punished.

When African American women condemn rather than support the victims of sexual harassment and abuse, we think we are separating ourselves from such women and thereby protecting ourselves from similar treatment. ("Women who are abused ask for it. Only bad women are treated that way.") In fact, we are paving the way for condemnation and disbelief when it is ourselves or our daughters who are abused. Very often, the women who are most vehement in expressing their disbelief

153

are in a state of denial about the abuse they have suffered. Ashamed of having been victims and of having remained silent about it, they wish to silence those women who remind them of their own pain and humiliation.

"What Is She Crying About? What He Did to Her Was Nothing, Really. He Didn't Rape Her"

Many African American women, in particular, do not consider verbal abuse a violation of their rights. Some of the women in the discussion groups and many of my students had a difficult time taking Hill's charges seriously because Thomas did not assault her physically. Her treatment was mild, according to them, even if it did occur in the workplace. She should have been able to handle it. Running the verbal gauntlet of the boys or men on the corner and being "felt up" in grade school are familiar experiences to every African American woman who grew up in the community. For too many African American women, and men, such behavior on the part of African American males is neither improper nor unacceptable. We seem to have a narrower definition than other groups of what constitutes proper and improper African American male behavior. Yet if a white man whistles and calls out to one of us, "I'd like to take you home, baby" or "I sure would like some of that," all of us, male and female alike, would quickly name the behavior. It's racist and sexist at the same time.

154

Here again, our socialization in a racist and sexist society and the multiple sources of our oppression are the keys to explaining why we accept inappropriate behavior from our men. Sexism within the African American community is so pervasive that it is hegemonic. We do not recognize it or name it when we see it. We reproduce it daily in our responses to it and in the way we raise our boys and girls. Sexism has become part of our "culture." It imbues the way strangers on the street, lovers, and other black men talk to and treat us—curse words, references to body parts, sexually explicit details of what they would like to do to us, the rough physical treatment during lovemaking. To reject the language, the playing around, and the lovemaking approach is to open ourselves up to more abuse: "Who do you think you are?" "You too good?" "You must like women." "You must think you white." We try not to see in such abuse the effort to dominate and control us through humiliation and disrespect. After all, these are brothers, and we face the same racist oppression. When most of us heard Hill describe what Thomas said to her, we instantly knew it was true. It sounded so familiar to us. How many of us have tried to ignore or laugh off this kind of treatment from a friend, schoolmate, coworker, or church member, hoping it would eventually stop? It never does. It often gets worse.

Because Hill continued to work for Thomas and because she "followed" him from the Department of Education to the Equal Employment Opportunity Commission, many Americans, European and African, male and female, found it difficult to believe that Thomas's remarks had offended her. As Hill explained during the hearings and subsequently with a greater sense of the victim's syndrome, she was in a vulnerable position in relation to Thomas. She hoped the behavior would stop. She felt it was her fault. Moreover, how would it look if her immediate supervisor, who was also the head of the department, did not write a letter of recommendation for her for a significant period and place of employment? Cordial relations had to be maintained for a considerable time after Hill's government employment. Thomas knew of his power and abused it.

Even when actual physical assaults occur, many African American men and women (like their European American counterparts) are not likely to believe the alleged rape victim. Witness the reaction on the part of many African American men and women of all ages to the Mike Tyson rape case. None of my African American female students believed Desiree Washington had been raped. Roughed up during foreplay or in the process of having sexual intercourse, perhaps, but not raped. "After all," one African American male student remarked, "what did she think she was going up to his room for? A cup of coffee?" Both Tyson and Thomas needed to assert power and control. Forced sex and explicit language were means to this end.

155

"How Could She Go Against a Black Man Headed for the Supreme Court?"

A majority of the women in one discussion group and many of the older women I talked with felt that Hill had betrayed the race by telling what had happened to her. One of my students shook her head and said, "They [the brothers] will point to Hill and say all we do is tear them down. We never build them up." Though most of the women were aware of Thomas's record at the EEOC, of his anti-Civil Rights agenda, and of the contempt he showed for his sister during the hearings, they still wanted him to be appointed to the Supreme Court. Many argued:

(4) He will change, discover his roots, upon being appointed for life. He will have no more political debts to pay.

(5) It's better to have a Black conservative on the Court than a white conservative. At least there's some hope with a Black.

(6) This is our only chance to maintain an African American presence on the Court. We have to support him, no matter what his views are.

(7) The elevation and advancement of one Black man serves all Black people.

Most startling to me was the anger and hostility of many women toward Hill. The complexity of our multiple oppressions is at the root of these feelings. Hill appeared to have chosen her identity as a woman over her identity as an African American. What's more, she did so publicly, for European Americans to see and exploit. She washed our dirty linen before the European American public. She broke the unity of the family and set herself up as the primary obstacle in the way of an African American man's ascent to the Supreme Court. She reinforced European American stereotypes about the sexuality of African American men *and* women.

The unveiling of Black sexual stereotypes caused tremendous pain and embarrassment for African Americans. We know that European Americans are extremely curious about Black sexuality. The hearings provided them with an opportunity to satisfy some of that curiosity. Many of us sensed that most European Americans viewed the testimonies of Hill and Thomas not as a confrontation about gender and power relations but as sexual entertainment. And it was Hill's deeds, not Thomas's, that made the "show" possible. Hill's charges against Thomas reinforced the stereotype of the sexually aggressive Black male. (Meanwhile, the charges and rumors about the Kennedys, George Bush, Bill Clinton, Franklin Delano Roosevelt, Gary Hart, Brock Adams, and so on, were statements simply about individual European American men.) Having failed to paint Hill with the brush of promiscuity, the senators accused her of fantasizing about sex. The next best thing. The point was that African American women, like African American men, are obsessed with sex.

More distressing for an elderly friend of mine were the graphic descriptions Hill was forced to give. My friend was torn. On the one hand, she was angry with the senators because she knew they would never have forced a European American woman to convey such details before the entire American public. On the other hand, my friend was angry with Hill for having gone along with it. She felt humiliated as an African American woman. Hill's testimony reinforced for my friend the slavery-era stereotype that African American women are at ease with everything about sex, including talking about breast sizes, penis sizes, and pubic hairs on Coke cans in front of their elderly parents and on national television. I feel my friend was right to be angry with the senators, Arlen Specter and Ted Kennedy alike. The objective of the Republicans was to demean and humiliate Hill. The Democrats just "got off" on her testimony. I must admit I, too, was annoyed with Hill for giving those European American men and the European American public such satisfaction. I remember yelling out at my TV set, "Tell them you will not repeat what you have already read in your statement just for their vicarious sexual gratification!"

"That Is One Brave Sister"

For reasons that are not completely clear to me, I found that the African American women who were most supportive of Hill were those whose age, education, and professional experiences most closely resembled hers: lawyers, academics, women working in the nonprofit and European American corporate sectors. At a discussion group consisting of such women, I found my ideological home. By the time this group met (in late October), most of us had discovered that not all our sisters shared our views. So, after affirming and building upon our own perspective, we spent some time talking about why we saw things differently from so many of our sisters. We speculated that perhaps Hill appeared too "white" or too assimilated for the tastes of many working and poverty-level African American women. Perhaps Hill was not like anyone they knew and, therefore, did not seem genuine. To many of these women, Hill has been privileged by an elitist education and profession. How could she possibly complain about a little kidding around by her boss?

What is at work here are increasingly different perspectives among African American women based on our education, class, and daily experiences. Though most of the women in this discussion group were from working-class or poor rural Southern backgrounds, education and income have now positioned us in a different arena of daily struggle in racist and sexist America. Our socialization often diverges from that of our working and poverty-level sisters. As professors in predominantly European American universities, as lawyers in a European American-controlled legal system, or as managers in European American corporations, we are confronted overtly and covertly every day with assaults on our intellectual capacities and our right to be where we are. Often, we are in positions of power and authority over European Americans, or we are in positions that demand at least formal respect from coworkers, subordinates, clients, or students. Many European Americans resent this and work diligently to undermine our self-confidence and boost their own. An African American woman or man who succeeds in this world might appear, like Hill, to be less "Black," but he or she is not. Most of us (and I would wager that Hill is one) have learned to switch our cultural personas depending on the dictates of the situation.

This is also a world in which collegiality is critical to keeping one's job and to advancement. For African American men, this means walking a tight rope with racist coworkers. For African American women, this means getting along with racist and sexist coworkers, some of whom might be Black. I can understand Hill's need to remain collegial with

Thomas. Though she is a Yale-trained lawyer, Thomas had the power to make her future job searches a rocky or smooth process. It is not unusual in this arena to ask for letters of recommendation from professors or superiors with whom one has not had contact for ten years or so.

At an earlier meeting of a group of African American women in a town south of Boston, I sensed that many were unsympathetic with (indeed, hostile toward) Hill because they could not identify with her. The women in this group were mostly nonprofessionals (city workers, clerks, homemakers), though some were professionals (teachers, nurses, social workers). They were organized around issues of concern to their community, issues related particularly to African American children. There was such disagreement at this meeting about Hill's charges that my head was spinning. The discussion was called to a halt after about an hour because the women realized they had to continue to work together on issues such as education, drugs, crime, police harassment, and racism. At one level, the decision to move on symbolized that gender issues could wait. At another level, it was clear to everyone that gender issues were too painful, too hot to handle. We were having trouble accepting and processing our differences. Though our ambiguous loyalties and identities were apparent, we did not know what to do with them.

Conclusion

These issues will not go away. We will be confronted more frequently in the future with sexual oppression within our community. Sometimes our awareness will go forward through outrage over specific events: the failure of most African American male leaders to speak out on Hill's charges or on the way she was treated by the Senate Judiciary Committee; the lack of response of leaders to the rape and brutalization of a New York African American woman just a few weeks before the European American Central Park jogger was raped, and to the acquittal of five European American St. John's University students for the rape of a Jamaican American female student; the misogyny of rap music; the attention given to the crisis of young African American males compared to the neglect of the crisis of young African American females; the "studding" of our young men who have few positive ways of exercising manhood.

Sometimes our awareness will go forward through slow realizations: the ultraconservative voting record of Thomas on the Supreme Court thus far has caused many African American women and men to pause and think. Perhaps it would have been better had he not been confirmed at all.

158

References

hooks, bell. *Ain't I a Woman: Black Women and Feminism.* Boston: South End Press, 1984.

The Year of the Woman or the Woman of the Year: Was There Really an "Anita Hill Effect"?

JULIANNE MALVEAUX

Only ten days separated the mo-   *159*
ment University of Oklahoma professor Anita Hill called a press conference on October 7, 1991, from the moment Judge Clarence Thomas was
confirmed as associate justice of the U.S. Supreme Court on October 16,
1991. In ten days, the nation witnessed conflicting allegations, dozens of
hours of comment and analysis, and, ultimately, the closest Supreme Court
confirmation vote in history. In ten days, Hill was transformed from a
private citizen to a public symbol. Some say that in these same ten days,
the Feminist Movement was given new life. The year 1992 was dubbed
the "Year of the Woman" because it saw the election of four new female
U.S. senators, including the first African American female senator, Carol
Moseley-Braun. Certainly, 1992 could not have been the Year of the
Woman had not Hill been the woman of the year in 1991.

The ripple effect of the ten public days of Hill-Thomas reverberated
for months. The Civil Rights Act of 1991, which specifically provided
civil rights remedies for acts of sexual harassment, was signed into law
on November 21, 1991, just a few weeks after the Senate confirmed Thomas
to the Supreme Court. Then-President George Bush had previously vetoed a version of the act weaker than the one he ultimately signed, many
say because of the attention Hill's testimony focused on sexual harassment issues. Reverend Jesse Jackson, in a singular act of hyperbole, described Hill as "the Rosa Parks of the 1990s." Books, articles, and con-

ferences were organized around Thomas-Hill, and Hill was honored as "Woman of the Year" by *Glamour* magazine.

The Senate, and especially senators Orrin Hatch, Arlen Specter, and Alan Simpson, vilified Hill. The stark visual image of three white men haranguing a black woman, of an all-male Senate Judiciary Committee sitting in opposition to a soft-spoken, self-contained African American woman, energized a movement. Indeed, to invoke the name of Hill is to twist a kaleidoscope and to raise questions about race relations, gender relations, feminism, sexual harassment, labor market policy, Civil Rights, Black conservativism. To call her name is to remind us of the confrontation but not the results; to call her name is to seek phantom solidarity without taking a position.

"Anita Hill"—does her name mean change/courage/audacity? Is the message an ambiguous one? Even those who identified with Hill and supported her courage have hesitated to deify her. Her belated act of courage, after all, followed a decade of silence during which careerist accommodationism was a stronger inducement than principle. Further, even though she has written and spoken about sexual harassment in the workplace since 1991, it is an area in which she had shown little interest before her accusations of Thomas. Her legal research and writing had focused primarily on bankruptcy and the uniform commercial code.

Will there be a lasting "Anita Hill effect"? The purpose of this essay is to consider the importance of Hill in shaping public policy, in revitalizing the Feminist Movement, and in altering the strained relationship between African American women and white Feminists.

160

At the University of Michigan's forum on women and politics in March 1993, I collided with Lynn Yeakel, a Pennsylvania Democrat who had made an unsuccessful bid for the U.S. Senate in 1992. Yeakel complained that her candidacy had failed to get sufficient support from African American women. According to African American congressional candidate C. Delores Tucker, Yeakel double-crossed her on an endorsement exchange and, as a result, lost Black women's support. But in an extraordinarily myopic and self-serving analysis, Yeakel cast her loss in terms of non-solidarity among women, then pulled out her trump card. "When I talked to Anita Hill . . .," she said, using the Black female law professor's name like a mantra, like a cross held to ward off offending vampires. That she had talked to Hill was presumed to have given her an imprimatur, a blessing, a sign that she should be all right for Black women.

"We should pull an Anita Hill on him," I heard another woman say, speaking of blowing the whistle on a man she found offensive. "Let's Anita Hill this," wrote *New York Times* columnist Anna Quindlen in February 1993, in reference to directing attention to badly neglected topics. Noun. Verb. Adverb. Icon. Mantra. Political effect.

The Anita Hill effect may have enlightened consciousness, but it did not guarantee Feminist consciousness on the part of women who were elected in the name of Hill. The "Anita Hill senators" are the women— Dianne Feinstein, Barbara Boxer, Patti Murphy and Carol Moseley-Braun— whose election was partly the result of women's heightened consciousness about the way Hill was treated by the Senate Judiciary Committee. While their ads proclaimed their outrage at Hill's treatment, their post-election actions suggest that Hill was as much a campaign device as Feinstein's slogan about 2-percent milk![1] I make this point not to criticize Hill, because my support for her actions in the October 1991 hearings remains unwavering. But I resist the attempt to deify her, to turn her name into a household word, some noun, some verb. Rather, I make the point because there are so many women who articulate support for her as a symbol for working women. Yet these women's actions do not indicate such support.

Anita Hill: Voices

After the dust from Hill's testimony settled, it appeared that those women who gained strength from her voice were not evenly distributed by race, class, and occupational status. Indeed, it was mostly professional women who stepped to the forefront with complaints about sexual harassment. Perhaps it is logical that these women should have been the first to benefit from the Anita Hill effect. They, like Hill, are well educated and articulate, able to present their cases and to explain themselves in a credible manner. However, it is important to note that the earliest recorded cases of sexual harassment in American workplaces were from the bottom of the occupational hierarchy, not the top.

161

Private household workers, clerical workers, hospital service workers, and restaurant staff all earn pay at the bottom of the occupational scale. They are as likely, if not more so, to be sexually harassed as their professional sisters. And they are more likely to be women of color. They don't make good copy, they are not necessarily articulate, and one can't build a movement or an "effect" around them. They are the voiceless women who may not have been empowered by the Anita Hill effect.

Whenever I think of Hill, I also think of Brenda Patterson, the plaintiff in *Patterson* v. *McLean's Credit Union*, one of the five cases that were part of the Civil Rights Act of 1991. We've never heard of the "Brenda Patterson effect" because the racial harassment Patterson experienced didn't rally women's groups around her. Yet the recurring racial hazing she endured was much harsher than the harassment Hill experienced.

The facts in *Patterson* are chilling. She was subjected to racial hazing in the workplace from the moment she was hired as an accounting clerk. According to court documents, her white supervisor told her that her coworkers would dislike her because she was Black. The only African American employee at her bank, Patterson was the brunt of an endless stream of racial remarks and workplace hazing. Her supervisors and coworkers told her that Black people were, by nature, slower than whites. Then they piled extra work on her to see if she could do it. She was ordered to dust and sweep the office, something no other accounting clerk had to do, and she was subjected to a constant barrage of obscene epithets.

Patterson was laid off in 1982, even though people who had been on the job less time than she had kept their jobs. She brought a lawsuit against her employers for denying her a promotion, for an unjustified layoff, and for racial discrimination on the job. She and her attorneys fought through District Court, to the Court of Appeals, and finally to the Supreme Court, which found, in 1989, that discrimination is not allowed at the point of hiring but is acceptable after hiring. This woman endured a decade of harassment and hazing, and she has yet to receive full satisfaction from the courts. Indeed, all her claims of racial harassment and discrimination have been dismissed, and the only pending action she has against McLean's Credit Union is based on whether she was unjustifiably denied a promotion.

People like Patterson have been jerked around by the judicial system and by legislators who choose to equate racial justice with quotas. Nothing in Patterson's case requests the establishment of quotas, just fair treatment. Until the Civil Rights Act of 1991 was passed, though, the law simply failed to address the sexualized racial hazing that Patterson experienced.[2] Patterson did not become a cause célèbre for Feminists, and outside Civil Rights circles (she was represented by the NAACP Legal Defense and Education Fund) her case was little noted. Yet it seems the precise kind of case that speaks to the nexus of race and gender in the workplace and more realistically reflects the occupational status of African American women.

Hill's testimony unleashed women's tongues and gave women voice. But the tongues unleashed were much like hers, the cultivated tongues of professional women who speak in modulated tones about workplace slights. Do these women speak for millions of other women who have no voice, no access to the media? Did the Year of the Woman trickle down? In my mind, the most enduring image of the Year of the Woman is the blow-dried group of female candidates who stood on a stage at the Democratic National Convention, wearing jewel-toned suits and smiling for the camera. They were the darlings of their party, the key to unlocking millions of women's votes for Democratic candidate Clinton. Not one of these women spoke to (or about) those millions of women who earn minimum wage. Not one of these women got past sexual harassment to the more basic issue of equal pay. Not one of these women mentioned the women who perished, a year before, in the chicken processing plant fire at Hamlet, North Carolina, because Imperial Foods locked a fire door to prevent theft. Jesse Jackson spoke about the plight of those women on the bottom, who bone chicken wings, clean toilets, earn the minimum wage. The voices raised because of the Anita Hill effect were not the voices of *these* women. Indeed, in the early days of the Clinton administration, there was palpable conflict between the women at the top and the women at the bottom.

Ain't I a Woman?: Anita, Zoë, the Corderos, and Lani

When President Clinton nominated Aetna attorney Zoë Baird for attorney general, her nomination was imperiled by the news that Baird and her husband had hired an undocumented Peruvian couple, the Corderos, to care for their children. Many argued that such lawbreaking, albeit "minor," did not disqualify Baird for the position, but she ultimately withdrew her name from consideration. What was interesting about the colloquy around the Baird nomination was the tendency of women to identify with Baird, not her household worker. More than 95 percent of all private household workers are women; nearly 40 percent are African American or Latina. White female pundits seemed inclined to shrug off Baird's transgression as the inevitable consequence of unavailable child care, ignoring the wage implications of paying someone $250 per week who sometimes worked more than twelve hours per day. If women's voices were amplified because of Hill, these voices were rarely used for women on the bottom. The core of opposition to Baird rested with African American women who, like University of Texas professor Barbara Jordan, made the case that lawbreaking is unacceptable, or, like Georgetown University law professor Patricia Williams, who indicated that the exploitation of an immigrant woman was of special concern to African American women who also experience this kind of exploitation.

163

The year after the Year of the Woman, then, the question was the same one Sojourner Truth raised when she asked, "Ain't I a woman?" Was Mrs. Cordero any less woman than Zoë Baird? Why did public sentiment not rally around her? Why was the case not named after her? Why was her name not invoked as an example of what happens when women are evaluated by institutional structures insensitive to us? Cordero, after all, was forced underground by the Baird attention. Her husband was swiftly deported. Baird, when last I heard, still held her corporate post at Aetna.

There was a disappointing silence from women's organizations about the plight of an immigrant woman whose workplace status was turned into a "Zoë Baird problem." There also has been a myopic cheering about gains some women have attained since Clinton became president in January 1993. To be sure, Clinton is a major improvement over twelve years of Reagan-Bush. In just six months, he lifted restrictions on abortion, the personal importation of RU486, and fetal tissue research, and he also signed the Family and Medical Leave Act. While these advances helped some women, they did little to improve the status of others. Was 1992 the Year of the Woman or the year of the *privileged* woman? For example, lifting the import ban on RU486 helps women who can personally bring the "morning-after" pill to the United States. Most working women aren't lining up to take a Concorde flight to get morning-after pills for their personal use. The company that manufactures RU486 doesn't want to distribute it here. Lifting the ban is a symbolic step that helps women at the top. Where is the relief for women at the bottom?

The issue of exclusion is far more pointed in Clinton's support of the Family and Medical Leave Act. To be sure, the President signed the bill that came to him from Congress, a bill that had been lingering for a full eight years since it was first proposed in April 1985. At the same time, given his stated principles of "putting people first," might not the president have indicated his support for a stronger bill than the one twice vetoed by Bush? The bill that Bush vetoed was a shadow of the legislation that was proposed in April 1985. At that time, the Parental and Disability Leave Act provided almost all employees eighteen weeks of unpaid leave for the birth, adoption, or illness of a child, along with twenty-six weeks for individual illness. The bill required employers to maintain health benefits during the leave, and to set up a study group to look into ways of providing salary replacement for those taking leave. But after two years of hearings, the bill was not voted on.

164

Since 1985, the Parental and Disability Leave bill has been modified to exclude those working for small businesses. In 1987, that was defined as those working for firms with fewer than fifteen employees; by 1992, that had been raised to those working for firms with fewer than fifty employees. The length of unpaid leave was reduced to twelve weeks in the 1992 version of the bill. New employees and part-time workers are also excluded from coverage. Because of the exclusions, only half of the labor force is covered by the Family and Medical Leave Act that passed in 1993, a major flaw of the legislation. Given changes in the structure of the labor market, unless this bill is substantially changed, most workers will not enjoy the benefits of family and medical leave. Further, since the leave currently mandated is *unpaid*, only those who can afford time off from work are better off than they were before the passage of the bill.

Clinton advocates cite the President's "good intentions" in noting that he has done better than Bush in promoting the issue of family and medical leave. But the president's treatment of attorney Lani Guinier indicates that good intentions are simply not good enough. A University of Pennsylvania professor, Guinier, formerly a Justice Department staffer and later an attorney at the NAACP Legal Defense and Education Fund, has devoted her career to dealing with racial justice and civil rights cases. Yet her nomination to be assistant attorney general for Civil Rights was torpedoed by a hostile right-wing press that described her in chilling personal terms ("Loony Lani" and "strange hair, strange name, strange views") and labeled her a "quota queen." Yet progressives suggest that her proposals for proportional voting expand the voting rights of both minorities and other interest groups in the electorate.

The Right was able to character-assassinate Guinier because her supporters, and especially the White House, were silent. I kept hearing people describe Guinier as a radical, but a balanced reading of her works suggests she is, at most, a thoughtful moderate who flails away at solutions to America's racial problems. She spoke with optimism about the election of Douglas Wilder as governor of Virginia, but the *Wall Street Journal*'s Paul Gigot chose to take her comments out of context and suggested that she had called Wilder an "inauthentic" Black. Instead, Guinier has said that non-African Americans can effectively represent African Americans "as long as the source of their authority, legitimacy, and power base is the Black community." Many have quoted her *University of Michigan Law Review* article out of context, attempting to portray her as some rabid rebel on a quota trip. But if I read this situation right, the "q" word is not *quota* but *quisling*, and the notion that the president's good intentions weren't good enough.

In the wake of Baird's botched nomination, Clinton nominated yet *165* another person, then distanced himself as the press hung her out to dry. The president has mealy-mouthed his way into appointing the "moderate" David Gergen as his communications director, but his treatment of Guinier suggests that this centrist can make room for a Reagan-advising Republican but not for an African American woman who is more than qualified to head the Civil Rights Division of the Justice Department.

Utah senator Orrin Hatch speaks of "minority rule," yet his party's filibuster of the president's budget is the best example of minority rule that I've seen in a while. Others speak of "quotas" and "race hate," but these are hard words to swallow from a Senate that confirmed Wib Hubbel to the Justice Department, the same Hubbel who only resigned from his Arkansas all-white-male club under pressure. Which quota is more objectionable, the quota that creates an all-white-male club or the thinking that explores paths to equal participation? Methinks the Senate doth protest too much and that Guinier's appointment would have hit them too close to home.

I am especially disturbed that some of the Senate Four, the women whose election has been attributed to the Anita Hill effect, were opposed to the Guinier appointment. The very women who stepped on the back of a Black woman to step into the Senate now seem willing to stab a Black woman in the back on the basis of a misreading of her writing.

According to some reports, California senator Dianne Feinstein directly petitioned the president to withdraw the Guinier nomination. The reluctance to support Guinier is at the root of the distance between Black and white women, a distance hardly bridged by the support of traditional women's groups for Anita Hill. This was a reluctance, though, that clearly transcended race. Illinois senator Carol Moseley-Braun was silent on the Guinier appointment, and the Congressional Black Caucus and the NAACP, though forceful in support of Guinier, were late in registering their outrage about her treatment by the White House.

In the aftermath of the Year of the Woman, just who qualifies for "woman" status? From the Baird case, we have learned she must not be poor or an immigrant. From the passage of the Family and Medical Leave Act, we have learned that she must work for a large company, one with more than fifty employees. From the treatment of Guinier, we have learned that she must not be vocal or thoughtful. So who benefits from the Anita Hill effect? The primary beneficiaries seem to be the "Anita Hill Four," those senators who were able to turn collective outrage into personal gain, whose contributions to women's equality have not yet trickled down to the rest of us.

Research on women's voices suggests that women are closer to Brenda Patterson than to Anita Hill in their concerns about workplace issues. According to the Ms. Foundation and the Center for Policy Alternatives, most women rank equal pay, child care, health care, and flex-time as far more critical concerns than sexual harassment and abortion.[3] In other words, the issues that generate headlines don't necessarily generate women's interest. This isn't to say that such issues aren't serious and important, but it is to note that most women are focused on *survival* issues. In the years after the Year of the Woman, it would seem that women leaders would ignore the sex, lies, and stereotypes and focus instead on those economic issues that affect women. In particular, passage of a minimum wage increase would have a particularly strong impact on working women since they represent two-thirds of those who work for poverty wages. Further, a focus on welfare reform, not welfare scapegoating (a two-year up-or-out training program didn't work for surplus engineers, so why should it work for poor women?), would be a focus on women and children. While many women agree that these are important issues, their agreement transcends the Anita Hill effect. Indeed, in many ways, the image that Hill presented during her testimony about Thomas was the antithesis of the image of a minimum-wage-earning, welfare-receiving woman. And thus, while some women declared themselves racially liberated because they supported Hill's allegations against Thomas, they hadn't moved a notch down their class mountain to examine the status of African American women occupationally less well situated than Hill.

The Anita Hill effect brought us senators, sensitivity, and symbolism. But the effect, like icing on a cake, seems stuck at the top of the occupational spectrum. It will take more than humming the mantra "Anita Hill" or invoking her testimony to transform the effect into gains for women at the bottom. And it will take more than solidarity around Hill to convince me that white Feminists "get it" from a Black woman's perspective.

Notes

1. The advertisement stated: "Two percent may be good enough for nonfat milk but not for the United States Senate."
2. The term *sexualized hazing* refers to the fact that Patterson's treatment was both race- and gender-based. She was spoken to in epithets that referred to both her race and her gender.
3. "Women's Voices: A Joint Project." *Ms.* Foundation and Center for Policy Alternatives. New York and Washington, D.C., September 1992.

For Pleasure, Profit, and Power: The Sexual Exploitation of Black Women

DARLENE CLARK HINE

Shortly after the Anita Hill-Clarence Thomas hearings, Harvard University sociologist Orlando Patterson wrote an op-ed piece for the *New York Times* in which he argued that the future Black U.S. Supreme Court justice was justified in denying all charges of sexual harassment made by University of Oklahoma Law School professor Anita Hill. Patterson's embrace of the politics of denial rested on his belief that even if the allegations of sexual harassment were true, the punishment—that is, the loss of the appointment—would far outweigh the severity of the transgression. He wrote:

> If my interpretation is correct, Judge Thomas was justified
> in denying making the remarks, even if he had in fact made
> them, not only because the deliberate displacement of his
> remarks made them something else but on the utilitarian
> moral grounds that any admission would have immediately
> .incurred a self-destructive and grossly unfair punishment.
> (Patterson 1991)

The fact that a liar, not to mention a harasser of a woman, would occupy a position on the nation's highest tribunal seemed inconsequential to Patterson.

Perhaps more than any of the other events of that emotionally draining weekend, Patterson's espousal of moral pragmatism and rationalized

deceit encapsulated vividly the centuries-long sexual harassment and exploitation experiences of Black women. Since the hearings, I have given
Patterson's comments considerable thought. The sexual exploitation of
Black women in the United States has a long and inglorious history that
persists to this day. Yet the true dimension and nature of this exploitation
remains shrouded in denial, metaphor, ignorance, and silence. Perhaps
as much effort has been expended to deny, rationalize, and ignore the
sexual exploitation of African American women by some European and
African American men, and by European and American women, as went
into the commission of these egregious offenses. Earlier, I had advanced
the idea that Black women's reluctance to discuss publicly their experiences with sexual abuse and exploitation grew out of the culture of dissemblance they had developed as a resistance or survival strategy (Hine
1988). A companion to this notion, however, is the politics of denial
practiced by European American men and women and African American
men. Dissemblance and denial combined in the larger society's mind to
obscure, nullify, or render unimaginable the possibility that a Black woman
could be raped, sexually exploited, and harassed.

Although the vast majority of Black women, for understandable reasons, remain silent, Hill belongs to a rather select group who have spoken
publicly about harassment and exploitation. These women braved a dis-
believing and hostile public. During enslavement, a few Black women
told of their sexual experiences in slave narratives, novels, poems, and
deeds.

The antislavery lecturer and poet Frances E. W. Harper wrote, in
a poem entitled "A Double Standard" (1896), the following stanza that
captures the pain and the price exacted for revealing that a Black woman
has been sexually active:

> Crime has no sex and yet to-day
> I wear the brand of shame;
> Whilst he amid the gay and proud
> Still bears an honored name. (Harper 1988, p. 177)

A quick perusal of library shelves yields other examples, such as Harriet
Jacobs' *Incidents in the Life of a Slave Girl* (1861, Jacobs 1988) and the
historical account of the murder trial of *Celia, a Slave* (McLaurin 1991).
To read both volumes is to glimpse the terror and humiliation slave women
endured and the lengths to which they went to protect their sexual selves.
In recent memory, there is the 1974 case of Joan Little, who killed Clarence Alligood, her jailer, as he tried to rape her. Like Celia, more than
a hundred years earlier, Little would also go on trial to face murder charges
and the death penalty for attempting to defend herself against a white
rapist. The intersections of race, gender, and class are deeply embedded
in all their stories.

Jacobs, Celia, Little, and Anita Hill all told stories of sexual harassment, met different fates because of their disparate responses, and encountered the politics of disbelief and denial. Few Americans wanted to hear the voices or confront the reality of the depth of violence and exploitation these shadow women endured. Few powerful European American males wanted to take them or their stories seriously. Almost no scholar wanted to go to the trouble of weaving into the basic fabric of America's largely mythological view of itself as the land of democratic egalitarianism and virtue the blood-soaked threads of Black women's exploitation. Why this disinclination to see or hear their stories? To do so, to take African American women seriously, would necessitate reckoning with the complicity of some white men, some white women, and some Black men in the enduring project to dehumanize and degrade the most nonprivileged and vulnerable segment of the American population. Ironically, however, to take black women seriously is also to recognize their culture of resistance and survival and the strength of their will to be free and sexually autonomous. In the case of Celia and Little, they were capable of killing.

Before proceeding, perhaps it would be useful to revisit briefly the experiences of these four Black women—Harriet Jacobs, Celia the slave, Joan Little, and Anita Hill. Perhaps retelling these resistance stories, and placing them in a larger sociohistorical and theoretical context, may motivate us to help African American women bring to an end this long reign of exploitation and terror. At least by engaging their stories, we empower and encourage present and future generations of Black women to continue the struggle for dignity and freedom from sexual exploitation in spite of the society's penchant for denial and disbelief.

Harriet Jacobs

In 1861, Harriet Jacobs, under the pseudonym Linda Brent, published *Incidents in the Life of a Slave Girl*, a narrative that even today generates controversy. One of the unique features of this narrative is Jacobs's personal testimony of the sexual harassment and exploitation she experienced as a slave. In the narrative of Jacobs's life, she identifies a Dr. Flint as her sole owner. Dr. Flint persistently harasses Jacobs and makes numerous attempt to lure her to his bed. Because she would not submit willingly and he refused to take her against her will, the sexual desires of Dr. Flint were never fulfilled. Most compelling is Jacobs's description of her creative means of resistance and ultimate escape from Dr. Flint's relentless entreaties and bribes for sex. Dr. Flint even threatened her at one point, saying that it was within his rights to kill her for resisting his advancements. For seven years, Jacobs secluded herself in a garret, assisted only by her grandmother. Before the hiding, Jacobs resisted Dr. Flint by voluntarily submitting to sex with another white man. "It seems less degrading to give one's self, than to submit to compulsion," she explained. "I knew nothing would enrage Dr. Flint so much as to know that I favored another; and it was something to triumph over my tyrant even in that small way" (Jacobs 1988, p. 85). But Jacobs's entreaties for understanding resonate throughout Black women's history. She confided,

> You never know what it is to be a slave; to be entirely
> unprotected by law or custom; to have the laws reduce you
> to the condition of a chattel, entirely subject to the will of
> another. You never exhausted your ingenuity in avoiding
> the snares, and eluding the power of a hated tyrant; you
> never shuddered at the sound of his footsteps, and trembled
> within hearing of his voice. (p. 86)

Eventually, Jacobs made a successful escape to freedom via the Underground Railroad.

Celia

In 1850, sixty-year-old Robert Newsom, a prosperous Callaway County, Missouri, farmer, purchased fourteen-year-old Celia, and over a period of years he repeatedly raped her and forced her to bear at least one child. Historian Melton A. McLaurin described the process quite succinctly: "a healthy sixty years of age, Newsom needed . . . a sexual partner. Newsom seems to have deliberately chosen to purchase a young slave girl to fulfill this role, a choice made the more convenient by the ability to present the girl as a domestic servant purchased for the benefit of his daughters" (McLaurin 1991, p. 81).

171

On June 23, 1855, a pregnant Celia repulsed Newsom as he attempted to force her yet again to have sexual intercourse. On that night of her resistance, Celia struck him twice with a stick. She then burned his dead body in the fireplace. After she was charged with first-degree murder, Celia's attorney asked the critical question: Did this Black slave woman have the right to defend her sexual self? Her counsel wanted specifically to receive a verdict that would establish that the master's economic prerogatives did not include the right of sexual molestation. Implicitly, he wanted an answer to the question: Was Celia a woman entitled to the right of self-defense assured all free white women under Missouri statute? He requested that the judge give the following instruction to the jury:

> If the jury believe from the evidence that Celia did kill
> Newsom, but that the killing was necessary to protect

herself against a forced sexual intercourse with her on part
of said Newsom, and there was imminent danger with such
forced sexual connection being accomplished by Newsom,
they will not find her guilty of murder in the first degree.
(Higginbotham 1989, p. 682)

The judge's negative answer came with dispatch, as he rejected the
lawyer's request and instead offered the prosecutor's instructions to the
jury:

If Newsom was in the habit of having intercourse with the
defendant who was his slave and went to her cabin on the
night he was killed to have intercourse with her or for any
other purpose and while he was standing in the floor talking
to her she struck him with a stick which was a dangerous
weapon and knocked him down, and struck him again after
he fell, and killed him by either blow, it is murder in the
first degree. (Higginbotham 1989, p. 682)

Armed with these instructions, the jury deliberated only briefly before finding Celia guilty of murder in the first degree, to be punished by
death. And just as U.S. Supreme Court judge Roger B. Taney would rule
in the famous March 6, 1857, *Dred Scott* case that a Black man had no
rights a white man was bound to respect, the Missouri courts declared
that in the eyes of the law, Black women, in particular slave women,
were not women. The court delayed execution until the birth of Celia's
child so as not to deprive the Newsom estate of the profit of Celia's rape.
The baby, however, was stillborn. This case lends special poignancy to
Sojourner Truth's often-repeated query, "Ain't I a woman?"

Newsom's daughters refused to comment on their father's abuse of
Celia or to respond in any way to her entreaties for help. Their silence
was in keeping with the politics of denial. For these plantation mistresses
to have aided Celia would have meant that they and other similarly situated white women had to acknowledge openly that their fathers, brothers, and husbands were rapists. Similarly, the Black slave with whom
Celia was involved ran away to avoid charges of collaboration in her rape
and any personal implication in the killing. As Orlando Patterson might
suggest, the punishment would have exceeded the friend's tangential involvement in the whole affair.

Joan Little

On August 27, 1974, the Beaufort County district attorney claimed
that twenty-year-old Joan Little, incarcerated on robbery charges on August 27, 1974, lured sixty-two-year old jailer Clarence Alligood into her

cell, stabbed him to death with an ice pick, and fled. One of the European American lawyers who helped to prepare the initial defense for Little saw in the case the opportunity to raise a number of legal and social issues, including "the right of a woman to defend herself against a sexual attack; prison conditions for women; the discriminatory use of the death penalty against poor people and Blacks; and the right of a poor person to an adequate defense" (Dees and Fiffer 1991, p. 164). Eventually, Little was freed, but not because anyone believed her account of Alligood's sexual attack against her. Ultimately, asserted one juror, the state failed to prove its case. Undoubtedly, had Little not attracted the assistance of the Southern Poverty Law Center and national media attention, the outcome might have been different. This acquittal, unfortunately, did not end her engagement with the criminal justice system. She was arrested in 1989 at the New Jersey entrance of the Holland Tunnel on weapons and stolen property charges (Dees and Fiffer 1991).

Anita Hill

I used to wonder how American history would read if it was told from the perspective of sexually exploited Black women. The Hill-Thomas sexual harassment hearings and the aftermath answered my question. As Hill spoke in her calm, controlled voice about the harassment and indignities she had suffered, she became a powerful metaphor for the telling of the Black woman's tale in America. As the Democrats on the Senate Judiciary Committee and a startled nation sat transfixed, Republicans Hatch, Simpson, and Specter let loose. The last voice that elite European American male power brokers want to hear in this society is the voice of the African American woman. Although their questions, innuendos, and demeanor sought to shatter her credibility, Hill persevered. In this last decade of the twentieth century, she opened the door through which all African American women must enter, or forever remain closeted in silence and secrecy, in denial and disbelief.

The magnitude of her courage to tell her story is revealed most effectively when viewed against the historical reluctance of Black women to draw attention to their inner lives. Because of the interplay of racial animosity, class tensions, gender role differentiation, and regional economic variations, Black women as a rule developed a politics of silence and adhered to a cult of secrecy. They cultivated a culture of dissemblance to protect the sanctity of the inner aspects of their lives. The dynamics of dissemblance involved creating the appearance of disclosure, or openness about themselves and their feelings, while actually remaining enigmatic. Only with secrecy, thus achieving a self-imposed invisibility, could ordinary Black women acquire the psychic space and gather the resources needed to hold their own in their often one-sided and mismatched struggle to resist oppression.

173

Pleasure, Profit, and Power

The sexual exploitation of a Black woman occurs on many different levels, as the above examples testify. On the physical level, she can be forced to give sex—that is, raped. This appropriation of her sex for pleasure and for profit reinforces male domination.

The profit gained from the sexual exploitation of Black women falls into two separate categories: economic and psychological. During slavery, Black women were sold as concubines or mistresses, and their offspring enriched the pockets of owners and lovers, for the child inherited the status of the mother. Obviously, there was economic incentive to possess a Black woman. But there was also the psychological or psychic profit gained from degrading and dehumanizing in one person the two characteristics most threatening to European American males: Blackness and femaleness. Domination of European American women meant control only of a subordinate sex, just as the control of African American men translated only into domination over race. With the African American woman securely under control, European American men imagined themselves true masters of the universe and all its inhabitants. Historian Joel Williamson offers a succinct summation: "By its very nature slavery created commanding imperious persons. Slaveholding planters saw themselves as the lords of their little earths, and of all the bodies dwelt thereon" (1980, p. 54). He reminds us that "however much white society might denounce as wretches those who used their power to extract sex from their slave subjects, it positively defended their right to do so, even under circumstances that were blatantly outrageous" (p. 54).

The achievement of total domination and the extraction of maximum psychological profit dictated the reduction of black women to something totally undeserving of human consideration. Accordingly, as Winthrop Jordan illustrates, white men demonized and villainized her sexuality and her femininity (1968). This process gave rise to an array of negative stereotypes. Deborah Gray White (1985) and Patricia Morton (1991) elaborate at length on the Jezebel, Mammy, and Sapphire stereotypes and how such negative depictions of Black women operate as invidious mechanisms of control. The victim was transformed into culprit as the Black woman became the ultimate "other." One of the common themes in the idea of otherness is objectification. As the other becomes object, it is perceived as a thing to be managed and possessed. The object is seen as dangerous, wild, threatening, but ironically it also inspires curiosity and invites inquiry, giving rise to intense desire for knowledge, possession, and domination. The corollary to the notion of woman as personification of nature is the conviction that it is man's responsibility to penetrate nature's mysteries. The Black woman came to exemplify nature, untamed, unknown, unmastered. That Black women were dark in color lent credence to notions that they were indeed more like nature, or even more

174

natural sites for European American men's explorations and aggressions (Jordanova 1989).

Profit, both psychic and economic, from the dehumanization and degradation of Black women cut across gender lines. White women gained from the exploitation of Black women in a culturally inscribed way. The slave and free Black woman's sexuality stood in stark contrast to the "ultra-feminine" images of Southern white womanhood. It is daunting indeed to unravel the interlocking images of the slave woman and her dominating European American mistresses, but we do know that European American female sexual status rose in proportion to the diminution of African American women. White women's virtue was protected as long as lustful passions could be released upon powerless Black women. Even today, popular culture is replete with a range of dichotomized images of the good white woman and the evil Black woman; the feminine white woman and the masculinized Black woman; the chaste, demure, virginal white woman and the sluttish, whorish, depraved Black woman; the dutiful housewife and the immoral, unmarried welfare mother.

Unraveling African American men's relationship to the exploitation of African American women is problematic. Black men won advantage because of the negative stereotyping of Black women. In bell hooks's accounting of the consequence of the scapegoating of African American women through matriarchal mythology, for example, European American men forged psychic bonds with African American men "based on mutual sexism." To be sure, matriarchal mythology often helped to deflect Black men's attention away from the serious social and economic policies and employment shifts that have worsened and today seriously impair their ability to provide for themselves and their families. For a long time, charges of matriarchal domination led to the conclusion that Black women were responsible for the "pathological status of Black families" and the demasculinization of Black men. Such accusations successfully deflected concern about growing economic and political disparities between white and Black males in the society. At the very moment in time that Black males bonded with each other and with white men in defense of Clarence Thomas, unemployment of blacks in general reached an all-time high. To the extent that justifiable anger over deteriorating economic, political, and social conditions is diffused into intraracial disquiet and conflict between African American men and women, elite European American males profit.

The Hill-Thomas phenomenon hit me hard. Actually, I cannot remember when an event affected me more deeply and profoundly. Of all the things that got to me during that tense weekend in October 1991, the most disturbing was the way the Republican members of the Senate Judiciary Committee treated Hill. Perhaps too deep a familiarity with the history of the sexual exploitation of Black women over the past four centuries on American soil ill prepared me for one more public assault. That

175

they were disrespectful is putting it mildly. She came to tell her story, to share her experiences, and to shatter the silence, to use her own voice in a quest for a fair hearing. Hill was scorned, ridiculed, threatened, and denigrated. As she left the chambers, I saw through my own tears and anger the shattered remnants of another African American woman's dignity. We stand on the threshold of the twenty-first century, and still African American women must seek, plead, even die, for the freedom, justice, and equality of opportunity so glibly promised to white males in the Constitution of the United States, to Black males in the fourteenth and fifteenth amendments and, for all intents and purposes, to white women in the nineteenth amendment to the Constitution. I wrestled with the same question that echoes across the decades of her unique history: What will it take for the black woman to be free and considered 'fully human? Black women will be free only when we are all brought to oneness as human beings, when we all love and care for one another simply because we are human beings and it is our duty and right. Yet an enlightened future is only possible if we are finally able to comprehend and to confront the damage that historic sexual exploitation has done to black girls and women. Further, we must fully understand the importance of close friendship and family ties among African American women. Only within the realm of these critical relationships can they receive the psychosocial support that has helped them escape the paralysis of being the country's greatest and most total victim.

Still, it would be naive to expect that a group of women so victimized and exploited have managed to escape with their identities intact. Actually, low self-esteem and virulent self-hatred afflict a great many African American women and preclude any possibility of mutual support in countless times and places. Divisive impulses were and continue to be fanned by the existing hierarchy of status and color privilege prevalent within the Black community, and by the often disastrous competition for male attention. While America has a penchant for blaming the victim, the victims often blame themselves and others similarly situated. This explains in part why so many Black women, if media reports and poll data are accurate, denounced Hill and supported Thomas.

Even so, the most fundamental tensions exist not among Black women but between Black women and the rest of society—especially European American men and women and, to a lesser extent, African American men. All are involved in a multifaceted struggle for control of Black women's productive and reproductive capacities and sexuality. But there are additional factors. Since sexual exploitation constitutes such a central force in the historical and contemporary lives of most black women, especially working-class or welfare-poor black women, they were undoubtedly astonished at what Hill described as constituting her experience with sexual harassment. In other words, Thomas's alleged allusion to pubic hair on his Coke can, for example, seemed mild in comparison to the rape, beatings, and verbal and psychological abuse that figure so prominently in poor Black women's daily lives.

Given our culture and history and the success of the politics of denial, it is encouraging to note that Black women are disproportionately represented among those who have filed sexual harassment suits in recent years. Sexual harassment and exploitation, whether for pleasure, profit, or power, are a significant concern of all women, but for Black women it is a cancer with which they have lived too long.

References

Dees, Morris, and Steve Fiffer. *A Season for Justice: The Life and Times of Civil Rights Lawyer Morris Dees*. New York: Scribner's Sons, 1991.

Harper, Francis E. W. "The Double Standard." In Maryemma Graham, ed., *Complete Poems of Francis Harper*, pp. 176–78. Oxford: University of Mississippi Press, 1988.

Higginbotham, A. Leon. "Race, Sex, Education and Missouri Jurisprudence: *Shelley* v. *Kraemer* in a Historical Perspective." *Washington University Law Quarterly* 67 (1989): 673–708.

Hine, Darlene Clark. "Rape and Inner Lives of Black Women in the Middle West: Preliminary Thoughts on Culture of Dissemblance." *Signs* 14 (Summer 1988): 912–20.

Jacobs, Harriet. *Incidents in the Life of a Slave Girl*. New York: Oxford University Press, 1988.

Jordan, Winthrop D. *White over Black: American Attitudes Towards the Negro, 1550–1812*. Chapel Hill: University of North Carolina Press, 1968.

Jordanova, Ludmilla. *Sexual Visions: Images of Gender in Science and Medicine Between the Eighteenth and Twentieth Centuries*. Madison: University of Wisconsin Press, 1989.

McLaurin, Melton A. *Celia, a Slave*. Athens: University of Georgia Press, 1991.

Morton, Patricia. *Disfigured Images: The Historical Assault on Afro-American Women*. New York: Praeger, 1991.

Patterson, Orlando. "Race, Gender and Liberal Fallacies." *New York Times*, Oct. 20, 1991, sec. 4, p. 15.

State of Missouri v. *Celia*. Index to Court Cases in Callaway County 496, file no. 4, 496 at 131, 1855.

White, Deborah Gray. *Ain't I a Woman? Female Slaves in the Plantation South*. New York: Norton, 1985.

Williamson, Joel. *New People: Miscegenation and Mulattoes in the United States*. New York: Free Press, 1980.

Clarence Thomas As Lynching Victim: Reflections on Anita Hill's Role in the Thomas Confirmation Hearings

ANGELA Y. DAVIS

Of the many statements Clarence Thomas made during his confirmation hearings, the most extraordinary—and perhaps, from his vantage point, the shrewdest—was his contention that he was the victim of a "high-tech lynching." Considering his previous denial that race had played any role in the process that led to his nomination, it also may have been the least anticipated. Following the position established during the Reagan-Bush era of "merit" as the so-called nondiscriminatory alternative to affirmative action, Thomas had represented himself as the best Supreme Court nominee by virtue of his past record as a jurist. Like the poet in Langston Hughes's manifesto "The Negro Artist and the Racial Mountain" (1926), Thomas called for color-blindness in those who presumed to judge him. They should not consider him a "Black judge" but rather a racially unmodified judge. His African Americanness, so he claimed, had nothing to do with the presidential choice that had brought him as far as the confirmation hearings. Under fire by the Democrats, who understandably leaped at the opportunity to use Anita Hill's charges of sexual harassment in order to publicly discredit him, Thomas chose to invoke a "racial" memory as his main rhetorical defense.

I want to examine briefly Thomas's self-presentation as a lynching victim, focusing on his reconfiguring of the "myth of the Black rapist" and specifically on ways it may have influenced interpretations of Hill's testimony. I will then raise questions both about the obsolescence of certain historical notions of the African American community and about contemporary constructions of community that problematize and challenge racial boundaries.

While Thomas evoked the African American community's past encounters with lynch mobs as a metaphorical allusion, the sheer force of the historical and racial implications of the term *lynching* is such that it can hardly be contained within the boundaries of metaphor. For those who have some awareness of African American history, memories of frightening repetitions of racist-inspired murders cling to the term *lynching*. During the three decades following slavery, the lives of more than ten thousand African American men and women were claimed by white lynch mobs, whose "low-tech" methods included ceremonial hangings, carnivalesque burnings at stakes, and vicious beatings to death (Wells-Barnett 1969). The lynching of Emmett Till in Money, Mississippi, in 1955 remains a prominent signpost in my own autobiographical memory.[1] As late as 1981, Michael Donald was lynched in Mobile, Alabama. His mother received the first major settlement in a lynching case—the assets of the Ku Klux Klan. The murder of Michael Griffith in Howard Beach, New York, in 1986 was referred to—even by then-Mayor Koch—as a "lynching."

When Thomas claimed to be the victim of lynching, he situated himself on a historical continuum that connects the racist murder of Michael Griffith in Howard Beach with the murders of newly emancipated slave women and men in the 1870s. Historically, most lynchings have involved groups of perpetrators, accomplices, and spectators who either directly witnessed the act or later sanctioned it. European American men were the perpetrators; European American women were often the accomplices—especially in cases where fraudulent rape accusations constituted the pretext for the lynching—and an entire population of white people were the spectators. In Thomas's case, the accused perpetrators were the European American men within the dominant political structure who are leaders in what is normally considered the more progressive of the two major political parties. The spectators were those who opposed Thomas for partisan reasons—though some were no doubt motivated by racism—as well as those of diverse cultural and ethnic backgrounds who opposed him for his politically conservative positions on issues such as affirmative action and women's right to reproductive choice. However, for the purpose of these reflections, I am primarily interested in the representation of Hill as an accomplice through a complex but easily accomplished reconfiguration of racial memory and gender stereotypes within that racial memory.

In representing himself as a lynching victim, Thomas not only placed himself in the company of those African American men whose lives were exterminated by lynch mobs but also placed Hill, by virtue of her gender, in the company of the European American women who collaborated in the lynchings of African American men, whether by active accusations of rape and sexual molestation or by acquiescence in such charges. How could Hill be considered an accomplice in a "high-tech" lynching? The charges of sexual harassment she raised against Thomas were formalistically equated with the charges of sexual assault some Southern white women had raised directly or by proxy—or had been coerced into raising—against African American men in the past. In constructing Hill as the female villain, the traditional racial lines that allowed for gender specificity only within the white community—"all the women are white, all the Blacks are men" (Hull, Scott, and Smith 1981)—were redrawn. Yet, in the redrawing of these lines, Thomas's conception redefined the Black community in masculinist terms that locate women such as Hill—women who refuse to prioritize the Black man to their own detriment—outside the African American community's boundaries and in the company of traditionally racist villains.

This conception of the African American community banishes African American women who challenge African American male supremacy by defining them as collaborators in racist attacks on African American men. Thus, as Hill's courageous stand against sexual harassment publicly dramatized our emergence as African American women from a gender-blind construction of community, she was—and this is the great fear feminism summons up in many African American women—defined as a traitor, as the enemy. This conception is nurtured by and revives historical stereotypes about African American women's presumed tendency toward emasculating behavior, vis-à-vis African American men. It thus attempts to confirm the old saying that "there are only two free people in the South: the white man and the African American woman." It also feeds the mystification spawned by contemporary discourse about African American men as an "endangered species." But these ideological notions are rapidly becoming historically obsolete. Even as they are revived, it becomes apparent that when Hill's testimony disrupted the conventional process through which Supreme Court justices are confirmed, African Americans were stricken with multiple and conflictual spasms that would forever alter the way we construct ourselves as a community.

As an African American feminist who passionately supports Hill's stand, I do not believe that feminist causes are served by ignoring the complex political and sociohistorical context within which Hill spoke out on behalf of all women. There were no simple deracialized gender issues. In telling a story of the sexual assertion of male power by an African American man, whose ability to act with impunity was greatly enhanced by the fact that his female target was also African American, that is, assumed to be sexually available to white and African American men alike, Hill ran the risk of excommunication. Chicana women recognize this logic of excommunication as similar to that which turned La Malinche into a mythical female traitor to the cause of la Raza. "As Chicanas embrace feminism," Norma Alarcon writes, "they are charged with betrayal a la Malinche" (1981).[2]

Hill's courageous stand on her own behalf, which many of us interpreted as a voice for the unrecognized victims of sexual harassment in the African American community, implicitly provided a voice for Latina, Asian, Native American, and Pacific Island women, whose multiple vulnerability to sexual harassment also has been historically cloaked by silence. In the process, Hill emerged as the most heeded oppositional voice, articulating white women's resistance to sexual harassment as well. The Tailhook revelations, leading to the firing of high-level officers in the Navy, is, in a very real sense, the revenge of Anita Hill.

Notes

1. Emmett Till was a 14-year-old young black man from Chicago visiting relatives in Mississippi when he allegedly made sexually suggestive remarks to a white woman shopper in a Money, Mississippi, general store. According to details given by Stephen Whitfield in his *A Death in the Delta*, Emmett Till was taken from the home of his uncle, Moses Wright, on August 28, 1955. He was severely beaten, shot, thrown into the Tallahatchie River. His murderers were arrested, tried, and convicted.
2. Alarcon defines "La Malinche" as a "subversive feminine symbol" in Mexican/Chicano tradition.

181

References

Alarcon, Norma. "Chicana's Feminist Literature: A Revision Through Maltinsin/or Maltinzin: Putting Flesh Back on the Object." In Cherrie Moraga and Gloria Andaluza, eds., *This Bridge My Back: Writings by Radical Women of Color*. Watertown, Mass.: Persephone, 1981, pp. 182–96.
Hughes, Langston. "The Negro Artist and the Racial Mountain." *The Nation*, June 23, 1926.
Hull, Gloria T., Patricia B. Scott, and Barbara Smith, eds., *All the Women Are White, All the Blacks Are Men, but Some of Us Are Brave*. New York: Feminist Press, 1981.
Wells-Barnett, Ida B. *On Lynching*. New York: Arno, 1969.

Of Metaphors and Meaning: Language, Ways of Knowing, Memory Holes, and a Politic Recall

LINDA SUSAN BEARD

All my life I had been looking for something, and everywhere I turned someone tried to tell me what it was. I accepted their answers too, though they were often in contradiction and even self-congratulatory. I was naive. I was looking for myself and asking everyone except myself questions which I, and only I, could answer. It took me a long time and much painful boomeranging of my expectations to achieve a realization everyone else appears to have been born with: That I am nobody but myself. But first I had to discover that I am an invisible man!

—Ralph Ellison (1947)

Why didn't someone write a piece about the mythic images of black women as mammies, jezebels, tragic mulattoes, hottentot venuses? The list of insulting degrading stereotypes goes on. . . . To my mind, as unfortunate and sad as they were, the events occurring the week of October 10th were a teachable moment. Why not take an opportunity to let the present serve as a guide towards interrogating the past?

—Vicki Crawford (1992)

As contentious as that October 1991, encounter between Professor Anita Hill and Judge Clarence Thomas became, in terms of the primary combatants themselves and among those secondary commentators who squared off against one another in print and broadcast media, there seemed to be one general area of agreement among several intellectual communities: that rules and unwritten understandings of all kinds had been broken in the Hill-Thomas affair, with disastrous results. The Senate itself vociferously demanded that a special counsel be charged with an investigation into the source of the news leak that had propelled Hill out of her self-chosen privacy. In the pages of the *ABA Journal*, eminent attorneys such as F. Lee Bailey castigated the Senate

Judiciary Committee for a process that revealed no "methodical, disciplined, cohesive attempt to pursue" the "truth" of the claims made by Hill or Thomas (Bailey 1992, p. 47). For Bailey and others, the hearings themselves indicated nothing less than "a [self-serving] failure of the machinery of confirmation" (p. 49).

Attorney Stuart Lefstein concluded his own commentary on the mishandling of the Thomas hearings with the recommendation of more energetic and vocal advocacy on the part of the legal profession vis-à-vis the Senate confirmation process itself:

> The bar must now vent . . . outrage by letting the Senate
> know in every imaginable way that the criminal abuse of
> one of its most important Constitutional functions
> [confirmation of Supreme Court appointments] will not be
> tolerated. It must insist that a special counsel again be
> employed—this time to conduct an investigation and
> hearing of the caliber envisioned by Bailey, to determine
> who lied under oath to the Senate and the nation. (Lefstein
> 1992, p. 115)

Such outrage did, in fact, surface in the pages of the Spring 1992 issue of the *Southern California Law Review*, a special issue devoted entirely to the legal and ethical significance of the hearings.

The legal profession did not constitute an isolated voice of public *183* and private self-censure, to be sure. The broadcast industry critiqued itself (and was roundly criticized) for the sensationalist commodification of the Hill-Thomas debate, the success of which *Advertising Age* could measure as scoring an impressive twelve points on the advertising index in its weekly "Cover Story" section for November 4, 1991 (p. 35). Gerry L. Spence castigated the televised packaging of the testimony as a response to, and an encouragement of, the public desire for sexually tintillating material (1992), while in the pages of the *New Republic*, Bob Cohn labeled the press coverage of the Hill-Thomas encounter a "dirt trail" (1992, p. 16). David Thomson, in an analysis of the hearings for *Film Comment*, drew provocative analogies between the visually constructed events in Washington and the structure of such motion picture successes as "Advise and Consent" and "Anatomy of a Murder" (1992). In the *Columbia Journalism Review*, William Boot offered a critical overview of the Hill-Thomas coverage as a case for indicting an irresponsible press community (1992). With greater indirection but equal seriousness, *Washington Journalism Review* editor Bill Monroe juxtaposed the Hill-Thomas press coverage of three major American papers—the *New York Times*, the *Los Angeles Times*, and the *Washington Post*—to raise prickly questions about a priori editorial positions and their effect on theoretically "objective" news reporting (1991).

Such professional scrutiny emerged, in large part, from a sense of dissatisfaction with processes that seemed to produce no clear, fixed result. Decisions based on faith in the credibility of either witness or in the well-intentioned structures of institutions and their procedural health seemed to many much less satisfying than the clarity of professionally cross-examined evidence or rigorously objective (and therefore uncontestable) reportage. When the dust cleared and commentators had the usually savvy hindsight of a year's distance from the heat of the battle, however, many still mourned what seemed to them the unfortunate inconclusiveness of the Hill-Thomas encounter. Gloria Borger, Ted Guest, and Jeannye Thorton, writing the several Hill-Thomas retrospective pieces of *U.S. News and World Report*, used the language of mystery to talk about the continuing "conundrum" (1992, p. 28). "One year after the showdown, a host of educated guesses substitutes for real knowledge about what happened between Clarence Thomas and Anita Hill" (p. 37), conclude the reporters, who characterized the hearings themselves as "a study in chaos and unbridled partisanship that failed to resolve the biggest questions" (p. 29).

Nowhere amidst such funereal nostalgia for an alleged certitude has there been a recognition that the Hill-Thomas confrontation was an epistemological crisis as well as an opportunity, a "teachable moment" for examining publicly what the nation thinks it knows, and the relation between that knowledge and the institutional language we speak. The old language ("mammies, jezebels, hottentot venuses," for example) represents received and not-yet-successfully-enough challenged assumptions and constructions about race, gender, class, or ideology; it could not begin to define, confine, or otherwise easily circumscribe Anita Hill, that ancient, ever-new, "new Negro." The attempt to come to terms with Hill in language battened on "the marrow of [an enslavement] tradition" resulted in a painful but pathetic exercise in contradiction. With her own brand of bitter humor, tempered in that crucible where gender and race always intersect, law professor Patricia J. Williams observed:

> Now as everyone knows, it is settled law in our land that witches are those who fly upside down. Thus it is that Anita Hill is dispositively a witch. Everything she touched inverted itself. She was relentlessly ambitious yet "clinically" reserved, consciously lying while fantasizing truth. Lie detectors broke down and the ashes of "impossible truth" spewed forth from her mouth. She was controlled yet irrational, naive yet knowing, prim yet vengeful—a cool, hotheaded, rational hysteric. (1992, p. 36)

The complexity of Hill's femaleness and her blackness proved to be—to use Allen Bloom's description of African Americans in the university, though with other ends than he intended—"indigestible" (Bloom 1987, p. 91). Reflecting on the hearings in her "Ain't Gonna Let Nobody Turn Me Around," Barbara Smith observed: "I can think of no other situation that has commanded the nation's undivided attention that so clearly illustrated the inextricable links between racism and sexism" (1992, p. 37). Nor did the Oklahoma law professor or the other Black witnesses fit racial stereotypes about a poor, politically radicalized monolith. In fact, Nina Burleigh's list of "winners and losers in the confirmation process" specifically included "black conservatives" who are "emerging as a new political force" (1992, p. 50).

The facile assignment of Hill to the gender corner and Thomas to the race section of the arena in their public boxing match proved to be specious, intellectually dishonest, and bankrupt. What many saw as the zero-sum result of the Hill-Thomas contest of wills was, in fact, a dramatic confirmation that the polar categories used to discuss the complexity of Hill's experiences as Black (as opposed to white) and as woman (as opposed to man) did not themselves compute. In underscoring the inadequacy of absolutist language and polar categories (of truth and fabrication, good and evil, maleness and femaleness, etc.) to address the nuanced complexity of Hill's multiple identities, the drama of this teachable moment called for a new calculus and a new vocabulary. In unconscious ways, many commentators recognized the severe limitations of traditional language and elected, instead, to make frequent use of metaphors and figures from the vocabulary of imaginative literature. Notwithstanding the generous invitation in *Plato's Republic* to return dramatic poetry from threatened exile should it be able to "show good reason why it should exist in a well-governed society . . . [where] it would be a sin to betray what we believe to be the truth," (XXXVII), that vocabulary somehow seemed to create a space to house the known, the unknown, and the felt.

185

II

It was well nigh impossible for many to talk about the riveting experience of the public struggle between Hill and Thomas in a vacuum, disconnected from slavery and Reconstruction history, the long practice of signifying in African-American oral tradition, or the complex interweavings of race, class, and gender. Nowhere in recent experience had the multifaceted intricacy of contemporary African American life been made more apparent, as if the double-consciousness DuBois predicted for our epoch in the very early days of this century had increased exponentially the closer we approached the twenty-first century. The painful intensity of a chorus of voices raised in support or in denigration of either of the two combatants only further complicated a sometimes tragicomic script which began as a disagreement between competing personal memories and interpretations of the past and ended in a national referendum, of sorts, on the manipulation of power, the ability of language to make meaning, and the power of appearances.

For an event so grounded in "history"—the saga that traditionally chronicles the actual and interactive activities of human beings—the Hill-Thomas exchanges of October 1991 seemed to demand a mythological reading. *Mythos*, that classical Greek term signifying both the imaginatively invented and the historically remembered, was operative throughout the Hill-Thomas hearings. The portrayal of Hill as a hallucinatory liar, a vengeful woman scorned by Thomas's and John Doggett's sexual disinterest in her, and/or an arrogant ice goddess without human sinews or feelings was but a latter-day recapitulation of Greek and Roman myths about Medusa, Medea, and pantheons of frustrated goddesses. The credibility gap many experienced while watching the devout, soft-spoken law professor articulate her charges clearly and gracefully was a function of the fact that Hill did not confirm others' mythic preconceptions, their ancient and new scripts, as it were, about her. Neither Sheba nor Hagar, Hill became incomprehensible—as if she were practicing glossolalia, speaking in languages inspired by trance, which her auditors could not possibly be expected to interpret:

We speak in tongues, when the words are not part of the
script. When we fail to remain solidly locked into our
preassigned roles. You can be Eliza on the ice floe.
Mammy in the kitchen. Tina Turner on the dance floor.
You can call on Jesus, that's O.K. You can fall on your
knees as if in prayer, unzip his pants and open your mouth.
But whoever heard of a hot-blooded Negress being sexually
harassed, much less offended? She must be delusional,
a.k.a. crazy! Or else she's just one of those jealous
vindictive black women—mad because she doesn't have a
man; mad because the man she wanted didn't want her;
mad because he married a white woman. No? Well, then
she's an innocent dupe of sinister forces—those professional
feminists, evil liberals—a dumb bitch! (Gillespie, 1992, 41)

It was historian Paula Giddings who reminded her sisters of the need for Black women to "invent themselves" rather than adopt the unusable pregeneric roles all too available for entombing them in others' constructs. Opening her *When and Where I Enter* (1984) with an epigraph from Anna Julia Cooper, Hill's intellectual and experiential foremother, and one from Toni Morrison's *Sula* (1973), Giddings hoped to equip Black women for their "complex task in the eighties" by reminding them of the lessons to be drawn from the previous century (p. 149). Other African American women had gone before them in the campaign to subvert mythological explanations of our and others' actions. Some, such as Ida B. Wells, had made use of the tools of investigatory journalism in order to discover the "truth" about lynching and other postbellum terrorism. Critic Hazel V. Carby, in her *Reconstructing Womanhood* (1987), reintroduced us to one such pioneer, Pauline Hopkins, who worked as a subversive iconoclast countering one myth about idyllic slavery with another in her turn-of-the-century novel, *Contending Forces* (1899).

The myths, the myth makers, and their critics entered the Senate Judiciary Committee hearings the moment Hill began a narrative peppered with sexual allusion, and at the very instant when Thomas resurrected the specter of Reconstruction violence rationalized as a response to sexual threat. With such direct references to Black women's sexual jeopardy and to mythic rituals of mutilation and death, the Hill-Thomas affair became a complex of cycling narratives within narratives, set in motion by the power of allusion. That few commentators could see the electronic Judiciary Committee gang-bang that transpired against Hill is itself a testament to the relative power of the sexualized myths about African American women, as well as the gender game in which, as Eleanor Holmes Norton noted, "race trumped sex" (1992, p. 44).

To the story of a battle between genders was added both intraracial and interracial clashes, vying definitions of identity, striking components *187* of class competition, competing epistemological claims about alternative ways of knowing, interactions between Hill and Thomas supporters and detractors, and tens of millions of spectator-participants in a world audience, competing over understandings of "truth." Hill's very appearance at the confirmation hearings, following the violent leak of privatized communication, added even more intricate choreography to the dizzying dance set in motion by Thurgood Marshall's resignation and the Bush administration's paradoxical and cynical recommendation of a Black anti-affirmative action politico to fill affirmatively the vacated "Black" seat on the Supreme Court. What had begun as Hill's private discourse, a lone unaccompanied melody that had been dismissed and trivialized by the Senate Judiciary Committee, became, as a result of someone else's decision to leak the story, a public theatrical event, a three-penny opera, with intricate and newfangled components of sung and spoken narrative and a brilliantly executed cakewalk.

As viewer-participants, we were literally treated to a story "not to be passed on," squarely located in that theater of history allegedly preoccupied with truth. Yet nowhere in recent popular experience have Hayden White's theories about the interconnections between the narratives of "history" and "fiction" been so wonderfully demonstrated (1978). Both

Hill and Thomas "plotted" different accounts of the events of their collegial history. In so doing, they produced historical narratives at war with each other. In the midst of the attempt to verify or to challenge the historicity of those competing recollections, both weavers-of-tales and those, like us, who insisted on creating commentaries about those remembrances, continuously discussed the Hill-Thomas affair in literary language as allegory, parable, myth, moral fable, high drama. "Fact" found itself embedded in metaphor, allusion, and irony. For many, there seemed to be no "truer" way, Platonically speaking, to talk about the affair, than to employ the language of myth.

An intense examination of language and meaning, the Hill-Thomas confrontation bore entirely too much resemblance to Ralph Ellison's timely novel of almost half-a-century ago, *Invisible Man*. Structured as an elaborate contest in which the rules were continually being changed, both Ellison's novel and the Senate hearings alternated between the search for the transparent and the quest for the opaque amidst the extraordinary complexity of an African American "I am."

> On the way to work one late spring morning I counted fifty
> greetings from people I didn't know, becoming aware that
> there were two of me: the old self that slept a few hours a
> night and dreamed sometimes of my grandfather and
> Bledsoe and Brockway and Mary, the self that flew without
> wings and plunged from great heights; and the new public
> self that spoke for the Brotherhood and was becoming so
> much more important than the other that I seemed to run a
> foot race against myself. (p. 371)

188

Replete with an all-male, all-white panel of primary voyeurs at a masochistic, gender-focused battle royale, and a small cast of two, recalling the archetypes in Ellison's novel—variously resuscitating the Invisible Man, Bledsoe, Rinehart, Tod Clifton, Norton, Trueblood, and the Ras families (of Exhortation and Destruction)—the October debate made discourse and its manipulation pivotal. Thomas's continual and literal evocation of the wisdom and exemplary power of his own maternal grandfather, Myers Anderson, seemed to offer a concrete example of the legacy of the invisible man's "grandfather's curse" (Ellison 1947, p. 17). That ancestor had left his grandson concrete deathbed advice about succeeding in a Jim Crow world:

> Son, after I'm gone I want you to keep up the good fight. I
> never told you, but our life is a war and I have been a
> traitor all my born days, a spy in the enemy's country ever
> since I give up my gun back in the Reconstruction. Live
> with your head in the lion's mouth. I want you to overcome

'em with yeses, undermine 'em with grins, agree 'em to death and destruction, let 'em swoller you till they vomit or bust wide open. (p. 16)

Thomas's skillful evasion and deflection of questions regarding his judicial opinions on such politically explosive issues as *Roe* v. *Wade* appeared as a disingenuous and contemporary use of such a strategic survival-through-accommodationism. Moreover, the marked change in Thomas's verbal disposition toward the Judiciary Committee following Hill's testimony and the substitution of a provocative Ramboesque assault for his earlier nonconfrontational deflection did not simply undermine the seemingly compliant character of his earlier rhetorical style. What the marked change in discourse actually did was to underscore the fact that we were in a realm far removed from the literal, one in which prosaic "truth" would be almost irrelevant, even as it confirmed the necessity of having powerful patrons who could help shape the contours (and the interpretive reception) of one's discourse.

That the public encounter between Hill and Thomas was, in fact, extraliteral and symbolic is clear in the language very often used to describe the confrontation. For some, it was "a Rorschach test" (Jordan 1992, p. 1), a metaphoric "political soap opera" (Monroe 1992, p. 30), and the raw material from which enduring myths are made (Safire 1991). This was underscored, almost daily, by the numbers of people who alluded to that testimonial weekend as a profound ethical crisis, a historically memorable occasion, and a turning point in both public and personal life. In her musings on Hill-Thomas, Rebecca Walker, daughter of Alice Walker, noted: "I am sick of the way women are negated, devalued, ignored. I am livid, unrelenting in my anger at those who invade my space, who wish to take away my rights, who refuse to hear my voice. . . . I begin to realize that I owe it to myself . . . to push beyond my rage and articulate an agenda" (1992, p. 41).

For others, Hill was the contemporary avatar of the glorified spirits of Eleanor Roosevelt, Harriet Tubman, Sojourner Truth, and Rosa Parks. Quite a few commentators considered Hill to be, at best, a collaborator with a corporate Machiavellian system extorting the politic savvy of female "corporate conformists" (Boo 1991, p. 48). Many others viewed the law school professor, "the lone black woman . . . out in the hills and dales of Oklahoma" as a willing participant in a white feminist-engineered "ploy . . . to derail the nomination of Thomas" (Hare and Hare 1992, p. 39) For most commentators, whatever their individual responses to the supposed veracity, character, or speculative motivation of either contender in this late-twentieth-century battle of rhetorical symbols, the Hill-Thomas confrontation was a representation of something much more momentous than a disagreement about arguable recollections and interpretations of past events.

Karen Labacqz insisted that the matter of sexual harassment was a cover for a far more significant issue. She argued that the Hill-Thomas encounter was an embryonic allegory of ideas:

> It was not sexual harassment that was on trial in the Thomas hearings. Nor was it Clarence Thomas who was on trial. Much more than the truth of the relationship between Anita Hill and Clarence Thomas was on trial here. Much more than the question of sexual harassment was on trial here. Listening to the Senate panel, one would have thought that the only significant question was: did Clarence Thomas sexually harass Anita Hill some ten years ago? But that is not really the question. . . .

> It was Anita Hill and the credibility of women that was on trial. This was the real issue. Could Anita Hill be believed? And, through her, could other women be believed? This is the issue that, like a bad dream, lingers into one's waking life, bringing a sense of danger and dis-ease.

It is this difference between the literal and the figural, or symbolic, which may account, in part, for Hill's own retrospective account of her disappointment with the reception of her testimony. In an interview in the *Washington Post*, published immediately after her departure from Washington, Hill observed: "There were times when I did want to leave. . . . I did not think we were at a fact-finding hearing. There were several moments when I thought they were doing something other than trying to establish the facts" (1991, p. A24). Shirley Wiegand, Hill's traveling companion and law school colleague, addressed their expectations similarly: "We knew we were up against a lot, but we really had no idea how brutal it would get. . . . Anita and I viewed ourselves and our mission in overly simplistic terms, as two farm girls who were taking the truth to Washington. When we got there, it became apparent that the truth was not relevant, so Anita packed the truth up and took it home" (p. A24).

In one of her re-rememberings, as a member of a sexual harassment and policymaking panel at the National Forum for Women State Legislators, Hill referred to the existence of sexual harassment as "the nature of the beast" (1992, p. 32). She specifically targeted the problem of definition: "Men tend to have a narrower definition of what constitutes harassment than do women" (p. 33). Yet she coupled her epistemological inquiry with a mythic reference: increasing men's "*body* of knowledge."

Timothy M. Phelps and Helen Winternitz (1992) employ gaming metaphors to depict Thomas as the diligent student of power broker-mentors John C. Danforth, C. Boyden Gray, Dan Quayle, and George Bush.

190

Only a century earlier, Frederick Douglass in *Life and Times* (1892) had complained that white abolitionists, such as George Foster and John A. Collins, attempted to manipulate Douglass-as-text in their insistence that he provide only the prosaic "facts" about his life in slavery, leaving the issue of interpretation in their hands (chap. 3). He had wondered aloud when the emancipated slave would own title to his own discourse about the slavery experience. In Phelps and Winternitz's reading of the power politics of the Thomas confirmation hearing, a savvy Thomas agreed to speak (or not to speak) with a symbolic logic. Bush could play a master trump: an African-American justice with loyalty to the right could help dismantle civil rights legislation while nullifying the expected charge that the Court was engaged in racist revisionism. Thomas's reward for helping to give the preeminent judicial arm of government the appearance of diversity would be none other than an associate justice seat on the High Court.

The confrontation between the law professor and the jurist was, almost from the beginning, often described in literary language as allegorical, metonymic, synecdochic, or ironic. Interpreters of the significance of the dispute between the two Yale Law School alumni insisted simultaneously on the historicity of the event and on the centrality of metaphor, particularly in Thomas's memorable allusion to Reconstruction-era lynching. The tropes metonymy and synecdoche surfaced as players in their own right. These implicit metaphors allow the substitution of an attribute or characteristic for the name of an object, permit a reference to one thing by mentioning something with which it has become closely associated, or allow the use of a part to signify the whole. Such was the role of frequent references to "Thurgood Marshall's seat" (Smith 1992, p. 93), Coke cans, "Long Dong Silver," "high-tech lynching," Pin Point, Yale, *Roe* v. *Wade*, and Uncle Thomas (and Uncle Thomasina).

In *People* magazine, Virginia Lamp Thomas, Clarence Thomas's wife, described the ordeal of her spouse's "trial by fire" in the language of another literary genre, that of a morality play—an allegory about the quest for salvation and the passage through dangerous territories of temptation and evil. In the early morning hours following Hill's own graphic testimony, Virginia Thomas recalled her husband's request: "I need you to call your two friends from your Bible-study group, and their husbands, and get them here with me in the morning to pray." Her reflection continues: "Clarence knew the next round of hearings to begin that day was not the normal political battle. It was spiritual warfare. Good versus evil. We were fighting something we didn't understand, and we needed prayerful people in our lives. We needed God" (p. 111). The final "word" of the article is a stroke of genius, marrying written and visual text in a single instance. It is a snapshot by Harry Benson depicting a lovingly victorious couple, in the comfort of their living room, reading together from the Bible. The caption serves a triumphalistic purpose: "Clarence was raised a Catholic, Virginia a Methodist. They attend an Episcopal church together. 'We've gotten closer to God,' she says" (p. 116). Thus gloriously ends the moral contest against the implicitly demonic forces that clearly propelled Hill, whom Virginia Thomas describes as "one of the shadow people" (p. 116), into the combat.

Virginia Thomas successfully reconfigured an embarrassing *fabliau*—that medieval satiric tale in verse that celebrates the bawdy—into a moral fable. The lens to be used in "reading" the event ought to be tinted by an awareness of global and allegorical struggle. Those lovers of Greek mythology who spoke of Hill as the scorned, fatal Medea and of Thomas as Prometheus (bound and unbound) were also casting the highly gendered duel between the two in an archetypal language with ancient mythic resonances. Such concern for the "big picture" presented by the Hill-Thomas confrontation emerged often in the rationale given by a sizable number of the more than 150 women running for political office in the 1992 campaign. Several specifically pointed to Hill-Thomas as the moment when they decided to "clean the House."

For many French readers of the weekly *L'Evenement du Jeudi*, Hill-Thomas was presented as a parable to help anchor the assertion that, in France, one in five women has been a victim or witness of sexual harassment in the workplace. The *Progressive Woman's Quarterly* (Summer 1992) made similar use of the October hearings to underscore the history of news reports about women. In an article entitled "How the Media Slants the Message and Other Reportorial Sins," Laura Sydell made connections between the hearings as presented in the press and the gender of those assigned to cover the testimony. Sydell discusses the stories that reporters subordinated, or dismissed altogether, in their coverage and the effect these editorial and plotting (in a narrative sense of course) decisions had on the news reports themselves. She outlines practices and patterns among the Washington Press Corps, who, according to Sydell, allow powerbrokers to provide the symbolic "spin" on many a controversial story, and hopes that a close analysis of the reports themselves will serve as a catalyst in the long overdue critique of news as an "objective" discourse of its own.

Whether "profane national passion play" (Williams, 1992, p. 36) or "spaghetti western" (Burleigh, 1992, p. 50), the Hill-Thomas affair was a study in negotiated power. Nancy Fraser yokes issues of mythic and actual power to the control of one's own narrative. In "Sex, Lies, and the Public Sphere: Some Reflections on the Confirmation of Clarence Thomas" (1992), she argues that one of the "morals of the story" is the need to make significant revisions in "the standard liberal view of the public sphere, since the categories of publicity and privacy are multivalent and contested, and not all understandings of them promote democracy." (p. 609) In other words, she demands a more complex and nuanced reading of the two spheres based on the lesson of the hearing itself.

If we examine the Thomas confirmation struggle more
closely, we see that the very meaning and boundaries of the
concept of publicity was at stake. The way the struggle
unfolded, moreover, depended at every point on who had
the power to successfully and authoritatively define where
the line between the public and the private would be drawn.
It depended as well on who had the power to police that
boundary. (p. 596)

Fraser recognizes that what such close attention to the details of definition—and the relation between literal and symbolic power—can bring
about is a paradigm shift, a more or less revolutionary new way of seeing
and, thereby, of knowing and being known. As Fraser indicates, the one
who controls definition (or meaning) controls.

III

Legal scholar Patricia J. Williams describes the role such catalytic
experience—when viewed in symbolic terms—can have in restructuring
both personal and professional histories. In fact, paradigm shifts are often
the result of such experiences. She targets the moment of conception of
that work:

193

A concise, modular, yet totally engaging item on the
"MacNeil/Lehrer News Hour": Harvard Law School cannot
find one black woman on the entire planet who is good
enough to teach there, because we're all too stupid. (Well,
that's not precisely what was said. It was more like they
couldn't find anyone smart enough. To be fair, what
Associate Dean Louis Kaplow actually said was that
Harvard would have to "lower its standards," which of
course Harvard simply cannot do.)

So now you know: it is this news item, as I sit propped up
in bed with my laptop computer balanced on my knees,
clad in my robe with the torn fringe of terry bluebells, that
finally pushes me over the edge and into the deep rabbit
hole of this book. (1991, p. 5)

Williams's scholarship, like that of professor Catharine Mac-
Kinnon, constitutes a new disciplinary focus altogether, critical legal studies,
a deconstructive analysis of the structure and assumptions of law itself.
Such interpreters of texts bring to the ultimate language of truth and pre-
cision a reading that asks about the nuanced assumptions of privilege
encoded in the law. It's as if such readings search for the mythological

elements buried beneath seemingly noncontestable "truth statements." Using techniques borrowed from contemporary literary critical theory, they uncover and thereby deconstruct the hidden texts within legal assertions. This is the exploration of the law-as-narrative, the extraordinary employment of the tools of the literary critic in the service of truth telling.

In addition to her theoretical critique of existing legislation, moreover, Williams simultaneously serves as one of many contemporary creators of narrative. Like those of us struggling to find a language in which to talk about, to transmit feeling about, and to analyze the Hill-Thomas drama, Williams seeks to help in the creation of a less positivist, less absolutist language and genre. We need a discourse as problematic as our multiple identities make our lives:

> I am trying to create a genre of legal writing . . . to fill the
> gaps of traditional legal scholarship. I would like to write in
> a way that reveals the intersubjectivity of legal
> constructions, that forces the reader both to participate in
> the construction of meaning and to be conscious of that
> process. Thus, in attempting to fill the gaps in the discourse
> of commercial exchange, I hope that the gaps in my own
> writing will be self-consciously filled by the reader, as an
> act of forced mirroring of meaning-invention. To this end I
> exploit all sorts of literary devices, including parody,
> parable, and poetry. (pp. 7–8)

194

Williams intermingles the autobiographical with her interdisciplinary observations and insights, all in the service of rereading (and reinventing) the law and legal discourse.

That the language and conceits of traditional literary study should be so potent in the creation of discourses such as law traditionally associated with the actual rather than the imaginative should be no surprise to those who witnessed the creation of the field of comparative narratology under the tutelage of such Virgilian guides as Hayden White. It was, in fact, White, the historian, who had argued:

> Understanding is a process of rendering the unfamiliar, or
> the "uncanny" in Freud's sense of that term, familiar. . . .
> This process of understanding can only be tropological in
> nature, for what is involved in the rendering of the
> unfamiliar into the familiar is a troping that is generally
> figurative. It follows, I think, that this process of
> understanding proceeds by the exploitation of the principal
> modalities of figuration, identified in post-Renaissance
> rhetorical theory as the "master tropes" (Kenneth Burke's

phrase) of metaphor, metonymy, synecdoche, and irony.
(1978, p. 5)

Thus, White could imagine "the historical text as literary artifact" shaped
by strategies of emplotment, a creative work comprised of "provisional
and contingent" representations (p. 81). Aware of the controversy that
would ensue from such an assertion, White continued: "Nevertheless . . .
in general there has been a reluctance to consider historical narratives as
what they most manifestly are: verbal fictions, the contents of which are
as much invented as found and the forms of which have more in common
with their counterparts in literature than they have with those in the sci-
ences" (p. 82). In such a dispensation, old boundaries between the fig-
urative and the literal, the "true" and the "fictive," the imaginative and
the actual, disintegrate.

It is in the rhetorical battle between Hill and Thomas that one locates an exemplary moment for testing the usefulness of White's notion
of history's literariness. From the beginning, the confrontation between
Thomas and Hill was a war of images, metaphors, and stereotypes manipulated in an adversarial and histrionic theater owned and operated by
puppeteers, with a cynical and venal memory of slavery and its aftermath.
The principal players in this ritualized "showdown" were cast as bipolar
opponents, an extraordinary marketing feat given the number of philosophical commonalities between the two conservative associates. Thomas's unbridled machismo, released suddenly and only, presumably, in
righteously indignant response to what he declared was unjust and invalid
accusation, was cast in opposition to Hill's ascendancy to a semiprivi-
leged place within the "cult of true womanhood" (Carby 1987, pp. 23–
34).

Pious, pure, submissive (Hull 1992, pp. 47–48), and domestic, Hill
nevertheless announced by her public testimony, that she had practiced
"the culture of dissemblance" (Hine 1989, pp. 912–20) by not confronting Thomas a decade earlier, and by making use of an established network, with Thomas as patron, for her own professional gain. Hill's critics
excoriated her for a host of contradictory reasons: for not having the moral
and ethical courage to walk away from personal insult and affront; for
playing a game of patronal influence with the Reagan and Bush admin-
istrations which necessitated collusion with her own deracination; for refusing to serve as a valiant role model for the Black women who would
follow her in the bureaucracies for which she worked. Some castigated
the law school professor for allowing herself to place a white Feminist
discourse about gender before the needs of her own race. Such large and
sometimes overwhelming demands underscore the impossibility of the Black
woman's role: failure is failure, and success is failure of another order.
R. Darcy and Charles D. Hadley address the impossibility of the Black
woman's position as mythic *or* as actual figure. Should she somehow

negotiate any liabilities connected with negative images of her race and gender (in situations of double jeopardy or, more precisely, interactive jeopardy), the successful woman must beware the pitfalls of the myth of Black matriarchy. Shirley Chisholm, the first Black female member of Congress, addresses this danger in the political realm: "[I]n a society that denied them racial manhood, I was threatening their shaky self-esteem still more. . . . To the black man—even some of those supposedly supporting me—sensitive about female domination, they were running me down as a bossy female, a would-be matriarch" (Chisholm 1970, p. 70).

Incapable of satisfying the demand that she successfully negotiate an imagistic minefield, the African American woman most often, argues Hine, stands alone. For all that is not known about her, "stereotypes, negative images, and debilitating assumptions fill[ed] the space left empty" (Hine 1989, p. 915). This woman, who stands in adversarial relation to European American men, European American women, and, often, African American men, sometimes hides within an enigma in order to "accrue the psychic space and harness the resources needed to hold [her] own in the often one-sided and mismatched resistance struggle" (Hine 1989, p. 915).

Both she and her herstorical narrative can, and most often do, disappear. In that supremely self-serving and cynical moment when Thomas arrogated to himself the role of lynch victim, figural language became the tool of conspiratorial amnesia. The *New York Times* (1991) argued confidently that no one should have been stunned by the

> surreal slogan . . . Clarence Thomas has always willingly benefited from his face and victimization. It's just that he has made his case slyly, in subtext, most recently with his sharecropper grandfather in the starring role. When he was director of the Equal Employment Opportunity Commission and under fire for undermining his agency, he accused his critics of indicting his grandfather.

Nell Irvin Painter's crisp, incisive commentary recounts statistics on lynching, beginning with 1882 and continuing to the early 1950s. Painter concedes that 95 percent of those who died at the hands of vigilantes were Black males. "But what of the invisible figure in this tableau?" she asks. "It is not by accident that in both the rape-lynch set piece and in Thomas's recitation, one figure in Southern society is missing: the black woman" (1991, p. 577).

In an oft-quoted citation, Hazel Carby charges that "the institutionalized rape of black women has never been as powerful a symbol of black oppression as the spectacle of lynching. Rape has always involved patriarchal notions of women being, at best, not entirely unwilling accomplices, if not outwardly inviting a sexual attack" (1987, p. 9). Nevertheless, the NAACP's April 1919 pamphlet did include a table listing the women and girls lynched, by state. The NAACP statistician indicated in a footnote that the number murdered (fifty colored and eleven white females) represented 1.5 percent of the total number of persons thus executed (2,522 colored and 702 white men). Though the numbers of lynch victims are very small, the number of Black women literally and figuratively lynched by the rope of sexual exploitation is enormous.

While the world recalls with fear and trembling the icon of the Black castrated male burning to death in a lynch mob's fire, federal judge A. Leon Higginbotham cautions the new justice about the responsibility of remembering. He tells Thomas: "You can become an exemplar of fairness and the rational interpretation of the Constitution, or you can become an archetype of inequality and the retrogressive evaluation of human rights" (1992). What will account for the difference? Higginbotham situates the locus of choice and of responsibility in the area of memory: "You . . . must try to remember" the ancestors "so that the sacrifices of all these men and women will not have been in vain" (p. 1026). Such recollections, Higginbotham implies, will remind Thomas that he is not orphaned, unmoored, or disconnected from a tradition upon which he can build. A Supreme Court justice and, above all, the grandson of a sharecropper must be "grounded in history" (p. 1013).

History, however, is not merely the allegedly objective recall of past events. History is also comprised of individual and communal mythologies, the sum of which enables a community to know and to understand its identity. Ida B. Wells had a potent understanding of the power of record and of long memory. She knew of the pervasive influence of myth. Conscious of the need to challenge the narrative lies that were being manufactured (in newspaper columns and in common parlance) to justify murder, theft, arson, and terrorism, Wells noted:

> The Afro-American is not a bestial race. If this work can contribute in any way toward proving this, and at the same time arouse the conscience of the American people to a demand for justice to every citizen, and punishment by law for the lawless, I shall feel I have done my race a service. Other considerations are of minor importance. (1892)

Wells dedicates the booklet to "the Afro-American women of New York and Brooklyn" whose efforts enabled her to publish her findings. Though much of her research reveals the systematic torture of many African-American men—a torture that often included, as Trudier Harris has demonstrated, a ritualized ceremony of physical and psychic castration—Wells herself is not confused about the intersection of race and gender.

African American women's literary history is a long trajectory of such intersections. In the pages of black women's slave narratives, the variables of identity (race, class, gender) surface in self-inventive languages that seek the complex truth of our experience in the literal as well as in the symbolic realm. According to Rosemary Bray (1991), the Senate Judiciary Committee made literal misuse of a single text, *The Exorcist*, in its attempt to identify truth. Far more useful, she argues, would have been a careful reading of the autobiographical and novelistic *Incidents in the Life of a Slave Girl*. In its pages, they would have discovered a multiple-identified narrator who, as both Linda Brent and Harriet Jacobs, could have moved them beyond the impasse of dysfunctional signs moving in every direction except toward understanding.

References

Bailey, F. Lee. "Where Was the Crucible? The Cross-examination That Wasn't." *ABA Journal* 78 (1992): 46–49.

Bloom, Allen. *The Closing of the American Mind*. New York: Simon and Schuster, 1987.

Boo, K. "The Organization Woman: The Real Reason Anita Hill Stayed Silent." *Washington Monthly* 23 (1991): 44–46.

Boot, William. "The Clarence Thomas Hearings: Why Everyone—Left, Right and Center—Found the Press Guilty As Charged." *Columbia Journalism Review* 30 (1992): 25–29.

Borger, Gloria, Ted Guest and Jeannye Thorton. "The Untold Story." *U.S. News and World Report*, Oct. 12, 1992, pp. 28–37.

Bray, Rosemary L. "Taking Sides Against Ourselves." *New York Times Magazine*, Nov. 17, 1991, p. 56.

Burleigh, Nina. "Now That It's Over: Winners and Losers in the Confirmation Process." *ABA Journal* 78 (1992): 50–53.

Carby, Hazel V. *Reconstructing Womanhood: The Emergence of the Afro-American Woman Novelist*. New York: Oxford University Press, 1987.

Chisholm, Shirley. *Unbought and Unbossed*. Boston: Houghton-Mifflin, 1970.

Cohn, Bob. "Dirt Trail." *New Republic* 205 (1992): 16–18.

Crawford, Vickie. "On the Clarence Thomas Hearings." *The Black Scholar* 22 (1992): 15–17.

Douglass, Frederick. *Life and Times of Frederick Douglass*. 1892. New York: Crowell, 1966.

Ellison, Ralph. *Invisible Man*. New York: Vintage, 1947.

Fraser, Nancy. "Sex, Lies, and the Public Sphere: Some Reflections on the Confirmation of Clarence Thomas." *Critical Inquiry* 18 (1992): 595–612.

Giddings, Paula. *When and Where I Enter*. New York: Morrow, 1984.

Gillespie, M. A. "We Speak in Tongues." *Ms.* 2, Jan.–Feb., 1992, pp. 32–33.

Hare, Nathan, and Julia Hare. "The Clarence Thomas Hearings." *Black Scholar* 22 (1992): 37–40.

Higginbotham, A. Leon. "An Open Letter to Justice Clarence Thomas from a Federal Judicial." *University of Pennsylvania Law Review* 140 (1992): 1005–1028.

Hill, Anita. "The Nature of the Beast." *Ms.* 2, Jan.–Feb. 1992, 32–33.

Hine, D. C. "Rape and the Inner Lives of Black Women in the Middle West: Preliminary Thoughts in the Culture of Dissemblance." *Signs* 14 (1989): 912–920.

Hopkins, Paula. *Contending Forces*. 1899, Carbondale, Ill.: Southern Illinois University Press, 1978.

Hull, G. T. "Girls Will Be Girls, and Boys Will . . . Flex Their Muscles." *Black Scholar* 22 (1992): 47–48.

Jordan, E. C. "Race, Gender, and Social Class in the Thomas Sexual Harassment Hearings: The Hidden Fault Lines in Political Discourse." *Harvard Women's Law Journal* 15 (1992): 1–24.

The Nation. "Judging Thomas." *Nation*, Oct. 28, 1991, p. 501, 503–4.

Kelly, J. (1991). Cover Story. *Advertising Age 62*: 35.

Labacqz, Karen. "Reflections on the Thomas Hearings." Newsletter of the Center for Women and Religion, Graduate Theological Union, Berkeley, Calif.

Lefstein, Stuart. "It's Not Too Late for the Crucible: Question of Perjury in the Thomas Hearings Will Not Go Away." *ABA Journal* 78 (1992): 115.

Monroe, Bill. "Anita Hill Explosion Also Hit the Press." *Washington Journalism Review* 13 (1991): 6.

Monroe, S. "Sex, Lies and Stereotypes." *Emerge* 3 (1992): 30–35.

Morrison, Toni. *Sula*. New York: Plume, 1973.

National Association for the Advancement of Colored People (NAACP). "Thirty Years of Lynching in the United States, 1889–1918." New York: NAACP, 1919.

New York Times. "To the Witness." Editorial letter to Anita Hill. *New York Times*, Oct. 17, 1991, p. A26.

Norton, Eleanor Holmes. "And the Language Was Race." *Ms.* 2, Jan.–Feb. 1992, pp. 43–45.

Painter, Nell Irving. "Who Was Lynched?" *Nation* 253 (1991): 577.

Phelps, Timothy M. and Helen Winternitz. *Capitol Games: Clarence Thomas, Anita Hill, and the Story of a Supreme Court Nomination*. New York: Hyperion, 1992.

Safire, William. "Myths of the Confirmation." *New York Times*, Oct. 17, 1991, pp. A19, A27.

Smith, Barbara. "Ain't Gonna Let Nobody Turn Me Around." *Ms.* 2, Jan.–Feb. 1992, pp. 37–39.

Smith, D. L. "The Thomas Spectacle: Power, Impotence, and Melodrama." *Black Scholar* 22 (1992): 93–95.

Spence, Gerry L. "Justice: The New Community." *ABA Journal* 78 (1992): 46–47.

Sydell, Laura. "How the Media Slants the Message and Other Reportorial Sins." *On the Issues* 23 (1992): 32–36.

Thomas, Virgina Lamp. "How We Survived." *People*, Nov. 11, 1991, pp. 108–116.

Thomson, David. "Our Process." *Film Comment* 28 (1992): 7–12.

Walker, Rebecca. "Becoming the Third Wave." *Ms* 2, Jan.–Feb. 1992, pp. 39–41.

Wells, Ida B. *Southern Horrors: Lynch Laws and Its Phases*. New York: New York Age Print, 1892.

White, Hayden. *Tropics of Discourse: Essays in Cultural Criticism*. Baltimore: John Hopkins University Press, 1978.

Williams, Patricia. J. "Silenced: The Bread and Circus Literacy Test." *Ms.* 2, Jan.–Feb. 1992, pp. 34–37.

———. *The Alchemy of Race and Rights*. Cambridge, Mass. Harvard University Press, 1991.

199

A Forensic Psychiatrist Reflects on Sexual Harassment

ROSALIND B. GRIFFIN

This essay presents a clinical perspective on sexual harassment within the framework of forensic psychiatry and draws upon my psychiatric private practice. As a subspecialty of psychiatry, forensic psychiatry interfaces with the legal system to assist in deliberations, findings, recommendations, and establishment of the mindset at the time alleged emotional injuries, criminal acts, or disabilities may have occurred in the workplace. Although the subject of sexual harassment is not new, it was propelled into national attention as a result of the Clarence Thomas hearings. It is critical that women be validated and empowered to address their rightful concerns within the medical-legal dimension of sexual harassment.

Both federal and some state laws are quite clear in delineating discrimination based on sex. Two types of sexual harassment are relevant to this discussion: (1) *Quid pro quo.* Unwelcome sexual advances and/or requests for sexual favors and/or "other verbal or physical conduct or communication of a sexual nature" which is explicitly or implicitly made a condition of employment, or is used as a factor in decisions affecting employment. (2) *Hostile work environment.* Unwelcome sexual advances or requests for sexual favors and/or "other verbal or physical conduct or communication of a sexual nature" sufficient to create an intimidating, hostile, or offensive working environment.

Medicine and law have worked together to satisfy and remedy allegations of sexual harassment when there have been emotional injuries.

Most of the injuries alleged by victims have been consistent with what is described by the *Diagnostic and Statistical Manual of Mental Disorders* American Psychiatric Association (1987) as "post-traumatic stress disorder." In essence, this disorder has several characteristic symptoms following a psychologically distressing event that is outside the range of usual human experience, such as chronic illness, business loss, or marital conflict. The stressor producing this syndrome would be markedly distressing to almost anyone and is usually experienced with intense fear, terror, and helplessness. The event may be one single episode, or the alleged harassment may take place over several months or even years. Characteristic symptoms involve reexperiencing the traumatic event as though it were present in the immediate experience, in one of the following ways: recurrent and intrusive distressing recollections of the event; recurrent and distressing dreams of the event; sudden acting or feeling as if the traumatic event were recurring (includes a sense of reliving the experience, illusions, hallucinations, and dissociative episodes, even those that occur upon awakening or intoxication); intense psychological distress from exposure to events that symbolize or resemble an aspect of the traumatic event, including anniversaries of the trauma.

A sexually harassed victim tends to avoid anything associated with the event, in at least three of the following ways: efforts to avoid thoughts or feelings associated with the trauma; efforts to avoid activities or situations that arouse recollections of the trauma; inability to recall an important aspect of the trauma; markedly diminished interest in significant activities; feeling of detachment or estrangement from others; restricted range of affect (such as being unable to have loving feelings); sense of a foreshortened future (such as not expecting to have a career, marriage, children, or a long life). In the case of a married woman who has been the victim of sexual harassment, she fears that her husband will assume she is at fault for seducing the alleged harasser. Thus, there is a compounded stress endured in carrying the weight of the problem alone without the support of one's mate.

In sexual harassment cases, the most common traumas involve a serious threat to one's life or physical integrity and the usual sense of post-traumatic stress disorder. Generally, there is a threat of the loss of one's job or promotion if the sexual favors are not granted. As a result, the trauma may be experienced alone or in the company of groups of people. The stressors producing this disorder include natural serious physical injury or deliberately caused disasters, such as hysterical acting-out and insubordination. Some stressors frequently produce the disorder of regular torture; others produce it only occasionally. At any rate, the psychological effects may be long-term and cannot be handled safely with legal action against the aggressor as a way of remediating the physical ills and emotional injuries. This type of post-traumatic stress disorder apparently is more severe and lasts longer when the stressor is of human rather than natural origin.

The traumatic event may be reexperienced in a variety of ways. Commonly the person has recurrent and intrusive recollections of the event or recurring distressing dreams during which the event is reexperienced. Sometimes there is a loss of libido. This is generally related to self-blame on the part of the victim of sexual harassment. In some of these neurotic conflicts, there may be emotional liability for the continuation as well as the sustained act of harassment. Chronicity and duration of the sexual harassment were part of the Anita Hill-Clarence Thomas question. Why did she put up with it? Why did she follow him from one job to another? Why did she not turn him in earlier? There may have been self-serving reasons for her not wanting to destroy him. However, often when sex is involved in the "forbidden zone" (Rutter, 1989), women view themselves as being able to heal the aggressor. The "forbidden zone" may be the workplace, the church, the psychiatrist's office, the lawyer's office, and so on.

It should be explained here that no matter what our childhood experience has been like, we all have, to one degree or another, unhealed wounds. We start from childhood and grow into adulthood to face the prospect of healing our life wounds. No matter how hopelessly our families have dealt with these injuries, we all hope for restoration of what has been lost. It is here that we turn to the forbidden zone for sexual conquest, in the unrequested, unsolicited professional relationship, to replace what has been lost. Women who engage in forbidden sex with their bosses describe this "unmeasurable nonsexual value" they felt the relationship had obtained before any sexual behavior took place. These women were trying to account for why they participated in sex or tolerated sexual innuendos with their mentors despite knowing how unhealthy it was. They also cited the strong influence of cultural factors in their upbringing that steered them toward complying with the sexual desires of rescuing, powerful men.

The woman as healer of such men tries to sublimate the identity of the symbolic depriving mother. Such a woman becomes more tolerant and more generous in reacting to the man's sexual references, innuendos, and advances. She may feel that this will disengage her from the symbol of the cold, unloving mother which may have caused the destruction of the mother's marriage or romantic liaison. However, this thought that the woman is the healer of the ailing male is a neurotic, imaginary one deeply seated in a psychological distortion of her own self-esteem. Clearly, no woman can heal a sexually deprived individual. One woman can only put a halt to the advances of the aggressor by whatever means she finds most effective. Clearly, the men in forbidden-zone relationships often have an expressed need to be healed through "the right woman," but in her subordinate role. When a man is healing or feeling his "wound" and the woman's sexuality becomes available to him through the protected, secret conditions of the forbidden zone, in this case the workplace, the tendency to avail himself of this opportunity can become irresistible. However, any sexual behavior by a man in power within what is defined as the workplace is inherently exploitative of a woman's trust. He is actually the keeper of that trust, and it is assumed that it is the man's responsibility, no matter what level of provocation or apparent consent by the woman, to ensure that sexual transgression does not take place. At any rate, women are generally considered vulnerable; they are mentees to powerful men who trust that their confidences will be safeguarded by wound-healing women.

For Black men to talk of their sexual power is considered their own way of enlarging their superiority. They do not actually take themselves seriously; they are trying to capitalize on the sexual stereotype of Black men as great and powerful, satisfying lovers. Black women may not take them seriously, either. However, in Hill's case, she felt that Thomas need not utilize this additional unsolicited description of himself; she was, in fact, becoming victimized. In any other social relationship, she might have laughed away this boasting as impotence and might have seen it only as a seductive means of trying to bridge the romantic distance between them. However, in the workplace, such unwanted sexual boasting by a superior is defined as sexual harassment.

203

Clinical Vignette

Ms. Gray had been happily married to her husband, a police officer, for several years. In the line of duty, he had killed a criminal. He was seeking psychotherapy for himself for overwhelming symptoms of grief and resolution of the conflict of his forced violence. During one of his sessions, he related that although his marriage had been a good one, his wife had been very distressed over the past year and had been crying and socially withdrawn. He felt she needed to be referred for psychotherapy as well.

I thought I would see Ms. Gray for conjoint therapy related to the stress Mr. Gray was enduring for having shot a citizen in the line of duty. He was eventually found not negligent, and it was determined that he had performed his duties according to the investigation conducted by his department. He nevertheless evidenced depression, increased isolation, and many features associated with regression and guilt. It was not unusual, then, for his wife to have a loss of consortium related to his ills. It was surprising, however, when she reported that she had been a victim of a separate ordeal apart from her husband's ordeal. She had been harassed by her boss for five years. She said that when she was pregnant with her last child, she thought the harassment would stop because she was no longer a sexually attractive object for her boss. However, when she returned from maternity leave, he resumed his advances.

Ms. Gray's boss had a reputation for being a lover of sorts and had "hit on" other people in the department. She was dismayed when he would call her into his private office at the end of the working day, assign her unusual and complicated projects to perform, and then manage to get physically close to her to the point of caressing her. He admitted that he found her attractive and lovable and asked if they could start a relationship. Since both were married, she used this as a tactful excuse for saying that she could not condone such acts, hoping that this would put a stop to his behavior.

He was at all times generally quite friendly and helpful, and because he was African American, he was considered a role model for many other aspiring African American executives in the department. Thus, she had much guilt about the possibility of destroying his career. At the same time, she felt that if she told her husband that she had gone over the edge of what would be considered minor, benign, and harmless physical involvement with him, such as allowing him to put his arms around her, the husband, who had recently been involved in a work-related homicide, might not be able to discern her behavior clearly as self-protective and exerting limits. She felt that her husband might be angered and provoked to kill the boss; she was distressed and silently harbored her anguish.

I saw Ms. Gray on two occasions to take a full history. She related numerous incidents in which she had told her boss repeatedly that she was not interested in him sexually. He had informed her that there would be cutbacks in the department, and if she were "nice" to him, he would protect her job. This was an economically critical time, because her husband's leave of absence from his job was already putting a dent in their income. She felt totally trapped. She could not turn to her parents for help because of her early-childhood distant relationship with her domineering father, nor could she turn to her friends who she thought would tattle or gossip about the boss whom she ambivalently respected. When she finally was able to obtain sick leave from her job, it was after I had referred her to an individual psychotherapist with a forensic background who would be prepared to help her fight this case under workers' compensation.

Ms. Gray had developed all the symptoms of depression: depressed mood most of the day, nearly every day; markedly diminished interest or pleasure in all, or almost all, activities most of the day, nearly every day; significant weight loss or weight gain when not dieting, or decrease or increase in appetite nearly every day; insomnia or hypersomnia nearly every day; psychomotor agitation or retardation nearly every day fatigue or loss of energy nearly every day; feelings of worthlessness or excessive or inappropriate guilt (which may be delusional) nearly every day (not merely self-reproach or guilt about being sick); diminished ability to think

204

or concentrate or indecisiveness nearly every day; recurrent thoughts of death (not just fear of dying); recurrent suicidal ideation without a specific plan, or a suicide attempt.

When the boss found out that Ms. Gray had filed a work-related injury claim as the cause for her leave of absence, he circulated a petition among his employees, 75 percent of whom were women, in essence asking them to support him as a credible, reliable, model employer who would not be guilty of any such wrongdoing as had been alleged by Ms. Gray.

When the lawsuit was filed alleging sexual harassment, Ms. Gray had implemented my recommendation that she confide in her husband and let him know that she had been sustaining this sexual harassment for several years. Ms. Gray had the wits and smarts to wire herself electronically, aided by her husband, to record conversations over several months indicating advances made by her boss.

During the depositions, Ms. Gray's boss profoundly and repeatedly denied her allegations; he stated that she was an unstable character and was undesirable to him, that he was faithful and loyal to his wife, and that he had signed petitions from his employees indicating that he could not be guilty of such actions. Then came the shocker. Ms. Gray's attorneys produced transcripts of all of the audio tapes: his asking her for a kiss, forcing himself on her, trying to give her a kiss, her saying no repeatedly, his offering to give her a promotion if she went along with him, and her statements that she felt she was worthy of a promotion but did not feel that she had to have sex with him. On the tapes, she came across as very frightened but direct, respectful, and firm. Her boss was later fired, and the lawsuit was settled out-of-court. The corporation wanted to quickly put as much distance as possible between him and their stated policy against such behavior.

This typical case indicates that we must acknowledge that a woman may be able to stop her boss's sexual advancement but with great loss to herself, her reputation, and perhaps even her finances. Many people tend not to believe the victim of sexual harassment and will side with the harasser if he has a suave way of smoothing over ills, taking people into his confidence, and appearing to be in need of sexual healing, a man to be pitied and supported. Nevertheless, he is a destructive intruder and a criminal and must be exposed for his antisocial personality disorder and his serious psychopathological problems.

Timing

We need to ask several questions about the timing of the disclosure of sexual harassment. It is assumed that there is always an opportune time. For instance, as soon as the first sign of sexual harassment occurs, the victim should run to the employment assistance office, the supervisor, or a law enforcement agency. However, such a knee-jerk reaction generally presents the victim as hysterical and oversensitive, and so it is to her credit that she waits until she has sufficient evidence to prove her case. Often it is unfortunate that she must be the one to prove her innocence and her victimization.

Returning to our clinical vignette, we can see how Ms. Gray became a victim when her husband was out of work, waiting to be proven innocent in the shooting accident. She clearly needed income to sustain herself and her family. The threats made by the boss that he could do away with her job made her more vulnerable and submissive. She did resist him and denies having sexual intimacy with him, but she was able to prolong the actual engagement by giving him one excuse after another, hoping that her job would give some final answer to her own security. So the timing of her vulnerability is another issue.

Timing is also critical when we consider why several people in the office would support a pledge acknowledging the innocence of a boss without interviewing the oppressed victim. The timing in this case appears to be related to all persons who are in need of a job and are afraid of losing favor with their boss. Further, the old saying "There is something about the distress of others that does not displease us" helps to explain why people believe the worst in others. Certainly there was jealousy that Ms. Gray may have manipulated her attractiveness in order to become the boss's favorite. Others may have wished to exchange places with her and would have welcomed his advances. There is no logical time, place, or opportunity wherein the boss may act on his aggrandized notion that he can have his pick of any woman at any time. Timing in this sense indicates that his premorbid personality is consistent with that of a person who is power-seeking and assumes entitlement to exploit another person's submissiveness.

Timing is related to the patient's unwillingness to share her feelings with her husband, knowing that he was himself already compromised in his mental functioning because of his own grief and guilt at having been forced to take a life. She thought she could bear these pressures herself and handle them without further burdening him. Releasing such information to her husband, she felt, might cause him either to deteriorate further or to act impulsively and aggressively against the boss and thus worsen their marital and legal situation. Fortunately, he proved himself to be caring, considerate, and loving; he saved his wife's trust in him by helping her endure what was an ordeal for her and by devising the scheme of taping her boss's advances. During the trial, the production of the transcripts and tapes caused the defendant's side to seek a settlement quickly in order to minimize and suppress any negative publicity to the organization.

Sexual harassment is often seen as something subtle, playful, or enjoyable in the workplace. Managerial intervention must set the tone for a vehement policy against any person's feeling oppressed or victimized by a coworker or a supervisor. This policy should be in place and acknowledged by all, and in a timely fashion.

Conclusion

Not every wrongdoing is exposed by the kind of electronic wiring that was used to trap Ms. Gray's boss. Not every stare or glance is captured in a still photo of the perpetrator of such subtle, graphic, or intimidating behaviors. The most atrocious part of a victim's sexual harassment is not being believed. It causes the victim to feel that she is psychotic, depressed, hysterical, isolated, and unsupported. The damage ranges from loss of employment, to loss of consortium, to adverse impact on her parenting ability, to negative effects on her ability to perform in a normal erotic relationship, to adverse impact on her ability to gain new employment.

A sociopathic character has disorders that cause him to lie and to blame the victim. He will seduce others, in a very charismatic way, to gain their trust in his folly. A sociopathic personality makes threats and may cause the victim to feel constant distrust and fear that she may be labeled a troublemaker. Whether Clarence Thomas qualifies as a sociopathic personality could only be determined by clinical analysis. However, in the future, using electronic equipment, video recording devices, and journal entries could make the victim appear less isolated and more credible in her allegations. Our victorious clinical case demonstrates that the victim can mount a challenge. Though Anita Hill was not as fortunate as Ms. Gray, we can envision the possibilities of the medical-legal dimensions of sexual harassment for African American women (and all women, for that matter) to validate and empower themselves.

References

American Psychiatric Association. *Diagnostic and Statistical Manual of Mental Disorders*, 3rd ed. Washington, D.C. American Psychiatric Association, 1987.
Rutter, Perter, M.D. *Sex in the Forbidden Zone*. New York: Fawcett Crest, 1989.

The Tongue or the Sword:
Which Is Master?

DENISE TROUTMAN-ROBINSON

The tongue is the sword of a woman, and she never lets it become rusty.
—Chinese proverb

If women possess the tongue as a weapon while men possess the *real*, tangible, double-edged, death-providing sword, then, in the words of Humpty Dumpty, "Which is to be master?" especially when the women are African American?

Research conducted on language and gender generally establishes a dichotomy. Men's language is characterized as powerful, and women's language is characterized as nonpowerful because of roles and positions that are constructed socially. This essay examines the correlation of race, gender, and language use to determine whether or not a different outcome evolves rather than the already established dichotomy. Specifically, when middle-class European American men engage in conversations with African American women, which group becomes master? Do African American women use the purported women's style of language, characterized as weak, indirect, and tentative? Do the power and dominance of European American men also obtain in their conversational interactions with African American women? This essay seeks to illuminate the question of language usage by examining the speech behavior of Anita Hill during her testimony before the fourteen-member, all-white-male Senate Judiciary Committee.

Power, Gender, and Language

Power is one element of human relationships. It arises in teacher-student, doctor-patient, customer-employee, employer-employee, parent-child, older sibling-younger sibling, and various other relationships. The powerful persons are those who control, who dominate relationships, and who exude strength.

In the United States and in other Western societies, men have power and can be construed as the "parliamentarians of power" (Lakoff 1990, p. 12). Viewed through this lens, men control social, economic, and political power; they are in control of decision and policy making; they have created and enacted the legislative and judicial laws; and they have determined the rules of the dominant written language. Men have maintained social, economic, and political power throughout U.S. history—as commanders-in-chief, members of Congress, Surgeon generals, Supreme Court justices, presidents of corporations, chairmen of boards, ministers in churches, and so on.

Language, as a correlative of social behavior, imitates and interprets power. The language of persons in power will be accepted as powerful. This list reconfigures Lakoff's discussion, showing characteristics of powerful and nonpowerful language:

Powerful language	*Nonpowerful language*
Direct speech	Indirect speech
Orders, commands:	Mitigated orders: "It's
"Open the door."	stuffy in here."
	"Please open the
	door."
Decisive	Indecisive Questions:
Assertions: "You can	"Could you open the
open the door."	door?" "Open the
	door, won't you?"
Interruptions	Few or no interruptions

Because men are the "parliamentarians of power," men's language (vis-à-vis women's language) is the language of power.[1] Men's language is characterized as direct, assertive, decisive, and strong; it is equivalent to all of the features listed above under "Powerful language." Women's language is identified as indirect, tentative, and weak; it employs all the the features listed under "Powerless language." Analyses of conversations between women and men indicate that men interrupt women more than women interrupt men. Men vivify their power by interrupting women's contributions to conversations. Interruptions, in this sense, are powerful forms of language because they are used predominantly by those in power and because the persons using them deny a full speaking turn to a conversational partner. Interruptions constitute the primary focus in this analysis of the speech behavior of Hill and one of her key interrogators.

After a preliminary dispute over a reasonable manner of proceeding, the senators of the Judiciary Committee agreed on an order of questioning with predetermined senators serving as primary questioners. Although any senator could have engaged in conversation with Hill at virtually any point, most senators abided by the prearranged order of speaking. Arlen Specter served as the key Republican questioner of Hill, while senators Biden and Leahy served as key questioners for the Democrats. After four rounds of thirty-minute questions from the Democratic and Republican principal questioners, other senators not designated as principal questioners were allowed up to five minutes to ask questions, alternating between Democrats and Republicans.

Data Collection, Procedures, and Analysis

The data analyzed for this study stem from a collection of transcripts, videotapes, and audio tapes of the interaction between Hill and the fourteen-member Senate Judiciary Committee. In particular, the analysis focuses on the conversational interchanges between Hill and her main antagonist, Specter. Two of the four conversational interchanges between Hill and Specter are analyzed below. In these two interchanges, Hill and Specter engage in battle, even though Specter claims that he does not regard the proceeding as adversarial.

After reading through the transcripts of Hill's testimony and making notes, the researcher viewed the videotapes of the testimony, making more extensive notations. Finally, the audio tapes were used to verify the transcript notations. Each instance of an interruption was counted and tabulated when it occurred in the data.

Interruptions represent one type of simultaneous speech (Sacks et al. 1974; Zimmerman and West 1975). Speech is classified as simultaneous when conversationalists speak at the same time. Interruptions are tantamount to simultaneous speech because the next speaker (Speaker B, for example) begins to talk during the current speaker's turn (Speaker A, for example), breaking off that turn. The literature on women and language establishes interruptions as characteristic of men's verbal behavior when they engage in conversations with women. Interruptions are breaches of the turn-taking system. Ideally, in a two-party conversation in some Western speech communities (including the speech community examined herein), Speaker A takes a turn, and at a relevant transition place (e.g., at the end of a sentence, clause, phrase, or word), Speaker B begins a turn, creating the conversational sequence ABABAB. Interruptions, then, are violations of a right (and an obligation) to speak. When Speaker B interrupts Speaker A, Speaker B violates the turn-taking system because Speaker A loses a turn to speak. Speech is interruptive when the next speaker breaks off the current speaker's turn at a nonrelevant transition place, within the boundary of a sentence, clause, phrase, or word. That is, interruptions occur at points where the current speaker does not complete a turn, whether the turn consists of a sentence, a clause, a phrase, or a one-word construction:

(1) *A:* I decided not to—

   B: Don't start **that** again.

In example (1), Speaker A begins a rightful turn yet does not complete that turn because of an interruption within a sentence boundary produced by Speaker B. Specter interrupts Hill in the following interchange:

(2) *Hill:* And I'm not sure what all that summarizes, but his sexual prowess, his sexual preferences could have—

   Specter: Which line are you referring to, Professor?

Example (2) qualifies as an interruption because Specter denies Hill a legitimate turn, breaking off her sentence before its completion.

Table 1 records the instances of interruptions in the first round of the Hill-Specter conversational interchange. Out of a total of thirteen interruptions, Hill interrupts Specter 69 percent of the time (nine times), while Specter interrupts Hill 31 percent of the time (four times). For example (see explanations of transcription notations at the end of this essay):

(3) *Specter:* "So then—
   Hill: I was very passive in the conversation.
(4) *Specter:* Well, let me—
   Hill: I don't understand who said what from that quotation.
(5) *Hill:* And at some point there might have been a conversation about **what might happen**. But—"
   Specter: Have been?

Table 1. Interruptions: Interchange 1

Hill	69% (9)
Specter	31% (4)
Total	100% (13)

During the first interchange, Hill violates the turn-taking system by cutting off Specter's obligated turn more times than would be expected. The findings here, in fact, reverse those reported in earlier studies. The present results suggest that Hill uses a more powerful speech style than Specter because of the greater occurrence of interruptions.

The distribution of interruptions for the second conversational interchange are presented in Table 2. Hill does all the interrupting (two times). Specter attempts to interrupt Hill's turn at two different points but fails in both attempts because Hill does not relinquish the floor. For example (see explanations of transcription notations at the end of this essay):

(6)   *Hill:*   "So I did do that in order to protect myself (.) but I did not write down any of the $=$"

     Specter: Well :::

     Hill: comments or conversations.

Example (6) would have qualified as an interruption had Hill's turn been cut off by Specter, yet in this exchange Hill does not stop speaking. She does not allow Specter's attempt to seize a turn to prevent her from completing a rightful turn. Specter begins a turn at a nonrelevant transition place, as is typical of interruptive speech. Instead of cutting off Hill's speech, however, Specter overlaps her turn, stopping apparently when he realizes that Hill will not relinquish her turn. Overlaps, in the present context, are viewed as attempted interruptions, interruptions that fail. The next speaker (Specter in this instance) begins speaking at the same time as the current speaker (Hill); the current speaker does not become silenced by the simultaneous speech but continues until her turn is completed. Thus, Specter's lack of interruptions during the second conversational interaction with Hill seems to be explained by Hill's refusal to allow him to usurp a turn.

The results from the second conversational interchange, then, manifest the same findings as those from the first set of data: Hill uses the powerful mode of speech. By combining the results from both sets of data, the latter point can be seen more clearly (see Table 3).

Out of fifteen instances of interruptions, Hill produced 73 percent (11); Specter produced 27 percent (4).

Table 2. Interruptions: Interchange 2

Hill	100% (2)
Specter	0% (0)
Total	100% (2)

Table 3. Total Instances of Interruptions

Hill	73% (11)
Specter	27% (4)
Total	100% (15)

The findings for both conversational interchanges dramatically contrast with previous findings on female-male conversations among European Americans. Hill does not use speech behavior characterized as "women's style"; her speech reveals not weakness but power, as measured by the greater occurrences of interruptions. These interruptions evince power in that the next speaker (Hill) takes over turns rightfully belonging to the current speaker (Specter). Hill infringes on Specter's right to finish a turn twice as many times as he violates her turn. Why does Hill use the more powerful style? Why do the present findings differ from previous ones?

One key area to examine for possible explanations is the intersection of language, gender, and race. Research conducted to date has not fully considered the impact of gender and race on language when the women are African Americans.[2] One way to illuminate this intersection of gender, race, and language is by examining two cultural habits, or "carryovers": the code of feminine politeness and agonistic behavior.

The code of feminine politeness is the implicit and explicit rules passed on to women in U.S. society concerning appropriate and inappropriate behavior. This code represents one form of women's socialization. During the eighteenth century, the code of feminine politeness, referred to as the "cult of true womanhood" or the "cult of the lady," decreed that true women were domestic, pious, pure, and submissive. Many women, aspiring to a new middle class, sought to show that they were true, moral women by upholding the cult idea. "A woman's place is in the home" became the modus vivendi during this time, since women of middle-class status who had formerly contributed to the family economy and single "Puritan girls" who had worked in factories dropped out of the labor force, giving more credence to serving as the family homemaker and family teacher of moral and social behavior (Giddings 1984).

This socializing phenomenon differs within women's speech communities, whereas there is a general assumption that the code is the same. One example of differences in the code of feminine politeness can be seen in the cult of true womanhood. African American women, during this time period, were obligated to work outside the home. Thus, the code of feminine politeness for African American women directly contrasted the Victorian ethic of domesticity. These women were not viewed as true

213

women, since domesticity eluded their grasp. In response to such exclusion, African American women created their own code. Of course, some overlap in the code exists across women's speech communities, regardless of ethnicity or race, since common women's experiences exist because of U.S. exigencies. For European American women, in general, the code dictates concealing true feelings and thoughts from those in power; in this sense, politeness remains uppermost in interactions between European Americans. In verbal interactions, politeness remains a central modus vivendi, because European American women have been socialized to wait their turn to speak and not to interrupt or violate another person's turn.

Among African American women, however, politeness norms differ. African American women appear to learn, at some point, how to tread the nebulous line between being polite and being assertive. Although the reproof, or its equivalent, "Don't be so womanish" is heard in many African American households, when African American females reach an appropriate age, they are expected to take on "womanish" ways. One mark of attaining womanhood is knowing when to be polite and when to assert oneself. This aspect of African American women's code of feminine politeness is passed on verbally or learned through nonverbal behavior.

This variant code of feminine politeness can be gleaned also, from Stanback's exegetical discussion of language and "black woman's place" (1985b). In explaining results from her study showing African American middle-class women using "smart talk" in conversation with African American middle-class men, Stanback posits such usage as stemming from the different spheres of existence for African and European American women. Having emerged within a social structure that required them to work double shifts—domestic (inside the home) and public (outside the home), unlike the single domestic shift of European American women—African American women learned and exerted assertiveness. This assertive verbal behavior reflected their real-world position and continues to do so. Because of the social structure of the United States, African American women have learned to be assertive and pass that characteristic on to succeeding generations via verbal and nonverbal behavior. The code of feminine politeness for African American women, then, teaches politeness as well as assertiveness.

Fannie Lou Hamer, whom Malcolm X described in 1964 as "the country's No. 1 freedom-fighting woman" (Mills 1993, p. 16), is one of many African American women who have exuded the African American women's code of politeness. She was daringly assertive, resilient, persistent, and outspoken. She defied Mississippi law and lynchings in order to become a registered voter. Even though she was arrested after attending a civil rights meeting and permanently injured in a jailhouse beating, Hamer became even more entrenched in the civil rights movement. She worked with college students in the 1964 Mississippi Summer Project and appeared on national television during the Democratic National Convention later that summer, appealing to a credentials committee to seat the Mississippi Freedom Democratic Party, of which she was a delegate. Her appeal was so moving, according to one reviewer, that Hamer "scared LBJ" (Mills 1993) into deceptive action. He called an impromptu news conference to deflect attention away from Hamer's evocative and emotive speech.

As an African American woman socialized in African American women's code of feminine politeness, Hill may interrupt Specter more often than he interrupts her because of the learned assertive behavior. The fact that Hill interrupts at all suggests boldness and self-confidence. Her conversational pattern indicates that she possessed enough assertiveness to take extra turns at talking.

Agonistic behavior, the second cultural habit, is behavior of struggle. It may provide an additional explanation for these results. Springing from its orality, African American culture displays a tradition of language usage that is agonistic, arising naturally out of being human. According to Ong (1982), when the human life-world is central, a natural consequence is to focus attention on human interactions, one of which is struggle. Within African American oral culture, language is used to display struggle, to engage listeners in a game of verbal and intellectual combat. Agonistic behavior is evident in the dozens, prayers, sermons, and toasts, even in written language (see Hughes and Bontemps 1958; Smitherman 1977; Troutman-Robinson 1989). Struggle takes place, for example, in playing the dozens, whereby agonists aim to win a verbal duel by creating the most insulting, humorous, spontaneous comments about the agonists' relatives, especially their mothers.

Agonistic behavior provides another avenue of learned assertiveness for African American women. If a group of people is engaged in a life-world of struggle in which winning is essential, boldness and an ability to defend oneself emerge as possible by products of that life-world. Particularly in verbal behavior, winning for African Americans has traditionally been key, as evidenced in playing the dozens (although, of course, winning is not always the end product). From this striving to cap or top verbal events, this cultural group learns and exudes confidence and boldness, traversing age and gender.

Research on the language of African Americans by sociolinguists has focused on male subjects, who have demonstrated their consummate skill as verbal artists. As typically associated with African American male Black English speakers, Hill, too, engages in verbal and intellectual combat. She uses a poised, calm style, which is not antithetical to verbal combat, although it does differ from the style of verbal combat described for African American male Black English speakers.[3] In the context of the Senate hearings, a calm, formal style is most appropriate, especially when those hearings become the "glue" of U.S. social and political attention to a nationally televised event. Hill's style shows both cultural preferences discussed above: politeness and assertiveness as well as agonistic behavior.

(7) *Specter:* I would press you on that (.) Professor Hill (.) in this context.

Hill: Uh-huh.

Specter: You've specified with some specificity about what happened ten years ago.

Hill: Uh-huh

Specter: I would ask you to press your recollection as to what happened within the last month."

Hill: (Z) And I have done that, Senator. And I don't recall that comment. I do recall that there might have been some suggestion that if the FBI did the investigation (.) that the Senate might get involved (.) that there may be (.) that a number of things might occur. But I really (.) I have to be honest with you (.) I cannot verify the statement that you are asking me to verify. There is not really more that I can tell you on that.

Specter: (Z) Well (.) when you say a number of things might occur, what sort of things?

Hill: May—may I just add this one thing?

Hill and Specter engage in battle here. Specter spews fighting words ("I would press you on that"), and Hill latches his turn, by allowing little or no gap between the end of Specter's turn and the beginning of her turn. Specter's words "press you" are explicitly confrontational. The perlocutionary force of those words (the effect on the listener) could be that of intimidation or trepidation. For Hill, however, the perlocutionary force is neither of those possibilities. Instead, her tone is calm and polite; she seems little affected by Specter's fighting words, tying in a minimal response during Specter's breath pauses. Her words, though not her temper, flare after Specter charges forward, pressing Hill's recollection: "I would ask you to press your recollection as to what happened within the last month." Hill responds with the retaliatory words "And I have done that. . . . And I don't recall that comment." She ends this turn at speaking with a seemingly capping sentence: "There is not really more that I can tell you on that." Hill asserts her position unhesitantly, retaining a polite

216

tone throughout her turn. She does not embed her comment in an alleg-edly weak, tentative style. For example, she does not say, "I think that I have done that" or "Haven't I done that?" or "I have sorta done that." She does not mitigate her response but uses direct assertions: "I have done that . . . I don't recall that . . . I cannot verify . . . There is not really more . . ." The use of "really" in this last assertion may be used as a hedge or may hold its denotative meaning of *truly*. In example (7), then, Hill's style is polite and assertive. She appears to win this pressing con-versational interchange.

Hill's apparent closure to the line of questioning causes Specter to pause briefly, yet he figures out a point of contention in the words "a number of things might occur" and fires back: "Well, when you say a number of things might occur, what sort of things?" The interesting point here is that Hill moves onto another focus, leaving Specter's question unanswered. She not only initiates a new direction for the conversation, but she also overlaps Specter's turn, using a speech act (taking a turn while simultaneously asking for or giving indication for a new focus in the discussion) that establishes a stronger conversational style for Hill.

Earlier research has focused on an error overlap, which is one type of simultaneous speech occurring because of a misanalysis of the end of the current speaker's turn. Error overlaps occur within the boundary of the last word of the current speaker's turn and are both permissible and excusable. For example:

(8) *Specter:* Well (.) you **did** teach civil rights law.

Hill: I did at one point.

In example (8), Hill produces an error overlap. She begins her turn si-multaneously with Specter's last word, "law." This error overlap does not violate the turn-taking system; the turn begins a little early because of an error in Hill's analyzing the end of Specter's turn.

The overlap produced by Hill in example (7) differs from the error overlap in example (8) because the former occurs before the last word. Hill begins a turn before a legitimate transition place in example (7): "May I just add this one thing?" She begins a turn earlier than the turn-taking system describes; she does not err in speaking but seems to usurp a turn. In this intentional overlap, where Hill seems to begin a turn in-tentionally sooner than the turn-taking system establishes, she shows as-sertiveness in taking the discussion into a new direction, exuding power in her conversational style.

Two more examples help to illustrate Hill's polite-assertive and agonistic style further.

(9) *Specter:* What's the relevancy as to when you got the assignment and how fast you made it for a new employer?

    Hill: [Forceful tone] Because it goes to whether or not I was slow in turning around a work product in a very fast-paced job situation.

(10) *Specter:* (Z) Professor Hill (.) as you know (.) the statute of limitations for filing a case on sexual harassment is 180 days.

    Hill: (Z) Yes.

    Specter: Right?

    Hill: (Z) Yes.

    Specter: (Z) A very short statute of limitations because of the difficulty of someone defending against a charge of sexual harassment. (.) Right?

    Hill: (Z) Well, it is a short turnover time. I'm not quite sure exactly why it is that short. That is one of the reasons that it is so short.

    Specter: (Z) Well, you're an expert in the field. Delaware State College versus Ricks? (.) 101 Supreme Court Reporter (.) in 1980 (Z) and Johnson v. Railway Express Agency (.) 421 U.S. Reports (.) comment about the short period of limitations because of the difficulty of defending against a charge of sexual harassment.

    Hill: (Z) But I don't believe **either** of those cases say that that's the **only** reason. [Strong, forceful tone] **And let me clarify something**. I consider myself to be an expert in contracts and commercial law (.) not an expert in the field of sexual harassment or EEO law. I do—I don't even teach in that area anymore.

Example (9) immediately precedes example (10) in the Hill-Specter speech exchange. Example (9), besides showing another intentional overlap, demonstrates a firm, assertive, and irrefuted response given by Hill, reminiscent of a Fannie Lou Hamer style.

As in example (7), Hill in example (9) shows a more powerful conversational style than Specter through the use of the intentional overlap. Again, she and Specter speak simultaneously (at the latch mark). After receiving and understanding the primary content of Specter's turn, beginning with "What's the relevancy" up to "and how fast you made it," Hill begins a turn ("Because it goes to whether or not . . ."), overlapping Specter's phrase "for a new employer." By speaking at this point in the exchange, Hill violates the turn-taking system by taking a turn at conversation before a legitimate transition place. She appears to begin a turn intentionally before her prescribed turn, showing assertiveness once again.

The response given by Hill in example (9) seems unassailable; Specter, in example (10), moves on to another line of inquiry. He lacks an apt retort and thus must move on to another topic. Hill's response comes forth smoothly, confidently, leaving Specter to pause, perhaps to figure out his next strategy. He appears to be in a position very similar to that of a person who has just lost a bout in an argument. The loser must pause, reflect, and figure out a next move. Hill caps or tops the verbal duel in examples (9), (10) (the full exchange of which does not appear above because of its length), (11), and others, by providing an apposite, unassailable retort, which is similar to the agonistic behavior used in playing the dozens. She engages in struggle and wins, displaying acuity in repartee. See also example (11) below.

In example (10), Hill caps the exchange through the use of additional manifestations of agonistic behavior. As in example (9), she shows skill in repartee. Specter begins the exchange in example (10) by pursuing questions that allude to the disparity between the seriousness of the sexual harassment charge and the amount of time that has lapsed (almost a decade) before any charge has been brought forth against Thomas. Although Specter does not overtly reveal this disparity intent, his line of questioning divulges his strategy. He begins this new topic by attempting to corner Hill on being cognizant of the brief period of time for which a sexual harassment case can be filed because of the difficulty of disproving charges of sexual harassment. Specter's strategy in projecting Hill as discreditable seems to be: (a) establish Hill's knowledge of the sexual harassment statute of limitations based on her prior experience in such court cases; (b) establish that the statute of limitations is short; (c) connect the short statute of limitations to the difficulty of defending against a charge of sexual harassment. If Hill agrees to each of the premises in Specter's syllogistic reasoning, she will implicitly discredit herself:

"As you know," a person has 180 days to file a sexual harassment charge. (major premise)

This time period is short because of the difficult defense against a sexual harassment charge. (minor premise)

Therefore, since you know that a person typically has a short amount of time (180 days) to file a sexual harassment

charge and you know that the short time period is because
of the difficulty in defending the case, why would you raise
a charge of sexual harassment when you know about the
difficulty Thomas would have in defending himself and you
know that the time limit has long passed? (conclusion)

Specter, however, does not succeed in creating a spurious view of
Hill. First, Hill does not accept the minor premise in Specter's syllogism,
even though she accepts the major premise: "Well, it is a short turnover
time. I'm not quite sure exactly why it is that short. That is one of the
reasons that it is so short." Second, the spurious creation fails because
Hill reinforces her rejection of the minor premise—"But I don't believe
either of those cases say that that's the **only** reason"—and she corrects
Specter's erroneous speculation: "**And let me clarify something**. I consider myself to be an expert in contracts and commercial law, not an
expert in the field of sexual harassment or EEO law." Hill's rejection of
the minor premise, then, does not allow the conclusion to be drawn. In
this way, Specter's attempt to create a falsified view of Hill's testimony
fails.

Struggle becomes apparent in example (11). Hill uses an assertive
tone as one piece of weaponry in the duel. At various points, she uses
increased emphasis as a verbal weapon, yet she continues to be poised,
in control of high emotions. Intellectually, she caps this interchange by
"setting the record straight":

220

(11) *Specter:*   (?) Well (.) I'll repeat the question again. Was there
any substance in Ms. Berry's **flat** statement that (.)
quote (.) Ms. Hill was disappointed and frustrated
that Mr. Thomas did not show any sexual interest
in her?

      Hill: (Z) No (.) there is not. There is no substance to
that. He did show interest and I've explained to you
how he did show that interest. (.) Now (.) she was
not aware of that. If you're asking me (.) could she
have made that statement. (.) She could have made
the statement if she wasn't aware of it. (.) But she
wasn't aware of everything that happened.

Again, Hill uses a firm tone of voice; she shows confidence in answering the posed question. That answer shows Hill's skill and cleverness
in her reply and in her ability to analyze language. The answer is direct
and relevant, and it exposes the weakness of Specter's question. Hill's
answer caps this interchange; her retort is clever, keen, and thorough,
leaving Specter at a loss for an appropriate response.

In example (11), Specter begins the sparring by stressing the word "*flat*," which seems to denote the meaning of *unequivocal* for Specter. Next, he begins the spar by introducing a cutting remark: "Ms. Hill was disappointed and frustrated that Mr. Thomas did not show sexual interest in her." Hill remains poised, answering Specter's question, moving on to the penetrating portion of the reply. Hill defeats Specter's attempt to win this part of the questioning by exposing the weakness of the Berry testimony. In uttering, "Now, she was not aware of that," Hill communicates that Berry was not aware that Thomas showed sexual interest in Hill; therefore, there is no substance to Berry's statement. This retort sufficiently shows the weakness of Berry's statement. The deductive syllogism does not hold true if one of its parts is not true:

Hill was disappointed and frustrated. (major premise)

Thomas did not show any sexual interest in her. (minor premise)

This reason helps explain why she would falsely make charges against Thomas. (conclusion)

Hill, then, rejects the minor premise, causing the testimony (the syllogistic argument) to fall apart.

She does not rest with this response yet moves on to the capping segment of the interchange. Hill provides Specter with a more reasonable question, which, she alludes, could have been the intent of his original question ("If you're asking me, could she have made that statement . . .") and proceeds to answer the question: "She could have made the statement if she wasn't aware of it." The semantics of this latter response shows Hill's intellectual alertness, her acumen in verbal combat. Hill acknowledges that Berry could have made the statement (in this sense recognizing possibility) particularly if she wasn't aware of the sexual interest. Besides, she adds, Berry wasn't aware of everything that happened in that job setting. These last two statements show Hill's skill in using language. She displays awareness of nuances of meaning in words, and she can deliver the final cutting line, which provides closure to the line of questioning. Specter has no vehicle of recourse, and Hill caps the conversational interchange.

In general, then, Hill's conversational style, which may be culturally toned with elements of assertive and agonistic behavior and which may be culturally passed on to succeeding generations of African Americans, may explain why she interrupts Specter's turns at speaking more than he interrupts hers.

Conclusion

In the verbal struggle with Specter, it is possible that Hill asserts more turns at speaking; that is, she interrupts more, thus uses a more powerful conversational style, because of culturally learned behavior. In order to win, she must actively assert her position and maintain it.

Overall, the data support the notion that the tongue *is* mightier than the sword. Hill used an assertive, confident, swift conversational style which may be characteristic of the larger speech community of African American women. In this study, power and dominance were transmuted to the African American woman, perhaps, as Stanback (1985b) has posited, because of historically and socially constructed roles of working in two spheres, domestic and public.[4]

The intuition of some African American female researchers (Etter-Lewis 1991, Nelson 1990, Smitherman-Donaldson and Griffin 1988, and Stanback 1985a and b) is that the linguistic patterns of African American women, because of the social construction of their reality, exist on a different semantic and pragmatic level of analysis. African American women have learned well that only the strong survive; their language, in turn, contains social manifestations of strong language. In light of the weak version of the Sapir-Whorf hypothesis, the findings in this study may not be totally unreasonable or surprising.

222

Transcription Notations

—   A dash indicates that speech was interrupted.

(.)   A period in parentheses marks a short silence.

(Z)   A Z in parentheses shows that latching occurs; little or no gap occurs between the end of the current speaker's turn and the beginning of the next speaker's turn.

=   An equals sign shows that there was no silence or pause discernible within one speaker's utterances.

.   A period indicates falling intonation.

?   A question mark indicates rising intonation.

bold   Boldfaced letters show emphasis, conveyed by either increased volume or pitch change.

:::   Colons mark the lengthening of the sound they follow.

[ ]   Brackets relay transcriber comments, not transcribed text.

Notes

1. All language used by all men is not powerful, of course. "Men's language" refers to the language of middle- and upper-class European American males.
2. The works of Stanback (1985a and b), Etter-Lewis (1990a; 1991), and Goodwin (1990) have contributed significantly to building a framework for when and where African

American females enter into the construction of women's language. Additional research is needed into the verbal behavior of African American females because the investigation of actual behavior will confirm or reject the hypothesis that a distinct "Black woman's language" exists and the hypothesis that African American women and female adolescents use the same linguistic patterns.
3. Although Hill does not use the same verbal style as many African American male Black English speakers, this finding does not suggest that African American women do not signify or play the dozens.
4. This latter point does not stem from nor find support in the claim of an African American matriarchy.

References

Etter-Lewis, Gwendolyn. "The Exceptions of the Exceptions: African-American Women in Higher Education." In *My Soul Is My Own*. New York: Routledge, 1993.

Etter-Lewis, Gwendolyn. "Voices from Within: Intertextuality in African-American Women's Oral Narratives." In *My Soul Is My Own*. New York: Routledge, 1993.

Etter-Lewis, Gwendolyn. "Black Women's Life Stories: Reclaiming Self in Narrative Texts." In Sherna Berger Gluck and Daphne Patai, eds., *Women's Words: The Feminist Practice of Oral History*. New York: Routledge, 1991.

Giddings, Paula. *When and Where I Enter: The Impact of Black Women on Race and Sex in America*. New York: William Morrow, 1984.

Goodwin, Majorie Harness. *He-Said-She-Said: Talk as Social Organization Among Black Children*. Bloomington: Indiana University Press, 1990.

Hughes, Langston, and Arna Bontemps, eds. *The Book of Negro Folklore*. New York: Dodd, Mead, 1958.

Lakoff, Robin. *Talking Power: The Politics of Language in Our Lives*. New York: Basic Books, 1990.

Mills, Nicolaus. "She Scared LBJ." *New York Times Book Review*. 1993, p. 16.

Nelson, L. "Co-construction in the Oral Life Narratives of African American Women." Unpublished paper, 1990.

Ong, Walter J. *Orality and Literacy: The Technologizing of the Word*. New York: Methuen, 1982.

Sacks, Harvey, Emanuel Schegloff, and Gail Jefferson. "A Simplest Systematics for the Organization of Turn-taking for Conversation." *Language* 50 (1974): 696–735.

Smitherman-Donaldson, Geneva, and Roslyn E. Griffin. "African American Women and the Challenge of New Realities." Paper given at Women and Power Conference, Dubrovnik, Yugoslavia, 1988.

Stanback, Marsha Houston. "Black Women's Talk Across Cultures." Paper presented to the Speech Communication Association, 1985a.

Stanback, Marsha Houston. "Language and Black Woman's Place: Evidence from the Black Middle Class." In P. A. Treichler et al., eds., *For Alma Mater: Theory and Practice in Feminist Scholarship*. Chicago: University of Illinois Press, 1985b.

Troutman-Robinson, Denise. "The Elements of Call and Response in Alice Childress' *Like One of the Family*." *Middle Atlantic Writers Association Review* 4, no. 1 (June 1989).

Zimmerman, Don, and Candace West. "Sex Roles, Interruptions and Silences in Conversation." In Thorne and Henley, eds., *Language and Sex: Difference and Dominance*. Rowley, Mass.: Newbury House, 1975, pp. 105–29.

Testifyin, Sermonizin, and Signifyin: Anita Hill, Clarence Thomas, and the African American Verbal Tradition

GENEVA SMITHERMAN

Jerene and Darlene come help me with the business . . . Plus, Darlene trying to teach me how to talk. She say US not so hot . . . peoples think you dumb. What I care? I ast. I'm happy. But she say I feel more happier talking like she talk . . . Every time I say something the way I say it, she correct me until I say it some other way. Pretty soon it feel like I can't think. My mind run up on a thought, git confuse, run back and sort of lay down . . . Bring me a bunch of books. Whitefolks all over them, talking bout apples and dogs. What I care bout dogs? . . . But I let Darlene worry on. Sometimes I think bout the apples and the dogs, sometimes I don't. Look like to me only a fool would want you to talk in a way that feel peculiar to your mind.

224

—Celie in Alice Walker's Pulitzer
Prize novel, *The Color Purple*, 1982

Speaking the Truth to the People

Several explanations have been advanced to account for the Anita Hill-Clarence Thomas phenomenon, both in terms of the conduct of the Thomas hearings themselves and in terms of public reaction to the hearings and the controversy. Such theories have ranged from the argument that U.S. senators lack sensitivity to and understanding of the dynamics of sexual harassment (they just don't get it); to the issue of Hill's and Thomas's credibility; to a recognition of the continuing cataclysmic significance of race over gender (it's better to be a sexist than a racist); to the ludicrous notion advanced by Orlando Patterson (1991) that Thomas was simply engaging in a "down-home style of courting" toward Hill. Attention has focused on the issue of sexual exploitation, the historical facts surrounding the Hill-Thomas relationship, and legal and social arguments about how to operationalize the construct of sexual harassment. For the African American community, however, the Hill-Thomas phenomenon raises issues far beyond the immediate problematic of sexual harassment in the workplace. This essay seeks to advance our understanding of these broader implications from the vantage point of the African American Verbal Tradition.

The rhetorical situation created by the Hill-Thomas conflict represents an excellent case study for revisiting the linguistics of the "Talented Tenth" (see Woodson 1925; Smith 1969; Smitherman and Daniel 1979). As articulated by W. E. B. Du Bois (1903), the notion of a Black talented tenth refers to the strategy for creating a leadership class by targeting societal resources to the development of the upper 10 percent of the community. This group of African Americans would then struggle for the uplift and betterment of the remaining 90 percent. Although their leadership has often gone unheralded, both as activists and as public spokespersons among the Talented Tenth, African American women have played a significant historical role in the Black struggle. At the dawning of the twenty-first century, with victory still on the distant horizon, African American women face a rhetorical dilemma in our continuing struggle to be free. As even greater numbers of African American women enter positions of influence and leadership, there is a critical need to reclaim a rhetorically effective voice that can, as Margaret Walker Alexander said long ago, "speak the truth to the people." The truth has to be spoken in a language that the people understand—with both their heads and their hearts. As the Greek story goes, when Demosthenes spoke, the people applauded, but when Pericles spoke, they marched. The people's response is a function of the speaker's adaptation of her language to the people. This is so because language is not mere words; nor can mere words, as they occur in conversation, dialogue, and speeches, be dismissed as just semantics. Rather, language plays a dominant—if not the dominant—role in the social construction of reality. Let us review the role of language in society generally and in African American society in particular.

225

Berger and Luckmann (1966) contend that language constitutes the most important content and instrument of socialization. Extending their paradigm, I posit that reality is not merely socially but also sociolinguistically constructed (Smitherman 1989). Social experience and even experience of physical, objective phenomena are filtered, apprehended, codified, and conveyed via some linguistic shape. This linguistic form exists in a dialectical relationship with cognition and social behavior. While Humboldtian (1963 [1810]) linguists and most Whorfians (1956 [1941]) perhaps overstate the case for language as the determiner of thought, consciousness, and behavior, language does play a dominant role in the formation of ideology and consciousness and in race, gender, and class relations—and in the sociolinguistic case study under examination here.

Language operates on the subtle, subliminal level, thus rendering it all the more effective in the sociolinguistic construction of reality. In U.S. popular culture, the number thirteen is considered bad luck, and so in most luxury hotels, guests sleep soundly in two-hundred-dollar rooms located on the fourteenth floor because the thirteenth floor has been sociolinguistically constructed out of existence. Manipulation of the sociolinguistic construction of reality by this country's power elites results in serious acts of linguistic trickeration, or what Lutz (1987) and other scholars refer to as "doublespeak." In countries the United States supports, the State Department decided that the term "killing" would be replaced with "unlawful or arbitrary deprivation of life"; nuclear strategists refer to the destruction of entire cities as "countervalue attacks"; and Bush and his military leaders made the Persian Gulf War palatable to U.S. citizens with such terms as "security review" to refer to the censorship of news reports and "collateral damage" to refer to civilians killed or wounded by "smart bombs" that were "servicing the target" (Committee on Public Doublespeak 1992).

Yet verbal operations on social reality can lead to progressive constructions. J. T. and Sam, two African American assembly-line workers at Detroit's old Jefferson Avenue Chrysler automobile plant extend the semantic space surrounding the word "nigger," going beyond a racial epithet to encompass the historical oppression of African slaves and the exploitation of any worker. They are talking about the large number of Vietnamese—"boat people," as many Americans derisively refer to them—who had sought refuge in the United States:

226

> *J.T.:* The Vietnam who didn't git off the boat, they was gon be the new nigguhs—for the Whiteys and us.

> *Sam:* Well, I wish they hadda come on out there to work, cause I'm tired of being the nigguh.
>
> (Smitherman 1976)

It isn't only in the semantic realm but also in syntax, discourse structures, speech acts, and verbal registers of communication that we can witness the subtle impact of language in constructing reality. Syntax can code a worldview. Power elites, aided by the media, make objects into subjects and use the passive voice, allowing those who commit an act to go unnamed. For example, the newspaper headline "Rioting Blacks Shot Dead" reverses the reality of who does what to whom and makes the individuals killed seem responsible for their own deaths. Making bad linguistic matters worse, everyday people often adopt these pernicious uses of language as their linguistic role models. For example, one of my students wrote, "The invasion of Grenada was officially approved," thereby permitting the agent, President Reagan, to escape unnoticed.

Consider the following interaction between a receptionist and one of her bosses in the outer office of a Black corporate setting:

Receptionist: Good morning, Mr. Jones.

   Mr. Jones: What's happenin', baby?

(Smitherman, in progress)

The receptionist, a Black woman, has used for her greeting the verbal register expected of a receptionist in a formal business setting. Her boss, a Black man, not only responds in Black English Vernacular (BEV) but also uses a BEV informal, socially intimate style, rather than a formal BEV greeting pattern. To be sure, in this country, the sociolinguistic rules allow the superior in a communication interaction to dictate the verbal styles and registers used in that interaction. So perhaps Mr. Jones, as the boss, is asserting his right to redefine this formal situation and recast it into an informal, more comfortable linguistic zone. Perhaps he wants to do so in the interest of cutting through the coldness and impersonality of the corporate world (in this instance, the Black corporate world). All of which he might have done by using the receptionist's first name, for instance, coupled with a more conversational form of the Language of Wider Communication—"Hello, [or Hi], how you doin' today, Barbara?" However, Mr. Jones code-switches to BEV. This asymmetrical ("down-home"?) greeting pattern is viewed by the receptionist as a sign of disrespect. In fact, however subliminal, Mr. Jones's greeting serves as an act of subordination, in essence, sociolinguistically putting the receptionist in her place, in terms of both class and gender. As she put it, "It's like he was saying, 'Since you are only a receptionist and a woman, I can talk to you any kind of way.'" (This interaction took place while I was waiting to see another of the corporate bosses, who had hired me as a consultant because the business was experiencing communication problems between staff and management!)

227

While African and European Americans share similar language norms and functions, there is an added dimension to the sociolinguistic condition of African Americans: the linguistic-cultural clash between the African American Verbal Tradition and that of European Americans. I am not simply referring to that frequently oversimplified issue about whether Black-English-speaking students should be taught "standard English." (For the record, I don't know of anybody—linguist or otherwise—who says they should *not*; the issue is how, when, and for what purposes such students should be taught "*the* standard.") I am talking about something more fundamental than the grammar of BEV—such as "She be looking good"—or the Black English pronunciation of "thing" as "thang." The African American Verbal Tradition clashes with the European American tradition because there are different—and, yes, contradictory—cultural assumptions about what constitutes appropriate discourse, rhetorical strategies, and styles of speaking. While the African American linguistic style has been described as passionate, emotional, and "hot" and the European as objective, detached, and "cold," we are seriously oversimplifying if we assert that one tradition is superior. What is not an oversimplification, however, is that African and European Americans have different attitudes about and responses to a speaker depending on whether she uses one style or the other.

The foregoing discussion is the vantage point from which this essay compares the linguistic styles of Anita Hill and Clarence Thomas in phase two of the Thomas confirmation hearings. AVT refers to the African American Verbal Tradition; LWC will refer to the Language of Wider Communication, that is, a language that facilitates communication beyond one's own speech community, i.e., in this country, European American "standard English." My thesis is that Hill used LWC, whereas Thomas used AVT, and that these contrasting styles had differential impact on African Americans.

While the language of the Chrysler workers and Mr. Jones, quoted above, illustrates obvious examples of BEV within the AVT, the rhetorical strategies and discourse modes of the AVT are more subtle. And they are powerful persuasive devices that can be used by a Supreme Court justice without the stigma generally attached to Black "slang" or BEV grammatical patterns. We shall examine four dimensions of the AVT that Thomas employed: signification, personalization, tonal semantics, and sermonic tone.

228

Signification

Signification, or signifyin', is the verbal art of ceremonial combativeness in which one person puts down, talks about, "signifies on" someone or on something someone has said. Also referred to as "joanin'," "cappin'," "soundin'," and currently "dissin'," this rhetorical modality is characterized by indirection, humor, exploitation of the unexpected, and quick verbal repartee. Sometimes done for just plain fun, signifyin' is also a sociolinguistic corrective employed to drive home a serious message without preaching or lecturing. For example, Malcolm X once began a speech this way: "Mr. Moderator, Brother Lomax, brothers and sisters, friends and enemies: I just can't believe everyone in here is a friend, and I don't want to leave anybody out." Without a direct frontal attack, Malcolm neatly put down his known enemies as well as those traitors in the all-Black audience—the "smiling faces" who sometimes "lie" (Smitherman 1986).

As various scholars have noted (e.g., Hurston 1935; Mitchell-Kernan 1972; Gates 1988), Signification has a long, honorable history in the Black experience and is strongly rooted in the African American Verbal Tradition. Black preachers are and must be adept signifiers. For example, one big-city preacher in a broadcast church service used extended signifyin' to dis his sacred and secular competition in the "blessing business," the business of dispensing advice, prayers, fortune-telling, symbolic artifacts, or other types of "mojo" that will help people achieve their desired goals. Such pretenders, so this preacher contended, are unqualified, either because they aren't successful themselves or because their "magic" demands too great an investment, such as traveling long distances or large financial donations. Simultaneously, the preacher is promoting and marketing his own power—his "thang" (also requiring a donation).

Preacher: I say this thang I got, this thang, yeah this thang, it ain' like what the other folks telling you 'bout.

Congregation: Yeah! Yeah! Tell about it! Say so! You on the case!

Preacher: This thang will make a way outta no way, and, listen to me church, you ain't got to go no long way to git it, not *my* thang.

Congregation: Yessuh! I hear you!

Preacher: You ain' got to catch no bus, you ain' got to fly no airplane, go no long ways, just come on over here and git this thang and help yo'self.

Congregation: Say the word! Talk about it!

Preacher: You see, like I was sayin', talk is cheap, plenty peoples go 'round sayin' what they gon' do for you and they ain' got nothin theyself.

Congregation: Look out now! Well, come on out wit it! Un-huh, un-huh!

Preacher: I say, what I look like askin' you to pray for me and you ain' got a pot nor a window!

Congregation: Watch yo'self, Doc! You gon' tell it in a minute! Go 'head, go 'head!

Preacher: Y'all know what uhm talkin' 'bout that's a word my grandmomma used to say. Come on over here to 14873 Puritan and git my thang!

(Smitherman 1986, p. 125)

229

Locating his rhetorical posture squarely in this tradition, Thomas's speaking style throughout the second phase of his hearings was rife with the verbal aggressiveness, indirection, and repartee of signification. From Giddayup, he comes on with an attitude, big-time, signifyin about the chain of events that have led to the reopening of the confirmation hearings:

> I have experienced the exhilaration of new heights from the
> moment I was called to Kennebunkport by the president to
> have lunch and he nominated me. That was the high point.
> At that time, I was told eye-to-eye that, 'Clarence, you
> made it this far on merit. The rest is going to be politics.'
> And it surely has been.

He concludes his opening statement by putting the Senate Judiciary Committee on defensive notice that racism is the name of this game, and he ain gon play in it, through this Signification: "I am a victim of this process. . . . I will not provide the rope for my own lynching."

Two of Thomas's best signifyin jabs occurred in the exchange between him and Senator Howell Heflin in his second appearance after Hill had testified. After Thomas boldly announced that he hadn't listened to Hill's testimony (which obviously is dumbfounding to Heflin), he and Heflin go at it, with Thomas's signifyin carrying the day:

> *Heflin:* We're trying to get to the bottom of this, and if she is lying, then I think you can help us prove that she was lying.
>
> *Thomas:* Senator, I am incapable of proving the negative. It did not occur.
>
> *Heflin:* Well, if it did not occur, I think you are in a position, certainly, your ability to testify to in effect to try to eliminate it from people's minds.
>
> *Thomas:* Senator, I didn't create it in people's minds.

The clear implication here is that Hill, the Senate Judiciary Committee, the news media, the person who leaked the FBI files, whoever, is responsible for planting this "scurrilous" charge against him in the public mind. So why should he be called on to eliminate it?

In the matter of the leaking of Hill's charges, Thomas gets in another good bit of Signification:

> *Thomas:* This matter . . . was leaked last weekend to the media . . . leaked to national newspapers [creating] a national forum . . . to discuss . . . allegations that should have been resolved in a confidential way.

Heflin: Well, I certainly appreciate your attitude toward leaks. I happen to serve on the Senate Ethics Committee, and it's been a sieve.

Thomas: Well, but it didn't leak on me.

In other words, don't even try it—don't deflect the power of my claim by suggesting that leaking is a general governmental concern; this one is personal, and it's killing me.

Personalization

The oratorical style of the AVT eschews the detachment and (presumed) "objectivity" of Eurocentric discourse. Personalization demands concreteness and specificity, not abstraction and generalization. In fact, there is distrust and suspicion of someone who is too clinical and distances himself or herself from phenomena and events that are under consideration. Do they care? Are they sincere? Well, if "they got religion, they oughtta show some sign." Some Afrocentric psychologists call this demand for personal involvement a "field-dependent" cognitive style (e.g., Wilson 1971; Pasteur and Toldson 1982). The style draws the audience into the arena of conflict; in so doing, the speaker seeks to establish a psychic bond. The theoretical abstract issue is thus brought right down front. Like, what if it was you, homey, how would you feel? Or in Thomas's words: "And how many members of this committee would like to have the same scurrilous, uncorroborated allegations made about him, and . . . then be drawn and dragged before a national forum of this nature . . .?"

Again and again, Thomas posed this same question in different forms. The ultimate personalization occurs when he likens his employees to family and implies that the committee should visualize their own reactions if a family member should turn on them. This exchange takes place with Thomas and Senator Leahy:

Leahy: Spoke of them really basically almost as family, the people that have worked for you . . . correct?

Thomas: Yes . . . Anita Hill came to me through one of my dearest, dearest friends. . . . They are family. My clerks are my family.

Leahy: Well, then, having done all this for Professor Hill and knowing now . . . and hearing her statement under oath, explicit as it was, the statements that you've categorically denied, to use your term, why would she do this?

Thomas: I don't know why family members turn on each other. I don't know why a son or a daughter or brother or sister would write some book that destroys a family.

(Like, you Senators know about that, don't you, like Reagan's daughter writing that book of hers?) Thomas, continuing to go straight for the jugular, signifyin even as he personalizes.

Tonal Semantics

Not only is AVT personalized, but it reflects impassioned language use and is characterized by a high-spirited style of delivery. The speech rhythms reflect emotional intensity. The voice itself, the choice of words, and the pattern of communication is high-energy, passionate, "soulful." Holt (1972) and Kochman (1981) refer to this as "expressive" style; I call it "tonal semantics" (Smitherman 1986). Kochman contends that this is a significant source of black-white communication difference and conflict:

> The black mode . . . is high-keyed: animated, interpersonal, and confrontational. The white mode . . . is relatively low-keyed: dispassionate, impersonal, and non-challenging. The first is characteristic of involvement; it is heated, loud, and generates affect. The second is characteristic of detachment and is cool, quiet, and without affect. (1981, p. 18)

Through emotion-laden words and the rhythmic repetition characteristic of the AVT, Thomas employed his dynamic verbal energy to superb rhetorical effect. The hearings were a "travesty," the charges "scurrilous," full of "sleaze," "trash," and "dirt" from the "sewer" of life. He is "stunned," "hurt," "confused," "abused," in "pain" and "anguish." He is being "pilloried" by this "debilitating," "Kafkaesque" "horror," beginning with "Charges . . . leveled against me from the shadows . . . drug abuse, anti-Semitism, wife beating . . . and now this." Ever since this occurred, Thomas's "days have grown darker," and he, his family, and his friends have endured "enormous pain and great harm." In fact, he asserts, "I have never in my life felt such hurt, such pain, such agony." Finally, he pulls out all the stops: "Yesterday I called my mother. She was confined to her bed, unable to work and unable to stop crying."

In the Tonal Semantics dimension of AVT, there is rhythmic, evocative repetition. This characteristic feature reinforces the high-spirited, emotional, expressive intensity of the Black speaking style. Thomas's rhetoric is shot through with this feature. An extended harangue by his boy, Senator Hatch, sets out the "totally offensive" Long Dong Silver pornographic story that Hill said Thomas discussed with her. Hatch laments the activation of the stereotype about the size of Black men's penises conveyed by the "Long Dong" metaphor, all of which has been used against Thomas. In obvious sympathy with Thomas, Hatch asks him, "What do you think about that?" Thomas replies: "I wasn't harmed by the Klan. I wasn't harmed by the Knights of Camellia. I wasn't harmed by the Aryan race. I wasn't harmed by a racist group. I was harmed by this process."

He continues:

> If someone wanted to block me from the Supreme Court of
> the United States because of my views on the Constitution,
> that's fine. If someone wanted to block me because they
> felt I wasn't qualified, that's fine. If someone wanted to
> block me because they don't like the composition of the
> Court, that's fine. But . . . I would have preferred an
> assassin's bullet to this kind of living hell.

Successive repetitions of key statements and/or phrases, ending with the punch of counterstatement—a classic rhetorical device in AVT. Thomas worked it effectively throughout the hearings. Hatch asks him if he ever thought he'd have to "face scurrilous accusations like those which you have refuted?" Thomas's tonal semantics answer:

233

> I expected it to be bad. I expected to be a sitting duck for
> the interest groups. I expected them to attempt to kill me.
> And yes, I even expected personal attempts on my life. . . .
> I did not expect this circus. I did not expect this charge
> against my name. I expected people to do anything, but not
> this.

Sermonic Tone

As scholars have demonstrated (e.g., Du Bois 1903; Woodson 1921; Mitchell 1970; Lincoln 1990), the Traditional Black Church has had a profound impact and influence on the African American Experience. For example, virtually all Black (male) leaders have come out of the Church— either the Christian or the Muslim, for instance, such as Reverend Jesse Jackson and Minister Louis Farrakhan. Being not simply a religious unit but the center of social life, the Church has influenced the development of AVT. Ordinary statements take on the tone of pronouncements and are given the force of the moral high ground; they are proclaimed with the profundity and moral sobriety of divinely inspired truth. This gives

Black speech its elevated, "fancy talk" quality. Thomas speaks of the "destruction of my integrity" and says that he "would not want to—except being required to here—dignify those allegations with a response." And "God has gotten me through the days since September 25, and he is my judge." (Not you Senators!)

Indeed, with the "help of others and with the help of God," Thomas has been able "to defy poverty, avoid prison, overcome segregation, bigotry, racism, and obtain one of the finest educations available in this country." Yet he has not been able "to overcome this process." Nonetheless, he reminds us that within the Judeo-Christian community of the saved, one can be sustained, as he has been, by "prayers said for my family and me by people I know and people I will never meet, prayers that were heard." (Jesus on the mainline and connected!)

Anita Hill and LWC

In contrast to Thomas's use of AVT, Anita Hill employed LWC. This style is low-keyed, clinical, dispassionate, unemotional. Despite the psychic wounds inflicted on her by Thomas, Hill exhibits no signs of anger, but methodically details his advances.

> His conversations were very vivid. He spoke about acts that he had seen in pornographic films involving such matters as women having sex with animals and films showing group sex or rape scenes. He talked about pornographic materials depicting individuals with large penises or large breasts involved in various sex acts. On several occasions, Thomas told me graphically of his own sexual prowess.

In contrast to Thomas's "scurrilous" allegations, she speaks of "unpleasant matters." Whereas her verbal accusations have visited "agony," "anguish," and "pain" upon him, his sexual verbalisms have only made her "extremely uncomfortable."

Hill remains stoically principled and refuses to personalize her assessment of Thomas, despite his sexual intimidation. She is undaunted by Senator Specter's attempts to rattle her when, for instance, he wonders why, if Thomas were such a bad fellow, did she give a high assessment of him?

> *Specter:* There is a report in the *Kansas City Star* . . . quoting you . . . 'the Clarence Thomas of that period . . . would have made a better judge on the Supreme Court, because he was more open-minded.' Now, how is it that you would have said that . . . considering all of the things you have said that he told you about at the Department of Education and also at EEOC?

234

> *Hill:* That opinion, Senator, was based strictly on his experi-
> ence, his ability to reason; it was not based on personal
> information. . . . I was trying to give as objective an
> opinion as possible . . . as a university professor . . .
> you have some obligation to try to make objective state-
> ments . . . based on his record as a public figure . . .
> not relying on my own private understanding and knowl-
> edge.

Nor does Hill have angry words of denunciation for the conduct and nature of the hearing, as does Thomas. Yet she had struggled to maintain her privacy and would not have come forth if someone hadn't leaked the information she had given in confidence to the FBI. Further, it is clear that *she* is the one on trial, not him; it is she who has been put on the defensive and discounted. Thus, she had every reason to feel as violated by the questioning as Thomas felt. Yet she maintains her objective, une-motional, depersonalized rhetorical stance. Her dialogue with Senator Deconcini is illustrative.

> *Deconcini:* Do you think, now having told your side and re-
> sponded to these questions, that your reputation from
> your standpoint could ever be fully restored?
>
> *Hill:* Not in the minds of many. Never. It will not be.
>
> *Deconcini:* . . . Is the committee more culpable for causing you
> to have to come forward? Is the press more culpable?
> Or is it all just a big bunch of stuff that we've got to
> deal with, and everybody's culpable?
>
> *Hill:* I think it's just the reality, Senator, of this situation,
> the nature of this complaint. And I cannot point my
> finger at any one entity, and say that you are respon-
> sible for this.

Finally, rather than signifyin, testifyin, or sermonizin, Hill remains cool and detached, even in the face of blatant attacks on her integrity and audacious attempts to impugn her character. Specter is most vicious and vociferous in this regard.

> *Specter:* Well, when you say you wanted to maintain a cordial professional relationship, why would you do that, given the comments which you represent Judge Thomas made to you. . . . Was it simply a matter that you wanted to derive whatever advantage you could from a cordial professional relationship?

> *Hill:* It was a matter that I did not want to invoke any kind of retaliation against me professionally. It wasn't that I was trying to get any benefit from it.

The Rhetorical Contest

The only tool Hill and Thomas had available to them was their language. Their rhetorical presentations had to substitute for standard legal evidence and judicial forms of proof.

Thomas did not simply revert to *race* in the construction of his proof. He also reverted to the race's *rhetorical paradigm*. His recourse to AVT accomplished two purposes: (1) It humanized him and created the mythology that he was like Sly Stone and Arrested Development's "everyday people." (2) Targeted at the weak side, his rhetorical stance was a verbal offense that put his enemies on the sociolinguistic defensive.

By using the age-old ethnolinguistics of the Black Tradition, Thomas became a person, rather than an abstraction, to African Americans. Even those who didn't like him, or his politics, grudgingly identified with his pain and his "down-home" personhood. When he describes the impact of all this on him, he brings the emotional suffering home with familiar concreteness:

> the last two and a half weeks have been a living hell. I
> think I've died one thousand deaths. What it means is living
> on one hour a night's sleep. It means losing fifteen pounds
> in two weeks. It means being unable to eat, unable to
> drink, unable to think about anything but this and
> wondering why, how. It means wanting to give up.

When Hatch asked him, "How do you feel right now, Judge, after what you have been through?" he came off just like your next-door neighbor:

> I'll go on. I'll go back to my life of talking to my
> neighbors, and cutting my grass, and getting a Big Mac at
> McDonald's, and driving my car, seeing my kid play
> football. . . . If I'm not confirmed, so be it—[I will]
> continue my job as a court of appeals judge, and hopefully

236

live a long life, enjoy my neighbors and my friends, my
son, cut my grass, go to McDonald's, drive my car, and
just be a good citizen, and a good judge, and a good father,
and a good husband.

The second critical function Thomas's AVT rhetoric served was to
sound a sociolinguistic clarion call to the Senate Judiciary Committee.
The African American Verbal Tradition is perceived to be aggressive,
threatening, intimidating. When Hatch posed the possibility of Thomas
withdrawing from the process, he said, "I'd rather die than withdraw. If
they're gon kill me, they're gon kill me . . . I never cry 'uncle,' and I'm
not going to cry 'uncle' today." (Like, kill me you Marilyn Farmers!)

It wasn't just the racial content, then, that Thomas introduced on
Capitol Hill. He did not talk about ropes and high-tech lynchings in the
restrained LWC style. It was the Black Expressive Style that sent them
all running for cover. It constructed the reality of a strong, angry African
American man (a "crazy nigguh") who might explode at any minute.
AVT upped the ante. As Kochman says, "Whites are constrained not only
by the higher level of energy and spiritual intensity that Blacks generate.
They are worried that Blacks cannot sustain such intense levels of interaction without losing self-control" (1981, p. 31).

Hill, by contrast, remained something of an abstraction, an unknown. Although many African Americans tried to empathize with her
powerlessness, she didn't provide any graphic specificity about her hurt
and feelings. For instance, when she told of being hospitalized for stress
during the sexual harassment period, she didn't try to make us *feel* her
pain the way Thomas did (he says he had lost weight, was only sleeping
one hour each night, had died one thousand deaths, etc.). Whether his
pain was real or feigned is ultimately irrelevant; he made it real. Hill,
though, didn't concretize her suffering. How did her stress manifest itself? Did she lose or gain weight? Did her hair fall out? Such personalization and use of emotional strategies, however, violate LWC conven-
tions.

The two contestants also contrast in terms of their rhetorical exploitation of family and family traditions. While Thomas constantly invoked his elders (his sharecropping grandfather's legacy, mother wit, etc.),
Hill never incorporated any talk about her family or the lessons and leg-
ends of her Blood. In fact, even though she brought her family members
with her, they remained just there, in the background like stage props.

Toward Twenty-first-Century
Womanist Language

A few days after the Thomas hearings ended, I sat among a group
of African American women, some of them from the hood, at a hair-
braiding shop. The hair braiding thing is an all-day affair. My well over

237

eight hours at the shop was my first introduction to the possibility that many African American women did not support Hill. So what if the Black men I talked to, heard and read about, supported Thomas and favored his nomination? "You know how a lot of the Brothas be, all nationalistic sometime, just when you need them to be critical," I reminded myself. And never mind those Black women demonstrating for Thomas on the day of the confirmation vote. "That's just an anomaly; besides, maybe he even paid them," I comforted myself. Surely most African American women understood and supported Hill's position, many having been subjected to such intimidation themselves. Certainly Black women recognized that Thomas's confirmation and the sure-to-be-regressive Supreme Court opinions his vote would solidify would be devastating, not only to the progress of women but to our children and the entire Black community. Surely this is how African American women are looking at this thing, I told myself.

That day at the hair-braiding shop let me know quick, fast, and in a hurry that I had another think coming. These Black women expressed strong negative reactions to Hill: "phony," "saddity" (stuck-up), "I don't trust her," they said, as they discredited her and her story. Even the couple of women who believed her said they could see why those Black women who testified for "Clarence" didn't like "Anita," that they found her kind of "strange," not like anybody *they* knew who had grown up in a poor family of thirteen children on a farm. I was to hear a similar refrain in a number of places—in my Traditional Black Church that Sunday; at a housewarming party I attended in the hood of another city; in the sauna at a city-owned community center in yet another city. I discovered that the opinions of everyday women, those who weren't the D's—i.e., Ph.D., M.D., J.D.—that I talked to in my personal travels around the country coincided with national poll data as well as with a pilot study done in Boston. (See essay by Grier in this volume.)

How do we account for these reactions—the strong Black support for Thomas, which actually *increased* after Hill's allegations, and the concomitant discounting of Hill herself? I want to suggest that language played a fundamental role in this construction of reality in African America. Suspicion and skepticism are common Black reactions to Black users of LWC rhetorical style. These perceptions exist simultaneous with the belief that one needs to master LWC in order to "get ahead." I call it "linguistic push-pull"; Du Bois called it "double consciousness." The farther removed one is from mainstream "success," the greater the degree of cynicism about this ethnolinguistic, cultural ambivalence. Jesse Jackson knows about this; so did Malcolm X and Martin Luther King; so does Louis Farrakhan. The oratory of each is LWC in its grammar but AVT in its rhetorical style.

Thomas capitalized on and ruthlessly exploited the African American Verbal Tradition for all it was worth. He seized the rhetorical advantage, swaying Black opinion by use of the touchstones of the Oral

Tradition and sociolinguistically constructing an image of himself as culturally Black and at one with the Folk. Hill, on the other hand, utilized
the European American rhetorical tradition in which she had been trained
and which she had mastered. Deploying the dispassion, logic, and verbal
forms of support of this tradition, she met white male adversity head on.
(Of course, Senator Heflin referred to her as a "meek woman," but I'm
sure he simply meant "meek" for a *Black* woman.) She did it all with
eloquence, grace, and style. But it was a *European* American, not an
African American, style.

Now, let us be clear because much is at stake here. In no way
should the analysis presented and the conclusion arrived at be construed
to be a condemnation of Hill. And it certainly *ain't* no celebration of
Thomas. Rather, the crucial lesson to be extrapolated from this sociolinguistic case study is this: African American women must fashion a language, building on and rooted in the African American Experience, that
speaks to the *head* and the *heart* of African America if we are to provide
the necessary leadership, not only for Blacks, but for the nation, in the
twenty-first century. In cautioning us to be wary of "uncritical acceptance
of Hill," bell hooks advises: "While it is crucial that women come to
voice in a patriarchal society that socializes us to repress and contain, it
is also crucial what we say, how we say it, and what our politics are"
(1992, p. 21). We are here concerned with the how. Is the African American Verbal Tradition the purview of Black men only? What are the discourse options available to Black women? Who is the Black woman, and
how *do* a Black woman sound? Hard, complex questions, requiring collective work to arrive at answers. Here, however, is a way we might
begin to chart the journey.

While there is an emerging Womanist paradigm, and while African
American women are fast at work recovering Black women's history, still
Toni Morrison's classic 1971 statement characterizes the current situa-
tion:

> For years in this country there was no one for black men to
> vent their rage on except black women. And for years black
> women accepted that rage—even regarded that acceptance
> as their unpleasant duty. But in doing so, they frequently
> kicked back, and they seem never to have become the "true
> slave" that white women see in their own history. True, the
> black woman did the housework, the drudgery; true, she
> reared the children, often alone, but she did all of that
> while occupying a place on the job market, a place her
> mate could not get or which his pride would not let him
> accept. And she had nothing to fall back on: not maleness,
> not whiteness, not ladyhood, not anything. And out of the

profound desolation of her reality she may very well have
invented herself. (p. 63)

As African American women, we need to ask ourselves: What is the
nature and linguistic character of this invented personna? Must everything
be cut whole from new cloth today, with no connecting threads to the
past? What are the African American woman's traditions that can be part
of the formula for the necessary rhetorical invention?

Given the construction of race, gender, and sexuality that Hill symbolized, coupled with the fact that *she* was the one on trial, she was in
an untenable, no-win situation. The only way to win in this kind of battle
is to jump outside the established logic and make winning irrelevant. Redefine the rhetorical moment as a forum for instruction. The issue of
sexual harassment in the workplace is not merely a middle-class white
women's issue. It is an even more crucial issue for women in the underclass, and for those in the working and un-working classes in the United
States, all of whom are disproportionately women of color. (See Malveaux's essay in this volume.) These women are highly vulnerable because they have fewer options than the female "D's." As for Thomas,
he is not bad news just because he might have been a sex harasser. His
is a retrogressive position that threatens the rights of *all* working and un-
working people. He is opposed to equity policies and affirmative action
for people of color. He is opposed to abortion. He supports the conservative agenda whole hog. Thus, here was a prime opportunity to "speak
the truth to the people," before, during, and after the hearing.

For the African American woman in leadership and struggle today,
construction of this twenty-first-century Womanist language requires that
we revisit the linguistics of leadership located in Black women's traditions and rhetorical archetypes—linguistic role models like Zora Neale
Hurston's signifyin Janie, Fannie Lou Hamer, Barbara Jordan, Ella Baker,
and others who come out of the Black tradition of struggle. The most
renowned speaker in this tradition is the great Sojourner Truth. In 1852,
she made her famous "And Ain't I A Woman?" speech at a Women's
Rights Convention in Akron, Ohio. She tells the white men gathered there
a thing or three about women's equality, including the right to vote. As
Arthur Huff Fauset describes the situation in his book, *Sojourner Truth*,
she is thinking:

> Who were these people anyway that they imagined they
> could make laws just to suit themselves—ministers, thugs,
> and barbarians? They with their laws about Negroes, laws
> about women, laws about property and about everything
> under the sun. . . . There was only one Lawgiver. He could
> make these picayune creatures fly, law or no law. He was

240

on *her* side; assuredly He was *not* on their side. (Fauset quoted in Davis and Redding 1971, p. 79)

Much has been made of the dramatic gesture of Sojourner Truth baring her breast in this famous speech to demonstrate that in spite of being forced to enact many male roles, she was indeed a woman. Yet more critically, this dramatic rhetorical gesture and the entire discourse itself are straight out of the African American Verbal Tradition, with Tonal Semantics, Personalization, Sermonic Tone, and, most of all, exhibiting the greatest Signification in the history of the tradition.

Den dat little man in black dar [pointing to a minister], he say women can't have as much rights as man, cause Christ warn't a woman. Whar did your Christ come from? WHAR DID YOUR CHRIST COME FROM? From God and a woman! Man had nothing to do with Him!

Yes, African American women do indeed signify. We also play the Dozens and "talk shit," but save that for another day. The point is that the AVT does not belong to the Brothas alone. African American women must appropriate the African American Verbal Tradition for the advancement of our children, our communities, and our people. We must build on the Womanist tradition of talk in the legacy of Sojourner Truth, Ida B. Wells, Frances E. W. Harper, and the many thousands gone. It is the only way to make sure we ain talkin in ways peculiar to our people's minds.

241

References

Berger, Peter, and Thomas Luckmann. *The Social Construction of Reality: A Treatise in the Sociology of Knowledge*. New York: Doubleday, 1906.

Committee on Public Doublespeak. *Quarterly Review of Doublespeak* 18 (January 1992).

Davis, Arthur, and Saunders Redding. *Cavalcade*. Boston: Houghton Mifflin, 1971.

Du Bois, W. E. B. *Souls of Black Folk*. New York: Fawcett, 1903.

Gates, Henry Louis, Jr. *The Signifying Monkey*. New York: Oxford University Press, 1988.

Holt, Grace. "The Ethnolinguistic Approach to Speech-Language Learning." In Arthur Smith, ed., *Language, Communication and Rhetoric in Black America*. New York: Harper, 1972.

hooks, bell. "A Feminist Challenge: Must We Call All Women Sister." *Z* (Feb. 1992): 19–22.

Hurston, Zora Neale. *Mules and Men*. New York: Harper, 1935.

Kochman, Thomas. *Black and White Styles in Conflict*. Chicago: University of Chicago Press, 1981.

Lincoln, C. E. *The Black Church in the African American Experience*. Durham, N.C.: Duke University, 1990.

Lutz, William. "Notes Toward a Description of Doublespeak." *Quarterly Review of Doublespeak* 13 (1987): 10–12.

Mitchell, Henry. *Black Preaching*. Philadelphia: Lippincott, 1970.

Mitchell-Kernan, Claudia. "Signifying, Loud-talking, and Marking." In Thomas Kochman, ed., *Rappin and Stylin Out: Communication in Urban Black America*. Urbana: University of Illinois Press, 1972, pp. 315–35.

Morrison, Toni. "What the Black Woman Thinks About Women's Lib." *New York Times Magazine*, Aug. 22, 1971, pp. 14–15, 63–64, 66.

Pasteur, Alfred B., and Ivory L. Toldson. *Roots of Soul*. New York: Doubleday, 1982.

Patterson, Orlando. "Race, Gender and Liberal Fallacies." *New York Times*, Oct. 20, 1991. sec. 4, p. 15.

Smith, Arthur [Molefi K. Asante]. *Rhetoric of Black Revolution*. Boston: Allyn and Bacon, 1969.

Smitherman, Geneva. *Language, Politics, and Ideology*. Work-in progress.

Smitherman, Geneva. "A New Way of Talkin': Language, Social Change, and Political Theory." *Sage Race Relations Abstracts* 14, 1 (1989).

Smitherman, Geneva. *Talkin and Testifyin: the Language of Black America*, rev. ed. Detroit: Wayne State University Press, 1986.

Smitherman, Geneva, and Jack L. Daniel. "Black English and Black Identity: Message to the 'Talented Tenth.' " *Journal of Educational and Social Analysis*, April 1979, pp. 20–30.

Smitherman, Geneva. "*The Language of Black Workers*." Unpublished manuscript, 1976.

Von Humboldt, Wilhelm. "Man's Intrinsic Humanity: His Language." In M. Cowan, ed., *Humanist Without Portfolio*. Detroit: Wayne State University Press, 1963 [1810].

Walker, Alice. (1982). *The Color Purple*. New York: Harcourt.

Whorf, Benjamin. *Language, Thought, and Reality: Selected Writings of Benjamin Lee Whorf*, ed. by J. B. Caroll. Cambridge: Massachusetts Institute of Technology, 1956 [1941].

Wilson, Reginald. "*A Comparison of Learning Styles in African Tribal Groups with African American Learning Situations and the Channels of Cultural Connection: An Analysis of Documentary Material*." Unpublished doctoral dissertation, Wayne State University, 1971.

Woodson, Carter G., ed. *Negro Orators and Their Orations*. Washington, D.C.: Associated Publishers, 1925.

Woodson, Carter G. *The History of the Negro Church*. Washington, D.C.: Associated Publishers, 1921.

Anita Hill, Clarence Thomas, and the Crisis of Black Political Leadership

LINDA F. WILLIAMS

Since the election of President 243 Ronald Reagan in 1980, Republicans have sought to create a new conservative Black political leadership as a dimension of their strategy to dramatically alter the ideological terrain of the United States. The task of this new Black leadership is to challenge traditional Civil Rights leadership which has dominated Black politics since the founding of the Niagara Movement in the early years of this century. With a new Black leadership, Republicans hope to secure a mass Black following that will (1) support a limited role for government in correcting the wrongs that have plagued African America since enslavement, and (2) simultaneously support an expansionist role for government in people's private, moral, and social lives. Throughout the Reagan-Bush era, it appeared as if the Republican strategy had failed. To be sure, there were occasional currents of conservatism in public opinion poll data during the 1980s, such as a relatively high level of Black support for the death penalty and prayer in the public school and Black antipathy to reproductive choice. However, most of the poll data throughout the 1980s demonstrated that Blacks were still highly committed to a liberal view of the role of government. They supported increased government spending in health care and housing; they supported affirmative government actions in providing equal and sufficient opportunities in jobs and schooling and in enforcing civil rights statutes. Thus, most analysts concluded that one community in which the so-called Reagan revolution had mightily failed was African America. Then, in 1991, along came the Supreme Court nomination of arch-conservative Black appeals court justice Clarence Thomas. With a majority of African Americans in the polls supporting Thomas from the day of his nomination, and with traditional civil rights leadership slow to oppose his nomination, conservatives began to crow that maybe, yes indeed, they had split Black America, and finally a substantial sector of African America was joining the Right.

This essay contends that the crux of the explanation for African Americans' reactions to Thomas's nomination and to the Hill-Thomas controversy is located in the crisis in Black leadership, and that it is a false reading to conclude that the Black conservative base has expanded. The Black mass continues to support a liberal view of the role of government, and, in fact, there are signs that forces to the left of liberalism have once again begun to grow among the Nation's Black population. The contradiction between the Black response to the Thomas saga and prevailing ideological tendencies in Black America is best understood by examining the failure of traditional Black leadership, which has fallen short on two fundamental counts. First, it has failed to adequately understand, much less explain to the mass Black public, the bifurcation of Black America along class lines. New social, economic, and political conditions in African America and the nation, and around the globe, have altered the playing field and render past Black leadership strategies obsolete. Second, traditional Black leadership has failed to address the long-run history of sexism not only within African America and the nation but also, critically, within African American leadership. New social dynamics, expanding social roles, and emerging new thought among Black women have altered the African American landscape and call into question traditional Black leadership's political programs, policies, and tactics. In developing this argument, Part One of this essay discusses the first phase of the Clarence Thomas confirmation process when the failure of traditional Black leadership was most evident in its inadequate grasp of the meaning of a class-divided African America. Part Two discusses the second phase of the Thomas confirmation process, beginning with Hill's accusations, the catalyst for bringing to the surface the long history of sexism in African America and for demonstrating the current usefulness of sexism as a divide-and-conquer strategy of the Right.

244

Beyond Skin Color: Thomas—No Natural Favorite of Black Leadership

When Thurgood Marshall's intention to retire was announced on June 27, 1991, it meant the departure of not only the Court's only African American but the last liberal voice from the era when Chief Justice Earl

Warren dominated a Court that substantially expanded the legal meaning of civil rights and liberties. Carefully vetting their appointments for ideological purity, both presidents Reagan and Bush had given the Court to the conservative movement, especially its far Right fringe element. In his final Supreme Court decision (handed down the day he resigned), Marshall expressed outrage at the current composition of the Court:

> Power, not reason, is the new currency of this Court's decision-making . . . scores of established Constitutional liberties are now ripe for consideration. . . . Tomorrow's victims may be minorities, women, or the indigent. Inevitably, this . . . will squander the authority and the legitimacy of this Court as a pro-tector of the powerless. (Phelps and Winternitz, 1992, p. 162)

In the press conference he held a day later, Marshall warned America not to be confused by the color of the skin of the nominee; what mattered, he argued, were principles of impartiality, judicial temperament, experience, stature, and other qualifications. For Marshall, it was clear that given the Court's close division between traditional conservatives (usually Justices Byron White, Sandra O'Connor, and David Souter) and its far right conservatives (usually Chief Justice William Rehnquist and Justices Antonin Scalia and Anthony Kennedy), another far right ideologue, regardless of color, or gender, for that matter, would virtually guarantee that the Court's efforts to right the wrongs of centuries of discrimination would not only be overturned but would eventually be obliterated. Indeed, at the very moment of Marshall's retirement, Democrats and moderate Republicans in Congress were still locked in their year-old bitter battle with the Bush administration over a civil rights bill that would restore the Court's infringements on such rights. Thus, the votes of the next nominee would matter significantly. To understand why Thomas became that nominee and especially why he was confirmed, one must go beyond the Bush administration's cynical choice of Thomas as a black man with the Right's ideology. Rather, one must focus analysis on the failure of Black leadership to mobilize Black opposition to the nomination, the resulting confusion of liberal leadership, the patriarchal nature of Black organizations, and the superior organization demonstrated by the Right in seizing upon these failings to fracture the potential coalition against Thomas.

When Bush announced on July 1, 1991, that Thomas was his nominee to replace Marshall, both the president and Thomas knew that the nomination was one most traditional civil rights leadership and Black elected officials would greet without enthusiasm. Thomas was in the first generation of African Americans who owed their success to the Civil

245

Rights Movement, and he had personally benefited from affirmative action when he gained financial assistance and admission to Holy Cross College in 1968 and later to Yale Law School in 1972. Yet Thomas had made a name for himself and had risen through conservative Republican ranks by attacking both civil rights leaders and civil rights legislation. He denounced "as dubious social engineering" the reasoning of the Supreme Court's all important *Brown* v. *Board of Education* decision outlawing segregation in public schools. He opposed affirmative action as a method for improving opportunities for Blacks and suggested, within a week of Reagan's reelection in 1984, that the Equal Employment Opportunity Commission, which he headed at the time, should abandon the use of goals and timetables. Thomas labeled these measures "a fundamentally flawed approach." He agreed with the Reaganite proposal that justice for African Americans could be achieved without government intervention, and he collaborated with Reagan's attorney general Edwin Meese to modify an executive order requiring that a portion of all federal jobs go to people of color.

As chairman of the EEOC, Thomas drastically cut back enforcement of the Equal Pay Act, the law that prohibits gender-based differentials in jobs that are equal or substantially equal. Notwithstanding the EEOC's obligation to enforce laws prohibiting gender- and race-based wage discrimination, he adopted a cramped analysis of Title VII's application to such discrimination that left the claims of many women unremedied. In spite of the proven effectiveness of class-action litigation, Thomas criticized the EEOC's reliance on that strategy and reduced the resources devoted to it—causing a substantial reduction in the number of class-action cases filed by the agency. Further, Thomas had made speeches, written articles, and endorsed reports attacking Constitutional protections of reproductive freedom that have enhanced the power of both African and European American women over their lives.

He vehemently criticized the welfare system, using a stunningly private example in a public news interview. He excoriated his own sister, Emma Mae Martin, who had stayed home in Pin Point, Georgia, caring for her children and her aunt and working at low-paying jobs. He characterized his sister as having "no motivation" for doing much of anything but getting "mad when the mailman is late with her welfare check." Left out of the discussion of his sister's plight was any mention of the many years she had worked, the conditions that forced her to turn to welfare, and the length of time the family had received welfare assistance. For Thomas, there was little space or respect for the intense struggle of women, including that of his mother and sister, who, when their husbands left or relatives fell ill, carried the burden for the family at great personal cost (King 1990).

With the legal philosophy of natural law, Thomas backed his opposition to government intervention for remedying discrimination and his strong support for the propertied.[1] His interpretation of natural law meant that people could look to God or nature for their rights, but not to government. Federal regulations of diverse kinds should be scrapped, freeing corporations from oversight and leaving the wealthy with their riches. In short, Thomas's position on the Black agenda was clear. He was an opponent of nearly everything most conservatives disliked and most Blacks liked—the minimum wage, rent control, equal pay for women, affirmative action, class-action litigation, and other proven remedies for discrimination (Williams 1990).

Neither Thomas's heroes nor close associates came from the ranks of traditional civil rights leadership. He was on record many times for attacking Marshall and challenging the leadership claims of civil rights leaders such as Benjamin Hooks of the NAACP, John Jacobs of the National Urban League, and Democratic presidential candidate Jesse Jackson. Thomas called them a thing of the past. Among Blacks, his best friends were people like Jay Parker, editor of the *Lincoln Review*, a quarterly magazine whose politics lie somewhere on the farthest fringes of the Right. The *Lincoln Review* featured pieces decrying economic sanctions against South Africa, calling for the outlawing of abortion, and demanding the repeal of the minimum wage. Parker, a highly paid lobbyist for the government of South Africa, had opposed the designation of Martin Luther King's birthday as a federal holiday. A member of the advisory board for the *Lincoln Review*, Thomas had written articles for the magazine, and while chairman of the EEOC, he had attended a dinner arranged by Parker to honor a South African dignitary whose job was to represent apartheid (Phelps and Winternitz 1992).

The most conservative of whites made up the bulk of Thomas's ardent admirers. For example, at Thomas's swearing-in ceremony at the EEOC, three of the most right-wing conservatives in the Republican party praised him as "the epitome of the right kind of affirmative action working the right way" (Phelps and Winternitz 1992, p. 197). They were Edwin Meese, Bradford Reynolds, then in charge of the Civil Rights Division of the Justice Department, and South Carolina Senator Strom Thurmond, who had formed the Dixiecrat party in 1948 in response to a civil rights plank in the Democratic party platform. Other ideological bedfellows of Thomas were the fundamentalist and evangelical Christians who compose the Library Court (a far-right coalition that specializes in crusading against abortion, gay rights, women's rights, pornography, and prayer in the schools), the Family Research Council (a conservative think tank and lobbying group that focuses on social issues such as opposition to abortion and specializes in attacking female-headed households), Phyllis Schlafly's Eagle Forum (first created to crusade against the Equal Rights Amendment and now opposed to sex education in the schools, gay rights, and even teaching children about the Holocaust), Beverly LaHaye's Concerned Women for America (which organized thousands of housewives to fight feminists and argued that submission is God's design for women), and fundamentalist preacher Pat Robertson's Christian Coalition. All of these groups vigorously supported Thomas and spent millions of dollars to secure his confirmation.

To most Blacks who knew anything about Thomas, he had clearly surrounded himself with an awfully strange group of bedfellows, people who had long been perceived as opponents, not proponents, of Black progress. The choice of Thomas, then, was clearly one the President knew would not find unanimous support among Black leaders. But the question from the start was: How much opposition? Would traditional Black leadership and organizations unite in opposition to Thomas? Or would Black leadership and organizations divide—some supporting him simply because he was descriptively Black, others opposing him because he was a conservative ideologue?

The Quandary of Black Leadership in the 1990s

Many Americans, if not most, feel comfortable, contented, and even proud when they see persons of their racial and/or ethnic origin holding public office. This has long been the role of "ethnic politics" in a country where class divisions are obfuscated and denied. People "feel they have come closer to acceptance when members of their group get honors and recognition" (Hacker 1992, pp. 203–4). What is true of most groups in the United States is perhaps even truer of African Americans. So long denied virtually all democratic rights and economic opportunities, a central goal of Black politics, since at least the late nineteenth century, has been to have Blacks in governmental positions. The belief is that if a Black American wins a prominent election or receives a public or private sector appointment, then Black people as a group will be symbolically empowered. This "descriptive representation" strategy has been the essential vision of traditional African American leadership for decades. For Black leaders steeped in this vision, the nomination of Thomas, then, represented a crisis of the first order.

Benjamin Hooks, executive director of the NAACP, is representative of traditional Black leadership's defense of Thomas's nomination. The line of argument had three main parts.

One element of the argument was that the crucial issue for Blacks was having a Black on the Supreme Court. Many believed that Thomas, even with his right-wing views, would serve his race better than most other candidates that the Bush administration might field. If Thomas were defeated, Bush would only come back with the nomination of an equally or more conservative Hispanic or European American. As Hooks put it, there "ought to be a Black on the Supreme Court" (quoted in Phelps and Winternitz 1992, p. 75).

Another thread of the argument was a refusal to accept just how far to the extreme right Thomas had swung. His political philosophy had been unstable over the years, and Black defenders scoured his past to find anything that might give them hope. Some argued that Thomas had once voiced praise for Malcolm X; that he had once supported affirmative action with goals and timetables; that he had even marched in civil rights protests in the 1960s; and that his days at the EEOC had not "grossly hindered minorities." As Hooks saw it, Thomas "was not completely without some good points" (Phelps and Winternitz 1992, p. 75).

The third and perhaps most important element of the argument, however, was that despite his conservative ideology, Thomas, nevertheless, was racially Black. He shared the Black experience of oppression and would sympathize with Black concerns once he was appointed to a lifetime job. Praising Thomas's vigor in a statement picked up by conservative groups, Hooks concluded: "If a Black or woman has been individually discriminated against or mistreated, he'll go to the ends of the earth to correct it" (Phelps and Winternitz, 1992, p. 75). Thomas, having experienced racial discrimination in Pin Point, Georgia, and elsewhere, was believed by African American leadership to be just such a man.

The central problem with the descriptive representation thesis and the attempt to fit Thomas into it was that it was based on a vision of African American with little meaning for the current realities of Blacks. The thesis that *any* Black could be counted on to defend the interests of *all* Blacks was substantially valid as long as Jim Crow segregation lasted. Segregation produced a sense of shared suffering based on racial oppression and a collective will to resist based on group identity. Segregation meant that all African Americans were severely punished for violations of Jim Crow laws and customs. Segregation dictated that Blacks, regardless of class, attend the same "mixed-class" churches, send their children to the same schools, and live in contiguous communities. Under segregation, African American professionals and other members of the African American middle class were connected to the Black working class and the African American poor by numerous ties. African American lawyers almost always had Black clients; Black physicians served Black patients; Black teachers and college professors taught in predominantly African American schools and universities. African American entrepreneurs depended upon the African American community for consumers and employees.

It was precisely the end of Jim Crow and the social and economic changes in African America wrought by the success of the Civil Rights Movement of the 1950s and 1960s that produced the need for a new vision of Black politics—and a Black conservative such as Thomas. The

249

net result of affirmative action, minority set-asides, other civil rights initiatives, and the heightened enforcement of these remedies, especially by
Black elected officials in local governments, was to expand the base of
the African American middle class. (The logic behind such efforts is located in Du Boisian notions of the "Talented Tenth," the belief that if
African America put its resources behind the upper 10 percent of the
group, that "talented" 10 percent would help uplift the remaining 90 percent.) By the 1990s, conspicuous distinctions in configurations of education, occupation, income, home ownership, and forms of recreation
indicated that African America was more bifurcated by class than ever
before. Statistical measures, such as the gini index of income inequality,
told a story of inequality growing faster among Black families than white
families in America's increasingly two-tiered society.

The development of a more class-divided Black America did not
mean that race or racism had actually declined in significance. Both daily
life and a vast array of studies, such as those conducted by the American
Bar Association, the Department of Housing and Urban Development, a
public commission reviewing the Rodney King beating, and the Washington-based Urban Institute continued to demonstrate that systemic discrimination based on race remains the order of the day in the United
States. Similarly, studies of violent acts of bigotry, e.g., those conducted
by the United States Justice Department and the Atlanta-based Klan-
Watch, showed that individual racism grew during the 1980s. What the
development of a more class-divided Black America *did* mean however,
was that bonds that once connected all African Americans had begun to
fray. Even the term "Black community" was up for debate. The structures
of accountability that the Black mass once used to influence and/or check
the actions of the African American middle class had begun to erode.
Conditions had been laid for a new type of African American leadership
to emerge, one that lived outside the Black community and had few personal contacts with African Americans. Descriptive representation no longer
worked with bureaucrats and politicians such as Thomas, who feel no
sense of allegiance to the historic Black freedom struggle (Marable 1992).

To be effective for the masses of African Americans, Black leadership must come to terms with the changing dynamics of race and class
that characterize the 1980s and 1990s. A more complicated race issue
means that Blacks have reached a moment of self-realization and uncer-
tainty, when the old beliefs can no longer be sustained, but the requisite
new insights have not been fully comprehended.

Black organizations and their leaders were woefully slow to respond
to Thomas's nomination at first, and later they were unusually splintered.
The leadership of the oldest civil rights organization, the NAACP, first
announced that it was stalled. Holding its annual convention only a week
after Bush announced the nomination of Thomas, the NAACP had an
opportunity for immediate impact on national perceptions of Thomas's

acceptability. Instead of seizing the opportunity to oppose a man who had time and again attacked the NAACP for its ideological principles and political victories, the organization wavered. Delaying its decision until the nomination was "evaluated as closely as possible," NAACP inaction provided the Bush administration with nearly a month to forge its own image of Thomas and to garner whatever level of support among African Americans it wanted.

The leadership of the National Urban League proved to be even less helpful in mounting any opposition to the nomination. On July 21, 1991, NUL head John Jacobs announced that his organization would remain "neutral" on the nomination. Shortly thereafter, Joseph Lowery, head of the Southern Christian Leadership Conference, actually announced his organization's support for Thomas.

Among those Black organizations with a firm national presence, only the Congressional Black Caucus announced opposition to Thomas. Critical of Thomas's stand on civil rights and denouncing him as unsuitable for a seat on the Supreme Court, especially that of Thurgood Marshall, the Caucus promised an "all-out war" to defeat the nominee. Such a war, however, never materialized. Although many of the politically powerful African American leaders attended the Caucus's lavish annual dinner, during the crucial weekend of phase one of the Thomas hearing, the nominee was not even mentioned in any of the speeches made that evening. "While serious dramas about the future of the Supreme Court were being played out elsewhere in the capital, the party went on, complete with a fashion show featuring gorgeous women" (Phelps and Winternitz 1992, p. 208).

Outside the Beltway, on regional and local levels, African American leaders proved to be just as derelict in providing leadership on the Thomas nomination. For example, in Alabama, where the Black vote was credited with making a significant difference in the election of senators who would vote on the nomination, Joe Reed's Alabama Democratic Caucus, perceived by many to be the most powerful African American organization in the state, never took a position on the nomination. Similarly, in Georgia, where Senator Wyche Fowler owed his victory to Black voters, Coretta Scott King, wife of assassinated civil rights hero Martin Luther King Jr., reportedly asked Fowler not to reveal her conversation with him about the nomination—making her position virtually meaningless for any public campaign regarding Thomas (Congressman John Lewis, personal communication, October 15, 1991).

Near the end of July, the NAACP finally announced its decision to "move full-court press" in opposition to Thomas. Yet the nearly month-long inaction by any national organization with claim to mass Black membership meant the absence of a signal from the African American community to European American liberal organizations (women's groups, People for the American Way, labor groups, Jewish groups, and others)

251

that usually ally with Blacks in political battles. Most critically, the Leadership Conference for Civil Rights (LCCR), an umbrella organization of some 180 groups representing the nation's broad civil rights community—from racial and religious minorities to women, the disabled, and the elderly—was essentially stymied since their Black member organizations[2] were split all over the political map, from delaying actions to neutrality to support. A confused and divided Black leadership meant that Thomas most likely would not face the sort of dangerous trial that arch conservative Robert Bork had undergone in 1987 when civil rights groups and an array of liberal groups had banded together early, energetically, and tightly to defeat his Supreme Court nomination. In phase one of the Thomas hearings, then, it was primarily the women's organizations (National Abortion Rights Action League, National Organization for Women, Women's Legal Defense Fund) and a few other liberal groups, such as People for the American Way, that took the lead and worked the hardest to defeat Thomas.

The nomination of a Black conservative to the Supreme Court had actually achieved something all of Reagan's attempts had never done: the fracturing of the civil rights establishment and its demobilization in a struggle over a controversial judicial nomination. This was the context in which the spirited organization and superior financial resources of the White House and the far right fringe of the conservative movement almost guaranteed Thomas a smooth nomination process. Given Thomas's lack of qualifications and stature to sit on the nation's highest court, the White House decided to package Thomas on the basis of his "character" as their chief selling point. Just as white reactionaries during Reconstruction had promoted the accommodationist Black leader Booker T. Washington as the right kind of Black "up from slavery," so the Bush administration in the late twentieth century recreated Thomas as the right kind of Black "up from poverty." By the time the NAACP decided to announce its opposition to Thomas, the Bush administration had already succeeded in transforming Thomas into a symbol of making it on one's own; of searing poverty turned to economic privilege; of self-reliance over "hand-out." Depicted as minimal were the benefits Thomas had personally received from affirmative action and from other gains of the civil rights struggle.

Given the vacuum created by the failure of Black leadership, coupled with the media's portrayal of the nomination process as an election campaign rather than a substantive hearing, the July 1991 polls showed that most Americans had apparently bought the White House's fairy tale. Not only the majority of whites (52 percent) but also the majority of Blacks (57 percent) favored the confirmation of Thomas.[3] That vigorous and sustained opposition from African American organizations might have made a difference is exemplified by declining support for the Thomas nomination in the August polls after the NAACP announced its decision.

For example, the Gallup poll found that while European American support for Thomas climbed, African American support slipped. In fact, those August polls indicated that Black opposition to Thomas doubled, rising from 18 to 37 percent (see Table 1). However, without Black leadership building sustained Black opposition and mounting an education campaign on the deeper questions of who Thomas actually was, what forces he really spoke for and represented, and what effect he would have on the Supreme Court and the nation—without such mass education, Thomas remained an almost totally unknown quantity to most of African America. In the deepening economic recession of the summer of 1991, African Americans as well as European Americans had other issues on their minds. Only a real all-out war by Black leadership could have resulted in shifting Black opinion.

Introducing Thomas to the Judiciary Committee, chief backer Senator John Danforth pointed out, "Not a single member of the Senate knows what Clarence Thomas knows about being poor and Black in America." Had the Senate had some people of color among its membership, Danforth would not have been able to get away with this (Phelps and Winternitz 1992). From the start, then, the limit of a Senate composed almost

---

Table 1. Thomas Confirmation—Trend.

QUESTION: *Would you like to see the Senate vote in favor of Clarence Thomas serving on the Supreme Court or not?*

	July 11–14	Aug. 8–11	Sept. 13–15	Oct. 10–13
Total				
Yes, favor	52%	56%	54%	53%
No, oppose	17	23	25	30
No opinion	31	21	21	17
Whites				
Yes, favor	52	57	54	52
No, oppose	16	21	23	31
No opinion	32	22	23	17
Blacks				
Yes, favor	57	46	54	67
No, oppose	18	37	32	24
No opinion	25	17	14	9

Source: *Gallup Poll Monthly*, October 1991, p. 20.

wholly of privileged, middle-aged and elderly white men was clear. Senate Democrats, the party to which Blacks had given more than 80 percent of their votes in presidential elections since 1964, apparently were stymied in how to challenge a Black nominee without looking elitist or racist. In the end, Democratic members of the Judiciary Committee allowed Thomas to elude tough questions, and Republicans threw him softball ones. Just how unprepared the club of old European American men was to deal with issues of race would become painfully clear in the unexpected part two of the Thomas hearings.

Enter Anita Hill

As the first phase of the Thomas hearing ended, it was widely agreed that Thomas would get a positive (albeit far from unanimous) vote from the Judiciary Committee and ultimately win a majority vote on the Senate floor. It was only when allegations that he had sexually harassed a former employee, attorney Anita Hill, and possibly other female subordinates, that doubts over his confirmation really took hold. In the fractious aftermath of Hill's allegations and Thomas's cynical but shrewd manipulation of the symbol of race during phase two of the hearings, that Black leadership, which had already proven its inadequacy in phase one, now virtually went underground. From the NAACP to the Congressional Black Caucus to the National Council of Negro Women, African American leaders tended either to give weak support to Hill, as did Jesse Jackson, or to refuse to comment, in order to give both Thomas and Hill the benefit of the doubt—which was actually impossible given their absolutely opposing versions of their history.

Meanwhile, polls showed that 82 percent of African American women reported that sexual harassment is a problem (50 percent saying it was a major problem), and nearly two out of five (36 percent) reported that they or someone they knew had been sexually harassed on their job.[4] Hill's charges rang true for hundreds of thousands of Black women who had been sexually harassed on the job, or who knew someone who had. Her charges also rang true for African American working-class women who had been the heroines of change in landmark cases of sexual harassment—Paulette Barnes, payroll clerk; Margaret Miller, proofing machine operator; Diane Williams, Justice Department employer; Rebekah Barnett, shop clerk; and Mechelle Vinson, bank teller trainee (Brownmiller 1991, p. 71).

Consider the many valid reasons for which Black leaders should have called Thomas to account for his conduct. Hill's charges were supported by four different credible witnesses. Her allegations might have exposed not only his character but also his lack of respect for the rule of law.[5] If true, her charges would have demonstrated that Thomas had perjured himself. These leaders could have pointed out that the accuser was also African American, that the symbol "Black" is not gendered. They could have indicated that to follow Thomas's suggestion, to just "let the whole matter go," would fit an equally heinous and embarrassing racial paradigm, that of ignoring the claims of sexual abuse brought by African-American women. At the very least, Black leaders could have pointed out the irony of Thomas's position, he who had so often claimed to be a firm *disbeliever* in utilizing race, now insisting that he was being accused because he was African American. But no such responses were forthcoming from African American leadership. Instead, in a stunning sleight of hand, they allowed Thomas to frame the issue as one of white racism, rather than that of a *Black woman* accusing a *Black man* of sexual harassment. Hill was left without support from a single national Black political leader—male or female—and she became a woman without race.

In this context, it is hardly surprising that Black support of Thomas grew dramatically during phase two of the hearings. Data demonstrate that African American support grew from a bare majority (54 percent) before Hill went public with her accusations, to a healthy majority during the reopened hearings (67 percent), to, indeed, 71 percent the night before the vote (see Table 1).[6] For the first time since Thomas's nomination, African Americans became substantially more likely than Europeans Americans to support Thomas's confirmation. There was also ample evidence in polling data to indicate that African Americans might reward elected officials who supported Thomas. While in September 1991, 75 percent of Blacks reported that a senator's vote in favor of Thomas serving on the Supreme Court would not affect their vote for the senator's reelection, by October 1991, only 52 percent of Blacks said a senator's vote would have no effect. In October 1991, 32 percent of Blacks reported that a vote in favor of Thomas would make them "more likely" to vote for a senator's reelection, while a scant month earlier only 10 percent had reported a favorable vote would make them "more likely" to vote for the senator. Even President Bush appeared to be getting a boost from the Thomas hearings.[7] While 44 percent of Blacks provided the president with a favorable rating in early October (before Hill), Bush's favorability rating among blacks shot up to 55 percent in mid-October after Hill; see Table 2).

On that holiday Monday, a day before the crucial vote for confirmation, the national offices of major civil rights groups were closed, but women's groups were fervently lobbying and planning a demonstration. On the day of the vote, not a single national Black organization held a demonstration at the capitol, or anywhere else, opposing Thomas for his decade-long opposition to the cornerstone of civil rights progress, and/ or on the basis of Hill's unresolved charges. Those African Americans, male or female, who remained vigorously opposed to Thomas's confirmation were left to demonstrate with the National Organization for Women and other predominantly European American women's groups. Among

Table 2. Views of Thomas during the Anita Hill-Clarence Thomas Hearings, October 10–13, 1991.

QUESTION: *How closely have you followed news coverage of the Senate hearings on the nomination of Clarence Thomas to the Supreme Court?*

	White	Black	Total
Very closely	28%	49%	30%
Somewhat closely	48	28	47
Not closely	23	24	23

QUESTION: *From what you may have seen, heard or read about the hearings, what is your impression of Clarence Thomas?*

	White	Black	Total
Very favorable	14%	14%	14%
Favorable	42	55	43
Unfavorable	24	14	23
Very unfavorable	7	8	7
Haven't followed hearings	5	2	5
No opinion	8	7	8

QUESTION: *University of Oklahoma professor Anita Hill charges Clarence Thomas with sexually harassing her when she worked for him in the early 1980s. Thomas denies Hill's charges. From what you have heard or read, whom do you believe more—Anita Hill or Clarence Thomas?*

	White	Black	Total
Hill	28%	34%	29%
Thomas	48	57	48
Neither (volunteered)	6	5	6
No opinion	18	4	17

QUESTION: *Would you like to see the Senate vote in favor of Clarence Thomas serving on the Supreme Court or not? Do you feel strongly about that or not?*

	White	Black	Total
Strongly favor	35%	55%	37%
Not strongly favor	17	12	16
Strongly oppose	21	21	21
Not strongly oppose	10	3	9
No opinion	17	9	17

Source: *Gallup Poll Monthly,* October 1991, p. 00.

the hundreds of mostly white women who demonstrated on the steps of the Capitol during the very moments of the Senate's vote on Thomas, there were fewer than ten Blacks. Across the Capitol's parking lot, however, hundreds of Blacks (a majority of whom were women) shouted and rallied in support of Thomas. Signs of "She Lied" and "Support Our Brother" were sprinkled heavily among the Black demonstrators for Thomas. Thus, George Bush, by now well accomplished in the politics of race, could rightfully conclude: "Judge Thomas has tremendous support from a broad section, a cross section, of America. And that across-the-board support includes minority communities, overwhelmingly supported in minority communities, I might add" (quoted in Phelps and Winternitz 1992, pp. 138–39).

Black Sexism in Historic Relief

From the start, sexism was centered in that most patriarchal of institutions, the Black church. Since practically all modern religions have an intimate relationship with patriarchy, the high level of religiosity among Blacks produced the background for beliefs such as "The head of the woman is man," and teachings such as "All wickedness is but little to the wickedness of a woman." The first Black organizations were dominated, directed, and controlled by Black men. The Negro Convention Movement, a series of Black political conferences beginning in 1830 in Philadelphia, almost always involved only Black men. Aldon Morris (1986) has chronicled the sexism of traditional civil rights organizations, such as SCLC, where women leaders, as politically sophisticated and experienced as Ella Baker, were relegated to secretarial positions whose duties included making the coffee and fetching the doughnuts. As of this writing, none of the best-known national African American organizations (the NAACP, the NUL, the SCLC, or CORE) has been led by a Black woman. Over time, the very cause of Black liberation became identified with the ultimate attainment of "Black manhood."

To be sure, there have always been a few African American leaders who spoke out against women's oppression. For example, Frederick Douglass supported the cause of women's suffrage in the early evolution of the suffragist movement, although he ultimately urged his followers to support the winning of Black male voting rights *first*, demonstrating at least a pragmatic inclination to ally with white male patriarchs.[8] W. E. B. Du Bois, more consistent in his support of women's equality, emphasized that the struggle for Black freedom must inevitably include the demand for the emancipation of women. In March 1941, he pointed out with pride that many more Black women were in the labor force than white women and enthusiastically supported the movement of women from the kitchens into the factory and business world. In January 1947, he urged African American husbands to "share housework" and to shoulder the burdens of child-rearing equally, and he authored a stirring endorsement of planned parenthood in *Birth Control Review* (1932), inviting Margaret Sanger (1934), a "birth-control pioneer," to contribute to the pages of the NAACP journal, *Crisis*. But Du Bois was atypical. Marcus Garvey's political approach toward African American women was a curious mixture of romanticism, sexism, and race nationalism (Marable 1983). Like other Black activists of the nineteenth century, Garvey identified the Black struggle with the attainment of manhood, the realization of a kind of masses' macho. Elijah Muhammad, founder of the Nation of Islam, warned Blacks that their women were unprepared for the "tricks the devils are using" to instill the idea of a false birth control in their clinics and hospitals. Muhammad contended that Black women were created by God to serve their husbands and sons, observing, "The woman is man's field to produce his nation" (quoted in Marable 1983, p. 83).

The 1960s and the rebirth of cultural nationalism proved to be an especially reactionary historical juncture for Black women's liberation. Indeed, in this era of the greatest enlightenment and progress of the race, the old attitudes that had negated the rights of African American women gained stronger ground. Minister Louis Farrakhan, of the Nation of Islam, wrote in *Essence*: "When the Black woman kills her unborn child, she is murdering the advancement of her nation" (quoted in Reid 1980, pp. 96–104). Although Malcolm X's views on Black women changed considerably toward the end of his life, like so many other male leaders, he usually thought of politics as the preserve of men only; sisters were an invaluable but secondary factor in the race war. From Malcolm: "You never can fully trust any woman. Too many men [have been] destroyed by their wives, or their women. Whatever else a woman is, I don't care who the woman is, it starts with her being vain" (Haley 1966, pp. 389–90). As bell hooks (1981) observes, "It is impossible to read [Malcolm's] *Autobiography* without becoming aware of the hatred and contempt he felt toward women for much of his life" (p. 109).

Malcolm X was not the only, and certainly not the worst, of the radical Black leaders of the 1960s on the issue of women's rights. Stokely Carmichael, leader of the Student Nonviolent Coordinating Committee (SNCC) in 1966, argued that young Black men had to assert themselves as males—politically and sexually. According to perhaps the most ridiculous nationalist of the time, Eldridge Cleaver (1968), there was little need for Black women to struggle because they already possessed "pussy power" (p. 61). The proper duty of African American women in the struggle for Black rights was clear: "The role of the Black woman in Black Liberation is an important one and cannot be forgotten. From her womb have come the revolutionary warriors of our time" (Staples 1970, p. 16).

Even Black women became justifiers of their subjugation as many began to sympathize with these views. Some went to great pains to distinguish themselves from white women who were seeking "liberation."

In *Ebony*, Helen King (1971) denounced "women's lib" as a white petty bourgeois fad that had little or nothing to do with the interests of Black women. At the founding convention of the Congress of African People in 1970, coordinator Bibi Amina Baraka set the tone of the Sisters' dialogue by first quoting cultural nationalist Maulana Ron Karenga: "What makes a woman appealing is femininity, and she can't be feminine without being submissive" (pp. 177–78). Amina Baraka (1972) went on to state that Black females had to internalize "submitting to their natural roles" by studying their attitudes toward their "man, house, and children." "Sisters" needed to take cooking classes, learn to create tasty recipes, and improve their personal hygiene.

Any attempt to be equal to the Black man was portrayed among most Black female cultural nationalists of the 1960s not only as an attempt to displace the natural order of Black male leadership but also as a distasteful imitation of white women. As Lucille Clifton (1974) put it in her poem "An Apology to the Panthers":

> i was obedient
> but brother i thank you
> for these mannish days.
> . . . brothers
> i thank you
> i praise you
> i grieve my whiteful ways. (pp. 67–68)

259

Against the voices of patriarchy that have dominated Black society and African American organizations, however, a vocal minority of women from Sojourner Truth to Angela Davis have always argued for women's equality. In the 1970s, a number of women emerged within the Black Movement to advocate reforms first suggested by the (white) feminist movement. To African American women pessimistic about the viability of joint political work with European American feminists, these Black women pointed out that the substantive political and economic advances acquired by women of color in the women's movement more than compensated for the very real problems and personal contradictions of certain petty bourgeois European American women leaders (Sedgewick and Williams 1976). Still, one can conclude that African American feminist leaders were largely ignored.

By the 1980s, many Black males had begun to decry the African American woman's status as a double token, a benefactor of affirmative action on the grounds of race and gender. Some concluded that African American women were now taking away newly won middle-income jobs from Black men. In the latter part of the decade, some African American men were calling for Black male schools; Black male conferences were

sponsored in some places; and there were calls to replace welfare programs targeted for Black women with programs targeting Black men.
Black leadership in the workplace, in street demonstrations, in electoral
politics, and in the bedroom was the province of Black men (Marable
1983, p. 99). Thus, in theory and in practice, long before Hill's accusations, the Black movement and Black leadership had been compromised
and gutted by their inability to confront squarely the reality of patriarchy.

When Thomas played the race card, claiming that Hill's charges fed
into the stereotype of the sexually hyperactive Black male, he created a
backlash. Even among African Americans who believed Hill, many felt
that she should have kept her mouth shut rather than publicly attack a
Black male in an all-white forum. Through Thomas' manipulation of the
symbol of race, Hill became "de-racialized" and partially erased. In an
ironic twist of fate, she became "Yale-educated female law professor" as
Thomas became "lynched Black man." In what would almost be comical
were not the fate of the Court, Blacks, and their nation at stake, Hill
became part of the *white racist* conspiracy against "a brother," a conspiracy supposedly led by the likes of liberal civil rights advocate Senator
Edward Kennedy, and Thomas became part of the *antiracist* protectorate
led by the likes of the founder of the Dixiecrats and once arch-segrega-
tionist Strom Thurmond.

Many African Americans refused to deal with the reality that Hill
would have had great difficulty taking legal action back when the harassment occurred, since it was not until 1986 that guidelines for protecting women against harassment were upheld by the Supreme Court. It
appeared that most African Americans hardly pondered the issue of "who
are our friends, and who are our enemies"—the likes of Kennedy, Metz-
enbaum, and Biden, or the likes of Thurmond, Hatch, and Simpson. They
refused to deal with the reality that although workers victimized by sexual
harassment now have ways to officially complain or sue, the vast majority
do not. It seemed that most African Americans failed to reflect on the
fact that no Black man had ever been lynched over what he did to a Black
woman. African Americans denied the reality that plaintiffs in most of
the landmark sexual harassment cases have been working-class *and* African American; therefore, sexual harassment is hardly a nefarious plot
cooked up by an elite European American women's movement to serve
middle-class professionals. Yet few speculated about the significance of
an African American woman making her charges in a society not only
dominated by white but white *male* values.

What was perhaps the most cruel blow of all was that it had long
been preordained where the African American community would come
out. A growing body of survey data indicates that African Americans are
even more, sexist than European Americans. For example, more African
American than European Americans feel that "married women should not
work." More Blacks than whites feel that a woman's place is in the home,

not "running the country." And more African Americans than European Americans have been reported to be antichoice in reproductive rights (Smith and Seltzer 1992, p. 100). Given the pervasive sexism in African America, the White House easily trumped the initial outpouring of women's support for Hill with the race card that Thomas played so well. Black leadership was now as much caught in its own sexist past as white Democrats were trapped by their own racist past. For whites, it was easier to support a Black man backed by the white establishment than to believe a Black woman challenging the establishment.

Rarely was the issue of Hill's accusations framed as being about both race and gender. The media portrayed all the angry women in response to Thomas's confirmation as white, and all the angry people in response to Hill's accusations as Black. The absence of the perspective of a *Black woman* reflected the almost complete absence of the African American female voice from political discourse. The American political realm was allowed to continue to resist the reality that discrimination or harassment can and often does occur *because* one is a woman of color. The statistical tables often compare the Black woman's earnings to the white woman's to show that the Black woman is not all that "bad off"; then the tables compare the Black woman's earnings to the Black man's to show that Black woman is not all that "bad off." Yet these tables never compare the Black woman's earnings to those of the white man, which would show that the African American woman is the worst off of the four typical race-gender groups. Similarly, a shifting base line of comparison existed in the Thomas hearings. Once the choice between race and gender was forced, then sex was represented by white women and race by Black men. Given Hill's de-racialization, she had entered a battle she never had a chance of winning in the context of sexist Black leadership and a sexist Black society in a racist nation.

261

The Aftermath of the Hill-Thomas Hearings and the Future of Black Leadership

Refusals to grow and change with the times mark the failure of Black leadership during the Thomas hearings. This failure must be listed as one of the key reasons Thomas was confirmed and the effort to pack the Court with conservatives on the far right succeeded.

Although it will be years before a full profile of Thomas's judicial philosophy can be drawn, he seems clearly aligned with the extreme conservative views of Justice Scalia on issues from affirmative action to workers' rights, women's rights, and immigrants' rights. In February 1992, Thomas issued a controversial decision on a case he had heard while still on the court of appeals, overturning the Federal Communications Commission's policy of giving preferences to women in granting radio and television broadcast licenses. Thomas asserted that the policy discriminated illegally against men. He agreed in a unanimous decision that a 1972 statute outlawing sex discrimination in schools allowed a Georgia high school student forced to have sex with a teacher to sue the school system. Yet he joined the other two most conservative justices on the Court, Scalia and Rehnquist, dissenting that the decision should have been much more limited than what the majority had decided. In another case, Thomas rejected even the Bush administration's view that organizers attempting to unionize a grocery store had access rights to a lot where workers parked their cars.

Perhaps most worrisome of all of Thomas's opinions so far are those concerning prisoners. In a move called "mind-boggling" in a *Washington Post* editorial[9] and earning him the title of "The Youngest, Cruelest Justice" in a *New York Times* editorial, Thomas dissented on a lawsuit brought by a Louisiana state penitentiary prisoner, Keith Hudson. He had been brutally beaten by a guard while handcuffed and shackled; the guards' supervisor watched, warning them "not to have too much fun." Seven of the justices, including Rehnquist and Kennedy, voted to approve a lower court's monetary award of $800 to the prisoner for violation of his Constitutional rights. Despite the fact that the beating loosened Hudson's teeth, cracked his dental plate, and caused bruises and swelling on his face, mouth, and lips, Thomas dissented, arguing that the beating did not violate the Eighth Amendment's ban on cruel and unusual punishment because the prisoner's injuries were not serious. Further, he indicated in his dissenting opinion that the majority decision was "yet another manifestation of the pervasive view that the federal Constitution must address all ills in our society." Justice O'Connor took Thomas to task, arguing that his dissent ignored "the concepts of dignity, civilized standards, humanity, and decency that animate the Eighth Amendment."

Thomas's opinions regarding prisoners on Death Row, even those who might not belong there, have been equally callused. When a witness whose testimony had convicted a Texas Death Row inmate, Justin May, recanted shortly before May was to be executed, Thomas voted with Scalia and Rehnquist to allow the state to execute May anyway, without any hearing. Fortunately for May, the majority of the Justices voted to stay the execution. Similarly, Thomas and four other justices refused to stay the execution of another inmate who also had produced compelling new evidence of his innocence. At the last minute, a Texas court stayed the execution so the appeal could be heard (Phelps and Winternitz 1992, pp. 427–30).

In phase one of his hearings, Thomas capitalized on the myth of descriptive representation in the context of prisoners' rights. He told the Judiciary Committee that he used to watch prisoners from his appellate office, and "say to myself almost every day, there but for the grace of

God go I." Undoubtedly such talk warmed the hearts of those Black leaders who insisted that Thomas, despite his reactionary ideology, is nevertheless Black. "He shares our experiences of oppression, and will sympathize with our concerns, once he's appointed to a lifetime job." Today they must face the sad and humiliating fact that Thomas is proving to be a very different man from what he pretended to be. A careful analysis of his evolving positions over the years would have demonstrated that he would be a justice with little or no connection to the Black freedom struggle.

By not addressing the long-term sexism in African America in the context of the changing status and conditions of women, Black leadership failed to illustrate the deficiencies arising from not just an *all-male* but an *all-white* Senate Judiciary Committee. By allowing Hill to be essentially de-racialized—a kind of white woman's Black—the primary message that came across was that "MEN," rather than "WHITE" men, by their white *and* male values, "just didn't get it." As the hearings ended, there was a growing sense of revulsion toward a predominantly male Senate but little or no discussion about an *all-white* Senate. While many addressed the difficulty of combating sexism, little discussion focused on the difficulty of combating racism *and* sexism. African American women, by virtue of their race and gender, are situated within at least two interacting systems of subordination—racism and sexism. Their experiences of racism are shaped by their gender, and their experiences of sexism are shaped by their race—this critical issue remained unexplored. Hill has been widely acclaimed by many leaders as the Rosa Parks of the woman's movement, revitalizing it even as the Black movement, in general, and traditional Black women's organizations, in particular, continue to appear confused.

What loomed so significantly beneath the surface and allowed the fracturing of the liberal constituency during both phases of the hearings was the separation of one kind of oppression from another. African American leaders missed a critical opportunity to explore and clarify how the powerful oppress *all* the powerless and divide the many in the interests of the few (privileged white males) by masking the intersections of race, gender, and class exploitation. Instead, Black leadership was virtually silent about the connections among all the "isms," which would have been a fundamental mechanism for combating the divide-and-conquer strategy of the Right.

The Thomas hearings and the Hill-Thomas confrontation pushed to the forefront a central question: Can the powerless in this country have a represented voice when the authority to which the Senate defers is male, white, heterosexual, and economically privileged?[10] The inadequacy of current African American leadership to address this crucial question has become starkly visible. In addition to its dereliction in responding adequately to the Thomas saga have been a series of other leadership failures

263

that highlight the crisis in traditional African American leadership. There was the regressive and sexist defense from some Black religious leaders of former heavyweight champion Mike Tyson when he was convicted of raping an African American woman. There was the failure of Black leadership to respond adequately to the May 1992 riots in Los Angeles that followed the verdict to acquit the four white policemen in the videotaped beating of Black motorist Rodney King. Lacking a grasp of class dynamics within race and insufficient comprehension of the post-1960s bifurcation of the Black "community," African American leadership is ill equipped to provide an understanding of and leadership to the many southcentral LAs in this nation.

In sum, among traditional African American leadership, there is no sense that a more progressive voice on politics and public policy must be articulated—one that recognizes that the political, economic, and ideological context for African American politics has changed fundamentally during the past decade; one that proposes programs and strategies to address the needs of a burgeoning African American underclass; one that recognizes the necessity for advancing a new strategic vision and tactical actions in challenging the system of white racism and corporate power; one that provides attention to contemporary realities and conditions confronting African America along race, gender, and class lines; and one that once and for all ends the male hierarchy of Black leadership. In the closing months of 1992, a diverse and growing body of African American progressives from across the nation met several times in Washington, D.C. Summoning a "New Niagara," they sounded a nascent call to rebuild the Black movement under new gender-balanced, class-oriented leadership. Reactions to the Thomas nomination and the Hill-Thomas controversy symbolically served notice on traditional African American leadership from both the Right and the Left. The future of African America and its leadership will depend on whether the friends and allies of African American women and the African American working class and poor have the courage to force the challenge.

Notes

1. "Ironically, it was the idea of the unfettered right of property that was used by the early Supreme Court to justify the holding of slaves" (Phelps and Winternitz 1992).
2. Early action was made impossible since Benjamin Hooks of the NAACP was chairman of the board of the LCCR.
3. The July Gallup poll found 52 percent of whites and 57 percent of blacks favored the confirmation of Thomas to the Supreme Court.
4. Survey, Greenberg-Lake: The Analysis Group Inc., June 1992.
5. As chair of the EEOC, Thomas was responsible for enforcing Title VII as well as the EEOC Guidelines prohibiting sexual harassment. Guidelines on Discrimination Because of Sex, 29 C.F.R., Section 1604.II (1990); originally enacted on Nov. 10, 1980 (45 Fed. Reg. 74,677 [1980]): "Harassment on the basis of sex is a violation of Section 703 of Title VII."

6. See Table 1 and *The Gallup Poll Monthly*, October 1991, p. 23.
7. See *The Gallup Poll Monthly*. Note, however, Bush's approval rating had declined to 36 percent by late October 1991.
8. Similarly, white women took contradictory positions on the race question. For example, in 1851, white suffragists protested the appearance of Sojourner Truth at an Ohio women's convention because they opposed both "abolition and niggers." In her debate with Douglas, Elizabeth Cady Stanton asserted that she would not trust "the colored man with my rights; degraded, oppressed himself, he would be more despotic with the governing power than even our Saxon rulers are. If women are still to be represented by men, then I say let only the highest type of manhood stand at the helm of State." Robert L. Allen, *Reluctant Reformers: Racism and Social Reform Movements in the United States* (Garden City, New York: Anchor Books, 1975), pp. 141, 153–154.
9. The *Washington Post* consistently stuck up for Thomas through the bitter hearings.
10. Here I rely on information gathered in a survey conducted by Greenberg-Lake: The Analysis Group, June 1992. Eighty-two percent of African Americans polled reported that the nation would be "better off."

References

Baraka, Bibi Amina. "Coordinator's Statement." In Amiri Baraka, ed., *African Congress: A Documentary of the First Modern Pan-African Congress*. New York: Morrow, 1972.

Brownmiller, Susan. "Heroines of Changes in Sexual Harassment." *Ms.* (September 1991).

Cleaver, Eldridge. *Soul on Ice*. New York: Delta, 1968.

Clifton, Lucille. "Apology to the Panthers." In Pat Crutchfield, ed., *Keeping the Faith: Writings by Contemporary Black American Women*. Greenwood, Conn.: Fawcett, 1974.

Hacker, Andrew. *Two Nations: Black and White, Separate, Hostile, Unequal*. New York: Scribner's, 1992.

Haley, Alex, ed. *The Autobiography of Malcolm X*. New York: Pathfinder, 1966.

hooks, bell. *Ain't I a Woman*. Boston: South End, 1981.

King, Helen. "The Black Woman and Women's Lib." *Ebony* (July 1971). pp. 68–76.

King, Patricia. "Clarence Thomas: On the Backs of Black Women." *Radical America 32* (1): 11–16, 1990.

Marable, Manning. *How Capitalism Underdeveloped Black America*. Boston: South End, 1983.

Marable, Manning. "Toward a Renaissance of Progressive Black Politics." Unpublished paper presented at Democracy and Its Discontents Conference, Washington, D.C., June 1992.

Morris, Aldon. *The Origins of the Civil Rights Movement*. Chicago: University of Chicago, 1986.

Phelps, T. H., and H. Winternitz. *Capitol Games: Clarence Thomas, Anita Hill, and the Story of a Supreme Court Nomination*. New York: Hyperion, 1992.

Reid, Willie Mae, ed. *Black Women's Struggle for Equality*. New York: Pathfinder, 1980.

Sedgewick, Cathy, and Reba Williams. "Black Women and the Equal Rights Amendment." *Black Scholar* 7 (1976): 24–29.

Smith, Robert, and Richard Seltzer. *Race, Class and Culture: A Study in Afro American Mass Opinion*. New York: SUNY, 1992.

Staples, Robert. "The Myth of the Black Matriarchy." *Black Scholar* 1 (1970): 8–16.

Hood, Elizabeth. "Black Women, White Women: Separate Paths to Liberation." *Black Scholar* 9 (1978): 45–46.

Williams, Patricia. "Clarence Thomas and the EEOC." *Radical America* 24 (1980): 17–20.

265

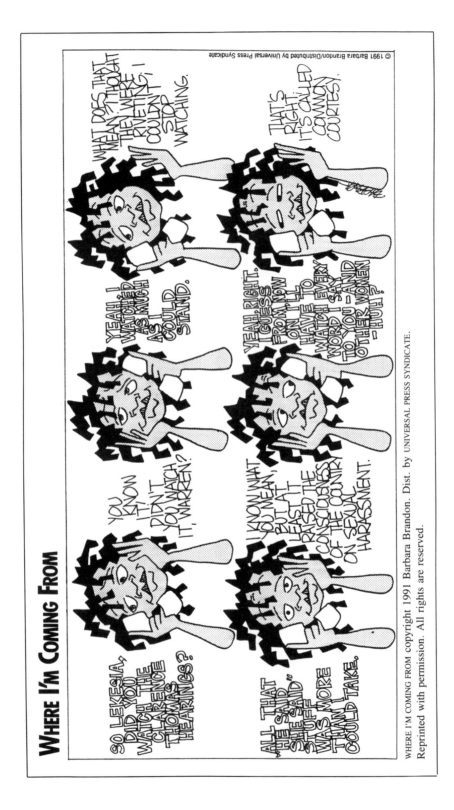

Contributors

Margaret Walker Alexander is a novelist and poet, perhaps best known for her novel *Jubilee* and for her book of poetry *For My People*. Professor emeritus at Jackson State University, she is considered the elder stateswoman among African American writers today.

Linda Susan Beard is Katharine E. McBride Visiting Associate Professor at Bryn Mawr College. Specialist in South African and African American women's literature, she has a reputation as a dynamic and innovative teacher, for which she has won Michigan State University's Teacher-Scholar Award and the State of Michigan Teaching Award.

Barbara Brandon is creator of "Where I'm Coming From," a cartoon strip about the lives, joys, and sorrows of nine sistas who reflect the diversity of contemporary Black womanhood. She is the only nationally syndicated (sixty newspapers) African American female cartoonist. The first collection of her work, also entitled *Where I'm Coming From*, was published in 1993.

Elsa Barkley Brown teaches in the Center for Afroamerican and African Studies and Department of History, University of Michigan, Ann Arbor. She is associate editor of the two-volume *Black Women in America: An Historical Encyclopedia* (1993). Her articles have appeared in *Signs, Sage, History Workshop, Feminist Studies,* and *Public Culture*. She was one of the organizers of the African American Women in Defense of Ourselves (AAWIDOO) campaign.

Patricia Coleman-Burns is director of the office of multicultural affairs in the School of Nursing at the University of Michigan. A longtime political activist and scholar, Dr. Coleman-Burns is a specialist in social movements and rhetorical theory. She is married to John Burns and is the mother of one son.

Angela Y. Davis has been teaching, writing, and lecturing about African American and women's social theories and practices for twenty years. She has also been active in a number of organizations concerned with issues of social justice. She presently teaches in the History of Consciousness Program at the University of California–Santa Cruz.

Toi Derricote is a poet and associate professor of English at the University of Pittsburgh. She has published *Natural Birth*, *The Empress of the Death House*, and, most recently, *Captivity*, now in its third printing. Reflecting on *Natural Birth*, Adrienne Rich said: "Her words touch the reader as life has touched her, soul and body. This is a strong, sensuous, original, courageous book." Derricotte's awards include two fellowships from the National Endowment for the Arts, the Distinguished Pioneering of the Arts Award from United Black Artists USA Inc., the Lucille Medwick Memorial Award from the Poetry Society of America, a Pushcart Prize, and a Folger Shakespeare Library Poetry Book Award. Her poems have appeared in *American Poetry Review*, *The Iowa Review*,

Callaloo, The Paris Review, Ploughshares, The Kenyon Review, Massachusetts Review, and in numerous anthologies, including *The Pittsburgh Book of Contemporary American Poetry, A New Geography of Poets*, and *New American Poets of the 90s*.

Gwen Etter-Lewis is associate professor of Linguistics at Western Michigan University. Her *My Soul Is My Own*, based on interviews and narratives from Black women in male-dominated professions in the first half of this century, was published in 1993.

Beverly Grier is an assistant professor of Government and International Relations at Clark University in Boston. Her area of research is African politics. Currently, she is working on the history of child labor in colonial Zimbabwe.

Rosalind E. Griffin, M.D., is a psychiatrist in a psychoanalytically oriented private practice for adults and adolescents in marital and family therapy. She is service chief of the Partial Hospitalization Program at Sinai Hospital in Detroit, where she treats hearing impaired patients, chemically dependent adults, and victims of domestic violence. Dr. Griffin has a subspecialty in forensic psychiatry and is clinical assistant professor at Wayne State University's School of Medicine. She is the mother of a son at Hampton University.

Darlene Clark Hine is the John A. Hannah Professor of History at Michigan State University. She is editor of the two-volume work *Black Women in America: A Historical Encyclopedia*, published in 1993. She is the author of several books, including *Black Women in White: Racial Conflict and Cooperation in the Nursing Profession, 1890–1950* and *Black Victory: The Rise and Fall of the White Primary in Texas*. In 1982, she directed the Black Women in the Middle West Project funded by the National Endowment for the Humanities. Dr. Hine's recent book is *Hine Sight: Black Women and the Reconstruction of American History*.

Nettie Jones is a writer. Formerly writer-in-residence at Michigan Technological University, she has authored two novels, *Fish-Tales* (1989) and *Mischief Makers* (1991). She is currently at work on a third novel, *Detroit: Beauty Within This Beast*. She is the mother of one daughter, Lynn.

Julianne Malveaux hosts *The Julianne Malveaux Show*, a Washington-based news and public affairs radio talk show. Her guests have included Eleanor Holmes Norton, Charles Rangel, Reverend Jesse Jackson, Ruby Dee, Ron Walters, and Susan Taylor. Dr. Malveaux is also an economist (Ph.D., M.I.T.), a writer, and a nationally syndicated newspaper columnist. She has written for *Emerge, Ms, Essence*, and *USA Today* and provides regular commentary on "CNN and Company" and PBS' "To the Contrary." She is a regular weekly contributor to the *San Francisco Sun Reporter*, where her column, "No Means No," won a 1993 award from the National Newspaper Publishers Association. A scholar of labor market and public policy theory, she co-edited *Slipping Through* *the Cracks: The Status of Black Women* (1986), and her *Sex, Lies and Stereotypes: Perspectives of a Mad Economist* was published in 1994. An activist and advocate, Dr. Malveaux is vice president of the National Child Labor Committee, board member of the Center for Policy Alternatives, and vice president of the National Association of Negro Business and Professional Women's Clubs.

Harriette Pipes McAdoo is professor in the Department of Family and Child Ecology, in the College of Human Ecology, at Michigan State University. Formerly, she was professor and acting dean at the Howard University School of Social Work. She has been a post-doctoral fellow at the Institute of Social Research and at Harvard University. Dr. McAdoo is past president of the National Council on Family Relations (NCFR), a director of the Groves Conference on Marriage and the Family, and a member of the governing council of the Society for Research in Child Development. Her awards include the Helms Award (Columbia University), the Outstanding Researcher of the Year Award (National Association of Black Psychologists), and the Marie Peters Award (NCFR). She is editor of *Black Families* and *Family Ethnicity: Strength in Diversity*, co-author of *Women and Children, Alone and in Poverty*, and co-editor of *Services to Young Families: Program Review and Policy Recommendations* and *Black Children: Social, Educational, and Parental Environments*. She is author of numerous book chapters and journal articles and serves on several editorial boards. Dr. McAdoo is the mother of two sons and two daughters.

269

Dianne M. Pinderhughes is professor of political science and Afro-American studies and director of the Afro-American Studies and Research Program at the University of Illinois Urbana-Champaign. Her *Race and Ethnicity in Chicago Politics: A Reexamination of Pluralist Theory* was published in 1987. She has also published numerous articles for the National Urban League's *State of Black America* and book chapters addressing issues of race, public policy, and electoral politics. Her awards include Postdoctoral Fellowships from the Ford Foundation's National Research Council, the Rockefeller Foundation, and UCLA's Center for Afro-American Studies. From 1988 to 1991, she was a University of Illinois university scholar. She has served as a council member of the American Political Science Association, the Midwest Political Science Association, and the National Conference of Black Political Scientists. She was president of the National Conference of Black Political Scientists from 1988 to 1989. Currently on leave from the University of Illinois, Dr. Pinderhughes is guest scholar in the Governmental Studies Program at the Brookings Institution.

Barbara Ransby is a faculty member in the department of history at DePaul University and serves as director of the Center for African American Research at DePaul. She is also a longtime community activist, freelance writer, and consultant to museums, foundations, and community agencies. She has lectured widely and published numerous articles on African American history, Black feminism, and social change movements in the United States. Prof. Ransby is a graduate of Columbia University and the University of Michigan and is currently completing a biography of the civil rights leader and radical intellectual Ella Jo Baker.

Geneva Smitherman is University Distinguished Professor of English and director of the African American Language and Literacy Program at Michigan State University. A specialist in sociolinguistics and African American speech, she is author of more than one hundred articles and papers dealing with Black speech and rhetoric, including the award-winning *English Journal* column, "Soul n Style." Her books include *Talkin and Testifyin: The Language of Black America* (1977), *Black Talk: Words and Phrases from the Hood to the Amen Corner* (1994), and the forthcoming *Educating African American Males: Detroit's Malcolm X Academy Solution*, co-authored with Dr. Clifford Watson. She is editor or co-editor of four additional books, including *"Ain't I a Woman?": African American Women and Affirmative Action*. Publicly active in the struggle for language and education rights for people of color, "Dr. G."—as she is affectionately known to students and friends—has appeared on several media programs, including *Oprah*, *Donahue*, *Today*, and *Dan Rather Special Reports*. She is the mother of one son, Robert Anthony.

Denise Troutman-Robinson is assistant professor of American Thought and Language and of linguistics at Michigan State University. Her research interests combine language variation with discourse analysis, including work on Black English speakers and African American women. She is the mother of a son and a daughter.

Susan Watson is a journalist and an award-winning columnist with the *Detroit Free Press*. She is a member of the Detroit Chapter of the National Association of Black Journalists. She is the mother of one son, now attending Howard University.

Linda F. Williams is professor of political science and government at the University of Maryland–College Park. She also serves as director of the Institute for Policy Research and Education in Washington, D.C. Dr. Williams is a specialist in African American politics and public policy.

Index

275

BOOKS IN THE AFRICAN AMERICAN LIFE SERIES

Coleman Young and Detroit Politics: From Social Activist to Power Broker, by Wilbur Rich, 1988

Great Black Russian: A Novel on the Life and Times of Alexander Pushkin, by John Oliver Killens, 1989

Indignant Heart: A Black Worker's Journal, by Charles Denby, 1989 (reprint)

The Spook Who Sat by the Door, by Sam Greenlee, 1989 (reprint)

Roots of African American Drama: An Anthology of Early Plays, 1858–1938, edited by Leo Hamalian and James V. Hatch, 1990

Walls: Essays, 1985–1990, by Kenneth McClane, 1991

Voices of the Self: A Study of Language Competence, by Keith Gilyard, 1991

Say Amen, Brother! Old-Time Negro Preaching: A Study in American Frustration, by William H. Pipes, 1992 (reprint)

The Politics of Black Empowerment: The Transformation of Black Activism in Urban America, by James Jennings, 1992

Pan Africanism in the African Diaspora: An Analysis of Modern Afrocentric Political Movements, by Ronald Walters, 1993

Three Plays: The Broken Calabash, Parables for a Season, and The Reign of Wazobia, by Tess Akaeke Onwueme, 1993

Untold Tales, Unsung Heroes: An Oral History of Detroit's African American Community, 1918–1967, by Elaine Latzman Moon, Detroit Urban League, Inc., 1994

Discarded Legacy: Politics and Poetics in the Life of Frances E.W. Harper, 1825–1911, by Melba Joyce Boyd, 1994

African American Women Speak Out on Anita Hill–Clarence Thomas, edited by Geneva Smitherman, 1995